GOOD
FOOD
FAST

GOOD FOOD FAST

A Menu Cookbook
by Anne Walsh
and the Editors of
Food & Wine

American Express
Publishing Corporation
New York

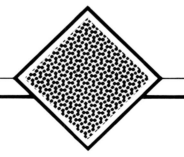

Menus pictured on the cover and the chapter openers are:
Cover: Special Occasion Dinner for Four (page 164)
Brunch & Breakfast: Southern Style Breakfast (page 16)
Poultry: Fourth of July Supper (page 56)
Meat: Spring Lamb Dinner (page 104)
Fish & Shellfish: Mid-Winter Weekend Lunch (page 150)
Ethnic: Chinese Family-Style Meal (page 184)

Good Food Fast
Editor: Stephanie Curtis
Art Direction and Design: Bette Duke
Photography: Thom de Santo
Food Styling: Andrea B. Swenson

American Express Publishing Corporation
Managing Editor/Books: Kate Slate
Marketing Director: Elisabeth Braun
Assistant: Diane Fernicola

Published by American Express Publishing Corporation
1120 Avenue of the Americas, New York, New York 10036

Manufactured in the United States of America

Library of Congress Cataloging in Publication Data
Walsh, Anne, 1936-
Good food fast.

Includes index.

1. Cookery. 2. Menus. I. Food & wine (New York, NY) II. Title.
TX652.W26   1985   641.5'55   85-11177
ISBN 0-916103-02-1

First Edition

TABLE OF CONTENTS

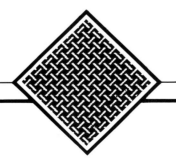

The Good Food Fast Pantry

Good Food Fast grows out of a lifetime interest in eating well. As the name implies, it is a collection of menus and recipes for food that is both good tasting *and* quickly prepared. My goal in writing this book has been to share with you discoveries that have shaped the way I cook today, and to pass on ways to create meals that are as delicious and attractive as they are quick and easy.

All of the recipes I've chosen to include have one thing in common: they are extremely practical for the busy cook. Some of the dishes are my adaptations of classic combinations and approaches, others are of my own invention, and others are variations on themes I have encountered while eating and cooking around the world.

I was born in England to an American family, all of whose members deeply appreciated fine food and were also excellent cooks, so I acquired an early interest in the subject. We moved around a lot when I was young—England, Caracas, Cincinnati, New York—and, as an adult, I lived in Paris for several years. Everywhere we went, we had the good fortune of having our kitchen graced with talented cooks. They hailed from such disparate parts of the world as Ecuador, Rome, Provence and Georgia, and I never tired of observing their skills and cooking styles.

In my "salad days," starting out on my own in New York in an art and design career, my culinary interests were reflected in my circle of friends. The "gang" included Francesco Ghedini, the late author of the now classic *Northern Italian Cooking*; W. Peter Prestcott, currently the Entertainment and Special Projects Editor of *Food & Wine* magazine, and noted food authority Michael Batterberry, who is also my brother.

We were an impecunious bunch in those days and rarely went to restaurants, unless a visiting parent came to town. We cooked for each other at our various pads in the winter, and in the summer we took turns in the kitchen of a rambling rose-covered cottage we all shared in the Hamptons. Few restaurants could have provided better fare. The food was imaginative, plentiful and varied.

Later, intrigued by my husband's interest in Zen and the tea ceremony, I learned about Japanese food and cooking techniques. The freshness, simplicity and economy of time and motion that characterize this cuisine have influenced my preparation of Western dishes ever since.

Several years ago, an important career change had another major influence on my cooking. I decided to give up a well-established art and design career to become a psychotherapist. The change involved intensive study at Princeton University, and later in New York, which required daily commuting from my home in New Jersey. Even though my spare time was stripped to somewhat less than zero during that period, I was not willing to stop creating appealing and good tasting meals for my husband and daughter. The result was that I discovered the preparation of many of my favorite dishes could be sped up and simplified, and, in many cases, the quicker versions were even better tasting than the originals.

There are a few things I always keep in mind when planning menus. I choose dishes that are visually appealing as well as flavorful. Contrasts in color, texture and temperature are also important in keeping a menu lively and interesting. Most of all, I don't want the task of preparing the menu to be overwhelming, so I usually simplify things by limiting the number of dishes I will prepare. And to make these simplified menus more lavish, I augment them with storebought extras such as pâtés, terrines, smoked fish, good cheeses, breads and desserts.

I hope these menus will help you and other lovers of good food to cook and enjoy delicious meals no matter how hectic your schedules. May you and those you cook for end every meal feeling relaxed, civilized and beautifully fed.

To achieve this goal without feeling harried or overworked, it's important not only to have a ready repertoire of good, fast recipes, but also to have a kitchen generously stocked, both with first-rate equipment and with a varied array of high-quality pantry goods.

Most cooks have their own quite personal and

frequently quirky lists of ingredients that they can't do without. My own such list includes Calamata olives, a hunk of Parmesan cheese, a knob of fresh ginger, unsalted butter, fragrant green olive oil, coarse salt, hot pepper sauce, a box of dried capellini, an enormous head of garlic, green and red onions, a lemon, a lime, an orange, clam and chicken broths and black peppercorns.

The following is a list of some other ingredients in addition to these—and such staples as flour, rice, pasta, eggs and milk—that are essential for making *good* food *fast*.

Pantry Staples

- COARSE (KOSHER) SALT: These salt crystals seem to stick to food, particularly meats, more readily than fine salt.

- SUPERFINE SUGAR: dissolves quickly and easily in cold drinks, marinades and sauces.

- BROWN SUGAR, WILDFLOWER HONIES, PURE MAPLE SUGAR: for a change from white sugar, these alternatives not only sweeten, but also contribute their own interesting flavors.

- EXTRA-VIRGIN OLIVE OIL, ORIENTAL SESAME OIL, WALNUT AND HAZELNUT OILS

- BALSAMIC VINEGAR, RICE VINEGAR AND OTHER FLAVORED VINEGARS: the first is dark, sweet and richly flavored, the second is milder and a little sweeter than most Western vinegars.

- CORNMEAL: substitute for flour or bread crumbs when dredging foods before frying. It's also good for quick breads, muffins and biscuits, as well as, of course, polenta.

- BULGUR, COUSCOUS, GRITS, WILD RICE: for a change from white or brown rice. The first three also have the advantage of being quickly prepared.

- CANNED WHITE AND BLACK BEANS, BLACK-EYED PEAS, CHICK-PEAS: all are good for

adding to quick soups, salads and hot side dishes.

- CANNED ITALIAN PLUM TOMATOES, TOMATO PASTE AND CRUSHED OR PUREED TOMATOES

- CANNED ANCHOVIES, SKINLESS SARDINES, TUNA IN OLIVE OIL, PICKLED HERRING IN WHITE WINE: good raw materials for impromptu meals, antipasto platters, salads.

- CANNED WATER CHESTNUTS AND BAMBOO SHOOTS: they add texture and flavor to main dishes and side dishes.

- CANNED OR BOTTLED CLAM, CHICKEN AND BEEF BROTH: quick stand-ins for homemade stocks to flavor sauces, soups and stews.

- CANNED SOUPS SUCH AS SHE-CRAB, SEAFOOD OR LOBSTER BISQUE: these are good for first courses and off-the-shelf lunches.

- SEMI-SWEET CHOCOLATE AND PRE-MELTED DARK CHOCOLATE: for desserts. The pre-melted variety saves cooking and cleaning up time.

- MAPLE SUGAR CANDY, STEM GINGER IN SYRUP, CANDIED VIOLETS AND CRYSTALLIZED ORANGE PEEL, GRAPEFRUIT PEEL AND GINGER: for adding flavor and garnishing desserts.

- JAMS AND JELLIES: including red currant, apricot, damson, quince and marmalade, all of which are particularly good flavors for melting to make quick sauces and glazes.

- HERBS AND SPICES: in addition to the standard herbs and spices, I always keep the following on hand: Madras curry powder, herbes de Provence, saffron threads, sweet and hot paprikas, and white, red, green and Szechuan peppercorns.

- SUN-DRIED TOMATOES: either the dried kind (which need reconstituting in hot water) or the

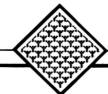

imported variety packed in olive oil.
- DRIED WILD MUSHROOMS

Garnishes and Condiments

- PICKLES: including cornichons, watermelon pickles, pickled onions, pickled walnuts, jalapeño peppers and Japanese pickles.
- OLIVES: including Calamata to add flavor to pastas and stuffed eggs, tiny black Niçoise olives for salads, Spanish and California olives for a milder flavor.
- ROASTED RED PEPPERS AND PIMIENTOS
- CHUTNEY: use it not only as a condiment with Indian food, but also in salad dressings and as an accompaniment to cold poultry or meat.
- CAPERS AND GREEN PEPPERCORNS PACKED IN VINEGAR OR BRINE: to brighten salads, sauces and a wide variety of hot dishes.
- HORSERADISH AND MUSTARDS: including Dijon-style and Pommery prepared mustards, English dry mustard and Japanese horseradish (wasabi)—for sauces, salad dressings and cold meats and fish.
- BOTTLED SAUCES: hot pepper sauce, for fire and flavor; soy sauce—I prefer the bright, fresher flavor of the light Japanese variety to the saltier Chinese type; A-1 or Worcestershire, for enriching and coloring sauces; oyster sauce for adding a rich unusual flavor to stir-fried vegetables and meats.

Refrigerator Staples

- UNSALTED BUTTER: it adds a fresher and better flavor than salted butter, and doesn't have the added sodium.
- CHEESES: including Parmesan, Cheddar,

Monterey Jack, Roquefort or Gorgonzola, and chèvre.
- LEMONS, LIMES AND ORANGES: have on hand not only for the obvious reasons, but for their zest: grated citrus zest sprinkled into stews, for example, lends a special flavor.
- GOLDEN DELICIOUS APPLES: although I favor tarter apples (such as Granny Smith) in many cases, the Golden Delicious is good for salads as it does not discolor when sliced.

In the Freezer

- ICE CREAM: the best brand available—with a few additions, it can be quickly transformed into an impressive dessert.
- FROZEN RASPBERRIES AND STRAWBERRIES: for desserts and almost instant sauces.
- WALNUTS, HAZELNUTS, CASHEWS, BLANCHED ALMONDS: (they stay fresh longer in the freezer) serve as an hors d'oeuvre, or sauté for garnishes, side dishes and desserts.

Wines and Liquor

- MADEIRA, PORT, SHERRY AND BRANDY: for flavoring soups, fruit and enriching sauces.
- SAKE: for marinades and sauces.
- BOURBON OR SOURMASH WHISKEYS: good over ice cream, in dessert sauces and in sauces for veal or pork.
- DARK JAMAICA RUM: especially good for flavoring sweet dishes.
- LIQUEURS: such as Kirsch, apricot brandy, orange liqueurs (Grand Marnier, Orange Curaçao, Cointreau), framboise, Kahlúa, Chambord, crème de cassis—for flavoring fruit and desserts.

—Anne Walsh

BRUNCH & BREAKFAST

Easy Early-Morning Elegance

**Fresh Orange Juice
Flavored with Orange Flower Water
and Lime***

◆

**"Lost" Muffins with Sour Cream and
Strawberries***

Honey-Glazed Broiled Ham*

Jamaican Coffee

*RECIPE INCLUDED

What Americans refer to as French toast is called *pain perdu*—literally "lost bread"—by the French. The method and the French name for this international breakfast favorite were the inspiration for my variation, "lost" English muffins soaked in milk and eggs before being sautéed.

The result is a golden, crispy crust on the outside and a warm, moist custardlike interior. When topped with sour cream and sweetened fresh strawberries, these make for a satisfying and quite filling meal on their own. But for those who want an even more substantial, rib-sticking meal, slices of honey-glazed baked ham go beautifully with the muffins.

Freshly squeezed orange juice flavored with orange flower water and lime juice makes a refreshing eye-opener.

THE GAME PLAN

- Preheat the broiler.
- Make the juice.
- Prepare the strawberries.
- Make the egg mixture and soak the muffins.
- Make the honey-lemon glaze for the ham.
- Sauté the muffins and, while they cook, put the ham in to broil.
- Garnish the muffins with the berries and sour cream and serve with the hot glazed ham.
- **If Time Allows:** The juice can be made ahead of time.

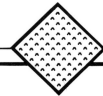

Two Servings

Fresh Orange Juice Flavored with Orange Flower Water and Lime

2 cups fresh orange juice
½ teaspoon orange flower water
2 teaspoons fresh lime juice

Divide the ingredients evenly between 2 tumblers or wine glasses, stir vigorously to blend and serve.

Honey-Glazed Broiled Ham

¼ to ⅓ pound pre-cooked ham steak, about ½ inch thick
1½ teaspoons lemon juice
1½ teaspoons honey

1 Preheat the broiler. Slash the fat along the edge of the ham in several places to prevent curling. Place the ham in a disposable broiler pan.

2 In a small bowl, blend the lemon juice and honey. Brush the ham steak with half of the lemon-honey mixture.

3 Broil the ham 3 inches from the heat source for 3 minutes. Turn and brush with the remaining lemon and honey mixture. Broil about 2 minutes more, until lightly browned.

"Lost" Muffins with Sour Cream and Strawberries

1 pint fresh strawberries, hulled
¼ cup sugar
3 eggs
2 tablespoons milk
1 teaspoon vanilla extract
Pinch of salt
2 English muffins, split
1½ tablespoons unsalted butter
¼ to ½ cup sour cream

1 Set aside 4 whole, unblemished strawberries for the garnish and slice the remaining berries. Place the sliced berries in a small bowl, sprinkle with the sugar, toss to coat and set aside.

2 In a large shallow dish, combine the eggs, milk, vanilla and salt. Beat together lightly.

3 Place the muffin halves, split-side down, in the egg-milk mixture and let them soak for 1 or 2 minutes, pricking them gently with a fork. Turn the muffins and soak another minute.

4 In a large skillet, melt the butter over low heat. Increase the heat to moderate, add the muffins and cook until golden brown, about 2 minutes. Turn and cook 1 to 2 minutes more, until browned. (The muffins should be crisp and golden on the outside and somewhat custardlike inside.)

5 Transfer the muffins to serving plates, top each half with sliced berries and a generous spoonful of sour cream. Garnish each with a whole strawberry and serve immediately.

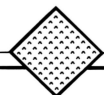

A Fireside Brunch

Aquavit Bloody Marys

Spinach and Avocado Salad*

Oyster Stew*

Russian Black Bread or Pumpernickel

Beverage Suggestion: Riesling from Alsace

———————————— ◆ ————————————

Oranges on the Half Shell*

Chocolate Cookies

*RECIPE INCLUDED

The dreary weekends of winter offer good opportunities to indulge yourself and friends in the inexpensive luxury of a warming brunch such as the one following. The entire menu can be readied in well under an hour. The foods—plump oysters, avocados, oranges—were selected to gladden the eye, cheer the palate and restore the spirits.

Some suggestions on procedures: first prepare the oranges for dessert only to the point of adding the liqueur and sugar. Next, prepare the salad, but dress the salad at the table. The final preparation should be the oyster stew, since the texture of the oysters is best when the stew is served immediately. The stew takes only a few minutes from start to finish. When shopping, select unsliced loaves of the freshest Russian black bread or pumpernickel available. Slice it just before serving.

The only danger-point in this meal involves the heating of the stew; do not allow it to boil or the half-and-half may curdle. If it does curdle, the presentation will be less appealing, but the flavor will be unchanged.

Bloody Marys made with aquavit or vodka are a good way to start this brunch. A dry, white wine or ice-cold ale will go well with the oyster stew.

———————————— THE GAME PLAN ————————————

- Prepare the oranges up to the point of adding the liqueur. Place on serving plates.

- Assemble the salad and make the dressing, but wait to dress the salad at the table.

- Serve the Bloody Marys.

- Make the oyster stew and serve immediately, along with the salad.

- Just before serving the dessert, sprinkle the oranges with liqueur and sugar, garnish and serve with the cookies.

○ **If Time Allows:** Halve the oranges and loosen the sections and make the salad dressing in advance.

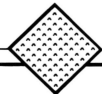

Four Servings

Oyster Stew

4 tablespoons unsalted butter
1 pint oysters, drained
1 quart half-and-half (or 2 cups light cream and 2 cups whole milk)
2 teaspoons salt
⅛ teaspoon freshly ground pepper
½ teaspoon paprika
3 to 4 tablespoons coarsely chopped celery leaves

1 Melt the butter in a large saucepan over medium low heat. Do not let it brown. Add the oysters and sauté them gently until their edges begin to curl, about 4 minutes. Pour in the half-and-half; add the salt and pepper. Heat almost to boiling, but do not allow the stew to boil.

2 Pour the stew into a warm tureen or into individual deep soup plates. Sprinkle with the paprika and chopped celery leaves.

Spinach and Avocado Salad

¾ pound spinach, stemmed and torn into bite-size pieces
1 large or 2 small avocados, peeled and sliced
Fresh lemon juice
4 scallions, sliced
6 tablespoons vegetable oil
3 to 4 dashes hot pepper sauce
Salt

1 Arrange the spinach on a serving plate or in a salad bowl.

2 To preserve their fresh color, place the avocado slices in a bowl, squeeze a little lemon juice over them, and toss until they are well coated. Arrange the avocado slices on top of the spinach. Sprinkle the scallions on top of the salad.

3 In a small bowl, combine 2 tablespoons lemon juice with the oil, hot sauce and salt to taste and whisk to combine. Pour into a serving dish and place on the table with the salad; dress the salad at the table.

Oranges on the Half Shell

4 large oranges
3 to 5 tablespoons orange liqueur, such as Cointreau, Grand Marnier or Triple Sec
Sugar
Sprigs of greenery, for garnish

1 With a sharp knife, cut the oranges in half crosswise and then cut about ⅛ inch of peel from the bottoms to provide the oranges with a flat base. Remove any seeds and loosen the sections with a grapefruit knife. Arrange the orange halves in a serving dish.

2 Sprinkle each half with 1 or 2 teaspoons of orange liqueur and top with a little sugar. Decorate with sprigs of greenery, if desired.

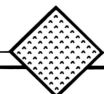

Southern-Style Breakfast

Sippin' Whiskey*

◆

Glazed Bacon with Walnuts*

Grits with Red-Pepper Butter*

Sliced Kiwis and Strawberries*

Shortening Bread*

French-Roast Coffee
or English or Irish Breakfast Tea

*RECIPE INCLUDED

Put on the skillet! Put on the lid!" and make yourself a Southern-style plantation breakfast. Sippin' Whiskey—bourbon stirred with a bit of marmalade and bitters and poured over crushed ice—gets things off to a glowing start.

Sweetened glazed bacon, crunchy with walnuts, and grits spiced with hot red-pepper butter are natural complements, decidedly "country" with a sophisticated twist. Refreshing sliced kiwis and strawberries follow, along with butter-rich shortening bread, which is delightful with a potent cup of steaming French-roast coffee or a strongly brewed English or Irish breakfast tea.

The glazed bacon with walnuts and the shortening bread—a rich cookie very similar to traditional Scottish shortbread—can be baked at the same time because they both require a 350° oven. Prepare the grits while the bacon is cooking. The shortening bread is best served at room temperature, so give it a chance to cool after you remove it from the oven. The crisp bacon should be eaten right away.

All this food is extremely simple to prepare, so the menu can be completed in next to no time. It is fine for breakfast, brunch or a late, late supper.

THE GAME PLAN

- Preheat the oven to 350°. Prepare the shortening bread dough and bake.

- Put the water for the grits on to boil. Slice the fruit and arrange on the plates.

- Start the grits. Prepare the bacon and put it in the oven to bake while serving Sippin' Whiskey.

- Prepare the Red-Pepper Butter and pour it over the grits just before serving with the hot bacon.

○ **If Time Allows:** The shortening bread can be made and the fruit sliced and tightly covered and refrigerated until serving time.

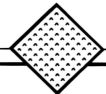

Four Servings

Sippin' Whiskey

6 ounces (¾ cup) sour mash whiskey or bourbon
4 teaspoons orange marmalade
⅛ to ¼ teaspoon Angostura bitters, to taste
Crushed ice
4 slices of orange, for garnish
4 sprigs of mint, for garnish

In a 2-cup measure, combine the whiskey, marmalade and bitters. Stir until the marmalade dissolves. Fill four old-fashioned glasses with crushed ice and pour the mixed toddies over the ice. Garnish each glass with a thin slice of orange and a mint sprig.

Glazed Bacon with Walnuts

1 pound sliced bacon
¼ cup packed dark brown sugar
1 teaspoon all-purpose flour
½ cup chopped walnuts

Preheat the oven to 350°. Arrange the bacon slices closely together but not overlapping on a broiler pan or fine wire rack over a dripping pan. In a bowl, combine the brown sugar, flour and walnuts; sprinkle evenly over the bacon. Bake until crisp and brown, about 30 minutes. Drain on paper towels.

Grits with Red-Pepper Butter

¾ teaspoon salt
¾ cup white hominy grits
1½ tablespoons unsalted butter
⅛ to ¼ teaspoon cayenne pepper, to taste
Chopped fresh parsley, for garnish

1 In a heavy medium saucepan, heat 3½ cups of water to boiling; add the salt. Stir in the grits, a little at a time. Return to a boil, reduce the heat and simmer, covered, for 25 minutes, stirring occasionally.

2 In a small saucepan or skillet, melt the butter and add the cayenne pepper. Pour the hot butter over the grits before serving. Garnish with a little chopped parsley, if you like, for added color and flavor.

Sliced Kiwis and Strawberries

4 kiwis, peeled and sliced
1 pint strawberries, hulled and sliced
Confectioners' sugar

Arrange kiwi and strawberry slices decoratively on individual serving plates. Pass a bowl of confectioners' sugar at table.

Shortening Bread

MAKES ABOUT 20 SQUARES

½ cup lightly salted butter
¼ cup light brown sugar
1½ cups all-purpose flour

Preheat the oven to 350°. Cream the butter and sugar together until light and fluffy. Mix in the flour until well blended. Form the dough into a ball; then roll it out to ½-inch thickness on a floured board. Using a sharp knife, cut into 1½-inch squares, or into attractive shapes using a cookie cutter. With a spatula, transfer to an ungreased cookie sheet and bake for 20 minutes, until pale brown. Let cool before serving.

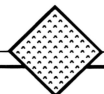

Winter Brunch for Company

Grapefruit with Brown Sugar-Rum Glaze*

◆

Broiled Halibut with Rarebit Sauce*

Green Salad with Anchovy-Leek Dressing*

Sautéed Tomatoes with Sage*

Hot Rolls or Toast

**Beverage Suggestion: Ale, such as
Ballantine's India Pale Ale, or a light red
wine, such as Valpolicella**

◆

Hot Coffee with Cream

*RECIPE INCLUDED

An ideal counterpoint to a chilly winter morning, this hearty company brunch serves four generously. It features fresh broiled halibut with a Cheddar cheese sauce, sautéed tomatoes flavored with sage and a green salad tossed with a piquant anchovy-leek dressing. A basket of crusty warm rolls or lightly buttered toast (flavorful sourdough is a particularly good choice) provides a nice foil for the rich rarebit sauce. Broiled grapefruit glazed with brown sugar and rum are appropriate either as an opening course or as a dessert.

A couple of do-ahead tips to help make preparation easy: the cheese sauce for the halibut can be prepared the night before, stored in the refrigerator and reheated shortly before serving. To easily handle last-minute cooking, first broil the grapefruit; leave the broiler turned on. Next, sauté the tomato slices and place them on a large, warm platter, loosely covered with foil to keep them warm. Broil the halibut, arrange on the platter with the tomatoes and spoon the rarebit sauce on top of the broiled halibut.

THE GAME PLAN

- Preheat the broiler.
- Make the rarebit sauce.
- Prepare the greens and dressing for the salad, but wait to toss together just before serving.
- Place the grapefruit in the broiler. Prepare the tomato slices.
- Remove the grapefruit from the broiler and serve. Meanwhile, place the fish in the hot broiler to cook.
- Sauté the tomatoes.
- Arrange the fish and tomatoes on a platter, top with the warm rarebit sauce and serve, accompanied by the salad.
- **If Time Allows:** The rarebit sauce and the anchovy-leek dressing can be made in advance. Store both covered in the refrigerator. Reheat the rarebit sauce just before serving.

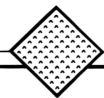

Four Servings

Grapefruit with Brown Sugar-Rum Glaze

2 grapefruit—halved crosswise, seeded and sectioned
4 tablespoons dark brown sugar
8 teaspoons dark rum

Preheat the broiler. Evenly sprinkle each grapefruit half with 1 tablespoon brown sugar and 2 teaspoons rum. Broil about 4 inches from the heat until the sugar is melted and bubbling, 3 to 4 minutes.

Green Salad with Anchovy-Leek Dressing

1 head of Boston lettuce, torn into bite-size pieces
½ small head of romaine lettuce, torn into bite-size pieces
¼ cup olive oil, preferably extra-virgin
1½ tablespoons red wine vinegar
⅛ teaspoon freshly ground pepper
8 flat anchovy fillets, cut into ⅛-inch pieces
1 small leek (white part only), thinly sliced

Place the Boston and romaine lettuce in a salad bowl. In a small bowl, whisk together the oil, vinegar, pepper, anchovies and leek. Pour over the greens and toss until well mixed.

Broiled Halibut with Rarebit Sauce

3 tablespoons unsalted butter
1 tablespoon all-purpose flour
¾ cup milk
¼ cup heavy cream
1 tablespoon Worcestershire sauce
¾ teaspoon powdered mustard
¼ teaspoon paprika
⅛ teaspoon cayenne pepper
1½ cups (about 6 ounces) shredded sharp Cheddar cheese
2 halibut, cod or tilefish steaks, cut 1¼ inches thick (about 1 pound each)
2 tablespoons fresh lemon juice
Chopped fresh parsley, for garnish

1 In a medium saucepan, melt 1 tablespoon of the butter. Add the flour and cook, stirring, over moderate heat without browning for 1 minute to make a roux. Whisk in the milk and cream. Bring to a boil, reduce the heat to low and simmer, whisking occasionally, until the sauce is thickened and smooth, 5 to 10 minutes.

2 Season with the Worcestershire sauce, mustard, paprika and cayenne. Add the cheese and stir until smooth. Remove from the heat and cover to keep the rarebit sauce warm.

3 Preheat the broiler. Arrange the halibut steaks on a lightly greased broiler pan. Dot with the remaining 2 tablespoons butter.

Broil about 4 inches from the heat for 5 minutes on the first side. Turn and broil for about 5 minutes longer, or until the fish is just opaque throughout.

4 Cut each halibut steak in half and transfer to a large, warm platter. Sprinkle with the lemon juice, spoon on the rarebit sauce and garnish with the parsley.

Sautéed Tomatoes with Sage

1 large tomato, cut into ½-inch-thick slices
2 tablespoons unsalted butter, melted
1 teaspoon crumbled sage
½ teaspoon coarse (kosher) salt
¼ cup yellow cornmeal
1 tablespoon vegetable oil

1 One at a time, dip the tomato slices on both sides in the melted butter. Sprinkle with the sage and salt; then coat well with the cornmeal.

2 In a large heavy skillet, heat the oil. Add the tomato slices and cook over moderately low heat, turning once, until lightly browned on both sides, 6 to 8 minutes.

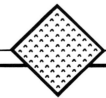

Jalapeño Frittatas for Six

**Salty Dogs* or Fresh
Grapefruit Juice in Salt-Rimmed
Glasses**

◆

**Monterey Jack and Pickled Jalapeño Pepper
Frittatas***

Apple Corn Muffins*

Puerto Rican Coffee

*RECIPE INCLUDED

A frittata, Italy's answer to the omelet, is traditionally served open-faced rather than folded over and has all ingredients mixed into the eggs before cooking. My version is slighty different; I've beaten jalapeño peppers into the eggs, sprinkled grated cheese over the top and reserved the remaining ingredients—black olives, avocado slices, scallions, jalapeño peppers and sour cream—to pile attractively on top after it has cooked. The result is an unusually colorful and fresh-tasting dish.

Like omelets, frittatas can be quickly made at the last moment—making them a good stand-by for when guests drop by unexpectedly; the variety of fillings is limited only by the imagination of the cook.

Some cooks make large frittatas for four to six and cut them in pie-shaped wedges. I prefer to make individual frittatas, or for two at the most. The eggs don't toughen as easily.

To make the cooking move along smoothly, assemble all of the ingredients ahead of time, mixing the eggs for each frittata in separate bowls.

THE GAME PLAN

- Preheat the oven to 425°. Prepare the muffin batter and bake. Take the muffins out and turn the oven up to broil.

- Assemble all the frittata ingredients and prepare the garnishes.

- Mix and serve the Salty Dogs.

- Make the frittatas, one at a time, and serve each immediately with the muffins.

- **If Time Allows:** The muffins can be made in advance.

Six Servings

Salty Dogs

Coarse (kosher) salt
3 cups fresh grapefruit juice
8 ounces (1 cup) light tequila
Pinch of superfine sugar
Ice cubes

1 Place the salt in a shallow dish. Dip the rims of six 6-ounce wine glasses in water, then in the salt.

2 Place the grapefruit juice, tequila, sugar and a few ice cubes in a cocktail shaker or a glass jar with a tight-fitting lid and shake vigorously. Strain into the salt-rimmed glasses and serve.

Monterey Jack and Pickled Jalapeño Pepper Frittatas

12 eggs
2 tablespoons minced, drained pickled jalapeño peppers
Salt
3 tablespoons unsalted butter
1⅓ cup grated Monterey Jack cheese

Accompaniments:
8 thin strips pickled jalapeño peppers
1 medium avocado, sliced and sprinkled with lemon juice
8 to 12 whole pitted black olives
2 tablespoons thinly sliced scallions
¼ cup sour cream

1 Preheat the broiler. In a small bowl, beat 6 of the eggs with 2 tablespoons of water and 1 tablespoon of the minced jalapeño peppers. Season with salt to taste.

2 In a 10- or 11-inch nonstick skillet, melt 1½ tablespoons of the butter over high heat until foaming but not browned. Tilt the pan to coat the bottom and sides well with butter.

3 Add the eggs, stir once with a fork and cook over high heat until the edges begin to set. Gently pull the edges of the eggs away from the sides of the pan so that the uncooked portion flows under the cooked edges. Continue in this manner until most of the liquid is set. The surface of the frittata should still be slightly runny.

4 Sprinkle the surface of the frittata with ⅔ cup of the cheese and place it under the hot broiler until the cheese melts and is lightly browned, about 1 minute. Divide in half, slide onto 2 warmed serving plates and garnish attractively with jalapeño pepper strips, avocados, olives, scallions and sour cream. Serve at once.

5 Repeat the process with the remaining ingredients.

Apple Corn Muffins

MAKES 12 MUFFINS

2 cups all-purpose flour
½ cup yellow cornmeal
⅓ cup lightly packed brown sugar
1 tablespoon baking powder
½ teaspoon salt
1 cup milk
1 egg, beaten
¼ cup unsalted butter, melted
1 large apple, preferably Granny Smith, peeled and coarsely diced

1 Preheat the oven to 425°. Lightly grease twelve 2½-inch muffin cups.

2 In a large mixing bowl, combine the flour, cornmeal, sugar, baking powder and salt and blend well. In a separate bowl, combine the milk, egg and butter and blend.

3 Add the apple and milk-egg mixture to the dry ingredients and mix lightly until the dry ingredients are just moistened; the batter will be slightly lumpy.

4 Fill each muffin cup about two-thirds full and bake for about 30 minutes, or until the muffins are golden and the tops spring back when touched.

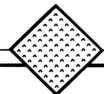

Fancy No-Fuss Breakfast

Sherry-Spiked Raisin, Date and Orange Salad*

◆

Nana's Scrambled Eggs with Tomato and Scallion in Buttery Croustades*

Crispy No-Fuss Bacon*

Coffee or English Breakfast Tea

*RECIPE INCLUDED

The centerpiece of this menu is my grandmother Nana's recipe for scrambled eggs with tomatoes and scallions heaped into buttery, brown croustades. It's an impressive-looking dish; those not in the know will think it required lengthy and elaborate preparation. Happily though, it's as quick and easy to make as it is pretty and delicious. Nana's secret is making quick croustades by hollowing out crusty hard rolls, brushing them with butter and toasting them in the oven.

Dates and raisins plumped in sherry and sprinkled over sliced oranges make a sweet, colorful salad, which may be served as a first course or a side dish along with the eggs and crisp bacon slices.

For the latter, four no-fuss methods for microwave, broiler and oven-cooked bacon are suggested. I much prefer these to pan-frying, which usually leaves me feeling somewhat fried myself.

THE GAME PLAN

- Combine the dates, raisins and sherry for the salad.
- Preheat the oven to 375°. Prepare the croustades and put them in to bake.
- Turn the oven up to 425° or to broil and cook the bacon according to one of the no-fuss methods.
- Assemble the salad.
- Sauté the scallions and tomatoes; add the eggs and scramble. Spoon into the toasted croustades. Serve hot with bacon and salad.
- **If Time Allows:** Assemble the salad and prepare the croustades for baking ahead of time.

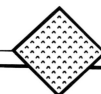

Two Servings

Sherry-Spiked Raisin, Date and Orange Salad

2 tablespoons chopped dates
2 tablespoons golden raisins
2 tablespoons sweet sherry
2 oranges, peeled and sliced into rounds
4 teaspoons brown sugar
Small bunches of green and red seedless grapes, for garnish

1 Place the dates and raisins in a small bowl; sprinkle with the sherry and let soak for at least 15 minutes.

2 Arrange the orange slices on individual serving plates and sprinkle with the brown sugar.

3 Spoon the dates, raisins and sherry over the orange slices. Garnish the plates with grapes and serve.

Nana's Scrambled Eggs with Tomato and Scallion in Buttery Croustades

2 hard rolls, about 3 inches in diameter
5 tablespoons unsalted butter, melted
1 or 2 scallions, thinly sliced
1 medium tomato—peeled, seeded and coarsely chopped
4 eggs, lightly beaten
Salt and freshly ground pepper

1 Preheat the oven to 375°. Carefully slice the top off of each roll and pinch out the soft centers, leaving a shell about ¼-inch thick.

2 Brush the insides of the rolls and the tops generously with 3 tablespoons of the melted butter. Place the rolls and tops on a baking sheet and bake until golden brown, about 5 minutes.

3 Meanwhile, in a medium skillet, heat the remaining 2 tablespoons butter over moderately low heat. Add the scallions and sauté, stirring, for 1 minute. Add the tomato and sauté 1 minute longer.

4 Stir in the eggs, season with salt and pepper to taste and scramble over moderately low heat until just set but still creamy. Spoon the eggs into the hot croustades and replace the toasted tops.

Crispy No-Fuss Bacon

Because of differences in water content and the thickness of slices, cooking time will vary from the times given in the following methods.

1 Broiled Bacon: For this, the quickest method, preheat the broiler. Place the bacon slices in one layer on a disposable aluminum broiler pan. Broil 6 inches from the heat source for 3 minutes. Using tongs, turn the bacon and broil 1 minute more. Drain the bacon on paper towels.

2 Oven-Fried Bacon: Preheat the oven to 425°. Line a baking sheet with aluminum foil. Place the bacon slices in one layer on the foil. Bake for 5 minutes. Using tongs, turn the bacon slices and continue to bake for about 4 more minutes. Drain the bacon on paper towels.

3 Baked Bacon: Preheat the oven to 425°. Line a baking sheet with aluminum foil and place a wire rack on top. Place the bacon slices in one layer on the rack and bake for about 10 minutes. Drain the bacon on paper towels.

4 Microwave: Cover the bottom of a glass or microwave baking dish with a sheet of plain white paper towel (colored towels bleed onto the food). Place the bacon strips in one layer on the paper towel and cover with a second sheet of paper towel. Cook on high power for 4 to 6 minutes.

Beet and Onion Salad with Escarole and Hearts of Palm Vinaigrette

PAGES 171 AND 119

Italian-Flavor Brunch

Campari Sunrises*

Spiced Walnuts*

◆

Baked Eggs Fonduta with Three Cheeses*

Cherry Tomatoes with Garlic and Parsley*

Beverage Suggestion: Barbaresco

◆

Italian Roast Coffee

Pears and Black Grapes

Amaretti Cookies

*RECIPE INCLUDED

Cheese and eggs are among the most natural and delicious pairings of ingredients imaginable, especially when baked over crusty Italian bread as they are here. This rich and creamy variation on the fonduta theme includes the traditional Fontina cheese, as well as Parmesan and Monterey Jack cheeses.

The cherry tomatoes add color and pizzazz to the menu. Toss all of the ingredients except the parsley together in advance if you can, so that the tomatoes have time to marinate. Sprinkle with the parsley just before serving.

Campari adds a rosy hue and a pleasant kick to fresh orange juice; it makes a perfect eye-opener to relax over, along with the spiced walnuts, while the fonduta bakes.

THE GAME PLAN

- Make the spiced walnuts.
- Prepare and toss together all of the ingredients for the cherry tomatoes except the parsley.
- Preheat the oven to 375°. Assemble the eggs and cheese and put in the oven to bake.
- Make the cocktails and serve while the fonduta is baking.
- Toss the tomatoes with the parsley and serve with the fonduta.
- **If Time Allows:** Prepare the cherry tomatoes in advance, reserving the parsley to sprinkle over the top just before serving. You can also beat the eggs, grate the cheeses and prepare the bread for the fonduta a little ahead, but wait until the last moment to assemble.

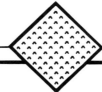

Four Servings

Campari Sunrises

Ice
6 ounces (¾ cup) Campari
Juice of 6 oranges (about 2 cups)

Fill four 8-ounce wine glasses with ice. Add a jigger (3 tablespoons) of the Campari to each and fill with the fresh orange juice. Stir and serve.

Spiced Walnuts

2 cups walnuts
¼ cup unsalted butter
½ teaspoon cumin
⅛ teaspoon cayenne pepper
¾ teaspoon coarse (kosher) salt

1. In a large heavy skillet, melt the butter over moderate heat. Add the cumin and cayenne and stir for 30 seconds.

2. Add the nuts and salt and cook, stirring, until the nuts are lightly toasted, about 3 minutes. Drain on paper towels.

Baked Eggs Fonduta with Three Cheeses

4 tablespoons unsalted butter, softened
1 garlic clove, halved
6 slices (1½ inches thick) Italian bread
¾ cup grated Fontina cheese
½ cup grated Monterey Jack cheese
¼ cup grated Parmesan cheese
2 eggs, beaten
1½ cups milk
¼ teaspoon powdered mustard
¼ teaspoon salt
¼ teaspoon freshly ground white pepper

1 Preheat the oven to 375°. Butter a 9-inch pie pan or round baking dish with a small amount of the butter and rub it well with the cut sides of the garlic clove.

2 Butter the bread slices on one side with the remaining butter and cut each slice into 4 quarters. Arrange the bread, buttered-side up, in the pan and sprinkle the cheeses evenly over the top.

3 In a mixing bowl, combine the eggs, milk, mustard, salt and pepper and beat together well. Pour the eggs evenly over the bread and cheese and bake for 25 to 30 minutes, until set and lightly browned on top. Cut into wedges and serve immediately.

Cherry Tomatoes with Garlic and Parsley

1 pint cherry tomatoes, halved
2 garlic cloves, minced
2 tablespoons olive oil
2 teaspoons fresh lemon juice
¼ teaspoon salt
⅓ cup coarsely chopped fresh parsley

In a large mixing bowl, combine the cherry tomatoes, garlic, oil, lemon juice and salt and toss well. Cover and chill until ready to serve. Just before serving, sprinkle the parsley over and toss.

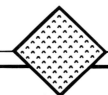

Chill-Chasing Brunch

Ale or Chilled Aquavit

Radish and Cucumber Tea Sandwiches on Pumpernickel*

◆

Sausages Braised in Ale*

Old-Fashioned Scalloped Red Potatoes and Onions*

Sautéed Apple and Lemon Slices*

Beverage Suggestion: Anchor Steam or New Amsterdam Amber Beer

◆

German Cookies

Clusters of Black Grapes

Coffee

*RECIPE INCLUDED

On blustery winter days, I like to cozy up to a plate of steaming sausages in ale, old-fashioned creamy potatoes and onions, and warm, buttery apple slices, slightly tart with lemon.

The cooking of this menu is almost as comforting as the supping; it's practically effortless and fills the kitchen with wonderful aromas.

Start preparing the potatoes and onions first. Then put the sausages on to simmer and proceed to sautéing the apples and lemons.

Pumpernickel tea sandwiches are good to nibble on as you sip some ale or swig a firey shot of aquavit. Homemade cookies and fruit make a nice dessert for this hearty meal. With all these comforting foods, who cares how much the wind howls outside?

THE GAME PLAN

- Preheat the oven to 350°. Steam the potatoes and onions.

- Make the tea sandwiches.

- Place the potatoes and onions in the oven to bake, and start cooking the sausages.

- Meanwhile, serve the ale or aquavit with the tea sandwiches.

- Start sautéing the apples and lemons about 10 minutes before the sausages and potatoes are ready to serve.

○ **If Time Allows:** The tea sandwiches can be made ahead and the potatoes and onions steamed and assembled with the remaining ingredients in advance.

Four Servings

Radish and Cucumber Tea Sandwiches on Pumpernickel

24 slices cocktail-size pumpernickel
3 tablespoons unsalted butter, softened
1 tablespoon prepared white horseradish, drained
2 teaspoons Dijon-style or Düsseldorf mustard
1 bunch of radishes (12 to 18), thinly sliced
½ of a large cucumber, thinly sliced

1 Lay the bread out on a flat surface and butter one side of each slice generously with the butter. Spread half of the slices with the horseradish and the remaining slices with the mustard.

2 Arrange sliced radishes on six of the horseradish-spread slices of bread and arrange sliced cucumbers on the remaining six horseradish-spread slices.

3 Top each sandwich with a mustard-spread bread slice. Cover with a damp paper towel and refrigerate until serving time.

Sausages Braised in Ale

1 pound large pork sausage links, about 1½ inches in diameter
1 tablespoon unsalted butter
1 slice of onion
1 bay leaf
½ teaspoon crumbled sage
3 peppercorns
1 bottle (12 ounces) of ale

1 Prick the sausages with a fork and place in a large skillet with ½ cup of water. Cover and simmer over moderately low heat for 5 minutes.

2 Pour off the fat and liquid from the skillet, add the butter and sauté the sausages, turning, until lightly browned all over.

3 Add the onion slice, bay leaf, sage, peppercorns and ale and simmer over moderately low heat for 15 minutes, turning the sausages occasionally. Season with salt if needed. Serve hot.

Old-Fashioned Scalloped Red Potatoes and Onions

1½ pounds small red potatoes, unpeeled and cut into ¼-inch slices
½ pound small yellow onions, peeled and quartered
Salt and freshly ground pepper
1 tablespoon unsalted butter
½ cup heavy cream
1 tablespoon chopped fresh parsley

1 Preheat the oven to 350°. Meanwhile, steam the potatoes and onions until fork tender, 10 to 15 minutes.

2 Place the steamed vegetables in a shallow, buttered baking dish and season with salt and pepper to taste. Dot with the butter and drizzle the cream evenly over the top. Bake for about 15 minutes, or until the cream is bubbling, thick and somewhat absorbed by the vegetables. Sprinkle with the parsley and serve hot.

Sautéed Apple and Lemon Slices

3 tablespoons unsalted butter
3 tart-sweet apples (preferably Granny Smith)—peeled, cored and sliced
4 thin slices of lemon, quartered

1 In a large skillet, melt the butter. When it begins to foam, add the apple and lemon slices and sauté over moderately low heat for 5 minutes.

2 Turn the fruit and continue cooking until the apples are tender but still somewhat firm and lightly browned. Serve hot.

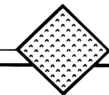

15-Minute Breakfast for Two

Honeyed Honeydew Melon Juice*

**Eggs en Cocotte with Black
Forest Ham***

Butterscotch and Lemon Toast*

French Roasted Coffee with Hot Milk

*RECIPE INCLUDED

From the moment you start the coffee brewing, this elegant little breakfast can be put together in about 15 minutes.

The butterscotch and lemon toast fill the kitchen with wonderful aromas and the eggs baked in individual ramekins with strips of rich Black Forest ham and chives on top should stir even small morning appetites. If you don't have Black Forest ham, a wide variety of ingredients can be substituted including Canadian bacon, small bits of bacon or sausage, sautéed chicken livers or asparagus tips. Take care to butter the ramekins thoroughly and not to overcook the eggs. The ramekins retain heat and continue to cook the eggs after they have been taken from the oven. Take them out when the whites are just set; the yolks should remain runny.

Break out your prettiest, most delicate china and some fine linen, and arrange a few wild flowers in a vase to make this effortless menu into a breakfast of splendor.

THE GAME PLAN

- Preheat the oven to 375°. Prepare the eggs and place the ramekins in the oven.
- Make the juice and toast the toast.
- Remove the eggs from the oven and turn the setting to broil.
- Finish the toast in the broiler.
- Sprinkle the eggs with pepper and chives and serve at once with the hot toast.
- **If Time Allows:** The juice can be prepared in advance. Stir just before serving.

Two Servings

Honeyed Honeydew Melon Juice

1 cup coarsely chopped
  honeydew melon
1 to 2 tablespoons honey, to taste
1½ tablespoons fresh lime juice
2 ice cubes
Lime wedges, for garnish

Place the melon, honey, lime juice, ice cubes and ¾ cup of water in a blender container and whir for several seconds until smooth and well blended. Pour into two wine glasses. Place a lime wedge on the rim of each glass.

Butterscotch and Lemon Toast

4 thin slices firm-textured white
  bread
Unsalted butter, softened
2 teaspoons dark brown sugar
1 teaspoon confectioners' sugar
½ teaspoon lemon juice

1 Toast the bread in a toaster.

2 Preheat the broiler. Spread the toast generously with butter. Evenly sprinkle 1 teaspoon brown sugar each over 2 of the bread slices. Sprinkle ½ teaspoon confectioners' sugar and about ¼ teaspoon lemon juice each over the remaining 2 slices.

3 Return the bread to the broiler and broil until the sugar melts and the edges are lightly browned.

Eggs en Cocotte with Black Forest Ham

4 eggs, at room temperature
2 tablespoons heavy cream
2 slices Black Forest ham, cut into
  2-inch-long julienne strips
Freshly ground pepper
1 teaspoon chopped chives or
  finely chopped scallions

1 Preheat the oven to 375°. Break 2 eggs into each of two well-buttered 6-ounce ramekins. Add 1 tablespoon of cream to each. Divide the Black Forest ham between the 2 ramekins.

2 Bake for 10 to 15 minutes, until the whites of the eggs are just set. The whites should be set, but the yolks still a little runny. Grind a little pepper over the top, garnish with chives and serve hot.

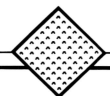

Hearty Country Breakfast

Spicy Hot Mulled Cider*

◆

**Country Omelet
with Cheddar, Spinach, Scallion and
Tomato***

Broiled New Potatoes with Thyme*

Toasted Pumpernickel

**Beverage Suggestion: Provençal Rosé, such
as Bandol**

*RECIPE INCLUDED

A hearty, fortifying country menu full of delicious fresh flavors! The omelet, heaped with Cheddar cheese, fresh spinach and tomatoes, was inspired by one I had at a cozy restaurant in a village on the Delaware River. It made a wonderful breakfast before setting off on a day of touring.

Contrary to popular opinion, omelet-making is not difficult, nor does it take long practice to master the art. I have seen butter-fingered novices prepare impeccable omelets when armed with a good nonstick skillet.

The proper pan of a size suitable for the number of eggs used—7 to 8 inches across the bottom for a 2- to 3-egg omelet—is one of the keys to success. A bit of organization helps also, especially when you're making omelets for guests. Measure all of the ingredients in advance and beat the eggs for each omelet in separate bowls before beginning.

Omelets readily qualify as "fast food" when prepared for no more than four guests. Beyond that number, I feel the cook stays too long at the stove.

THE GAME PLAN

- Make the cider.
- Assemble all the ingredients for the omelets, beating the eggs for each in separate bowls. Sauté the vegetable filling.
- Start steaming the potatoes. Preheat the broiler.
- Make the first omelet (toasting one portion of pumpernickel at the same time).
- Finish the potatoes and serve with the first omelet and toast. Keep the remaining potatoes warm while preparing the remaining three omelets, one order at a time.
- **If Time Allows:** The cider can be made in advance and warmed up just before serving. The potatoes can also be steamed ahead.

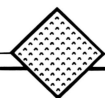

Four Servings

Spicy Hot Mulled Cider

½ teaspoon allspice berries
1 small stick of cinnamon
10 whole cloves
1 quart apple cider
4 julienne strips of orange zest
Freshly grated nutmeg

1 Tie the allspice, cinnamon and cloves in a small square of cheesecloth.

2 Pour the cider into a large noncorrodible saucepan. Add the spice sachet and warm over moderately low heat for about 10 minutes. Pour the cider into mugs with a strip of orange zest. Grate a little nutmeg into each mug and serve hot.

Country Omelet with Cheddar, Spinach, Scallion and Tomato

10 teaspoons unsalted butter
⅓ cup coarsely chopped, peeled and seeded tomato
8 teaspoons chopped scallions
5 ounces fresh spinach leaves, stemmed and torn into bite-size pieces

8 eggs
Salt
Freshly ground white pepper
½ cup grated sharp Cheddar cheese

1 In a small skillet, melt 2 teaspoons of the butter over moderate heat. Add the tomato, scallions and spinach. Sauté until the spinach wilts, about 30 seconds. Remove from the heat and set aside.

2 In a small bowl, beat 2 of the eggs lightly and season with salt and white pepper to taste. (For fast and easy preparation, put the beaten eggs for each omelet in a separate bowl.)

3 In a 7- to 8-inch nonstick skillet or well-seasoned omelet pan, melt 2 teaspoons of the butter over high heat until foaming but not browned. Tilt the pan to coat the bottom and sides with butter.

4 Pour in the eggs, stir once with a fork and cook over high heat until the edges begin to set. Prick the bottom of the omelet with a fork and gently pull the edges away from the sides of the pan so that the uncooked portion flows under the cooked edge. Continue in this manner until most of the liquid is set, about 20 seconds. The surface of the omelet should still be slightly runny.

5 Sprinkle 2 tablespoons of the cheese and one-fourth of the sautéed vegetable mixture over the omelet. Fold half the omelet over onto itself and continue cooking for 10 to 15 seconds more. Turn onto a warmed plate and serve immediately.

6 Repeat the process with the remaining ingredients to make 3 more omelets.

Broiled New Potatoes with Thyme

10 to 12 small new potatoes (about 1 pound), unpeeled
3 tablespoons unsalted butter, melted
4 sprigs of fresh thyme or ¼ teaspoon dried
Coarse (kosher) salt
Fresh coarsely ground pepper

1 Steam the potatoes until fork tender, about 10 minutes. Cut in quarters.

2 Preheat the broiler. Line a broiler pan or a baking sheet with aluminum foil and brush generously with some of the melted butter.

3 Place the quartered potatoes on the pan, brush generously with the remaining butter and sprinkle with the thyme, and salt and pepper to taste. Broil until lightly browned, 3 to 6 minutes.

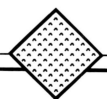

English Breakfast for Four

**Honeydew or Crenshaw Melon with
Lime Wedges**

◆

Parslied Eggs in Baked Tomato Shells*

Sautéed Mushroom Caps with Bacon*

**English Scones
with Crystallized Orange Peel and
Golden Raisins***

English Breakfast Tea or Coffee

*RECIPE INCLUDED

The English know about as well as any civilized people how to make breakfast a meal that warms the soul as well as the body. This English-style breakfast seems elaborate, but it requires only a short amount of time in the kitchen. The results are dazzling; it's a good choice for holidays and for entertaining.

Warm, baked tomato shells are an attractive way to present eggs. Here I've scrambled them, but poached eggs could also be served this way. The sautéed mushrooms and bacon add a substantial note and pleasing contrast. The warm fresh scones, studded with crystallized orange peel and golden raisins, are the crowning touch. Be sure to have lots of sweet butter on hand for the scones.

THE GAME PLAN

- Preheat the oven to 450°. Prepare the scones and put them in to bake.
- Meanwhile, prepare the melon, garnish with the lime wedges and set aside. Scoop out the tomatoes, salt and let drain.
- Remove the scones from the oven and keep them warm. Reduce the oven heat to 350° and bake the tomato shells.
- Meanwhile, start the bacon and mushrooms.
- Serve the melon.
- Sauté the scallions, add the eggs and scramble. Spoon the eggs into the tomato shells and serve at once with the warm scones, bacon and mushrooms.
- **If Time Allows:** The scones and melon can be made ahead. Reheat the scones before serving.

Four Servings

Parslied Eggs in Baked Tomato Shells

4 firm-ripe medium tomatoes
Salt
8 eggs, lightly beaten
3 tablespoons unsalted butter
2 scallions, finely chopped
4 tablespoons chopped fresh
    parsley
Freshly ground pepper

1 Preheat the oven to 350°. Carefully slice the tops from the tomatoes and scoop out and discard the seeds and pulp leaving a shell ¼ inch thick. Lightly salt the interiors of the tomato shells and invert them on a rack to drain for 15 minutes.

2 Place the tomatoes, still inverted, on a rack in a baking pan and bake for 7 to 10 minutes, until tender but still somewhat firm.

3 Season the eggs lightly with salt. In a large skillet, melt the butter over moderately low heat until it begins to foam. Add the scallions and sauté for 1 minute. Add the eggs and scramble over low heat until set but still creamy, sprinkling half the parsley over them just before they are done.

4 Spoon the eggs generously into each tomato shell, and sprinkle with pepper and the remaining parsley and serve hot.

Sautéed Mushroom Caps with Bacon

¾ pound mushrooms
6 slices of bacon, cut into 1-inch
    pieces

1 Wipe the mushrooms clean and trim the stems even with the caps.

2 In a large skillet, sauté the bacon until lightly browned. Remove with a slotted spoon and drain on paper towels.

3 Pour all but about 2 tablespoons of the bacon fat from the skillet and add the mushrooms in a single layer, stem-ends up. Sauté over moderately low heat until golden brown; turn and sauté 2 minutes more, until tender but firm. Drain off any liquid and fat.

4 Return the bacon to the skillet and toss with the mushroom caps over moderate heat until hot.

English Scones with Crystallized Orange Peel and Golden Raisins

1½ tablespoons diced crystallized
    orange peel
1½ tablespoons golden raisins
2 teaspoons sherry or Madeira

1½ cups all-purpose flour
1½ tablespoons sugar
1½ teaspoons baking powder
½ teaspoon salt
4 tablespoons unsalted butter, cut
    into small pieces
1 egg, beaten
½ cup milk or cream
Sugar, for sprinkling

1 Preheat the oven to 450°. Place the orange peel and raisins in a small bowl, sprinkle with the sherry and let soak for 15 minutes.

2 In a large mixing bowl, combine the flour, sugar, baking powder and salt. Cut the butter into the dry ingredients until the mixture resembles coarse meal.

3 Drain the orange peel and raisins and stir them into the dry ingredients.

4 In a small mixing bowl, beat the egg and milk together. Reserve 1 tablespoon of the egg-milk mixture for a glaze. Make a well in the dry ingredients, add the remaining egg-milk mixture and mix lightly with a fork just until the dry ingredients are moistened.

5 Turn the dough out onto a floured surface and knead for a few seconds. Pat the dough out into a ½-inch-thick round and cut into 6 pie-shaped wedges. Brush each wedge with the reserved egg-milk mixture and sprinkle lightly with sugar. Place on a greased baking sheet and bake 13 to 15 minutes, until golden brown.

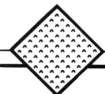

A Summer Brunch

Iced Ginger Beer with Rum*

◆

**Broiled Sea Trout with Watercress-
Watermelon Pickle Butter***

Steamed New Potatoes

Orange-Glazed Muffins*

Beverage Suggestion: Muscadet de Sèvre et Maine

◆

Coffee

*RECIPE INCLUDED

The English and Scandinavians, as well as sport-fishermen everywhere, know the pleasure of eating fish for breakfast.

One of my favorite dishes for a leisurely weekend breakfast is this broiled sea trout in a butter sauce flecked with watercress and watermelon pickles. Almost any firm-fleshed fish, including sea bass, scrod or red snapper, is delicious prepared with this simple sauce.

If you aren't lucky enough to have a dear little grandma who pickles and puts up watermelon rind for you, this pleasantly crunchy condiment can often be found in well-stocked supermarkets or specialty food shops. If they're not available, mixed sweet pickles can be substituted.

Prepare the muffins first and while they cook do the preparation work required for the fish, such as chopping the watercress and watermelon pickles. Start steaming the potatoes while serving the ginger beer and broil the fish last; it's best when taken straight from the broiler to the table.

THE GAME PLAN

- Preheat the oven to 400°. Prepare the muffins and bake.

- Meanwhile, prepare the fish fillets for the broiler. Make the watercress-watermelon pickle butter; keep warm.

- Make the orange glaze and spoon over muffins as they come out of the oven. Turn the oven up to broil.

- Start steaming the potatoes and serve the ginger beer.

- Place the fish in the preheated broiler and broil while finishing cocktails.

○ **If Time Allows:** The muffins can be made in advance and reheated just before serving.

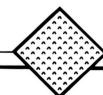

Four Servings

Iced Ginger Beer with Rum

Ice
6 ounces light rum
3 bottles (8 ounces each) ginger beer
4 wedges of lime

Fill four tall glasses with ice. Add 1½ ounces of rum to each. Fill with ginger beer. Squeeze a lime wedge over each, drop the lime into the glass, stir and serve.

Broiled Sea Trout with Watercress-Watermelon Pickle Butter

2 pounds sea trout or sea bass fillet, skinned and cut into four equal pieces
2 tablespoons unsalted butter, melted
Salt and freshly ground pepper
8 wedges of lemon
Watercress-Watermelon Pickle Butter
Watercress sprigs, for garnish

1 Line the broiler pan with aluminum foil and place it 3 to 4 inches from the heat. Preheat the broiler.

2 Brush each piece of fillet with ½ tablespoon of the melted butter. Season with salt and pepper to taste and squeeze a lemon wedge over each.

3 Place the fillets on the broiler pan and broil until just opaque throughout and the flesh flakes easily with a fork, 8 to 10 minutes, depending on the thickness of the fillets. (The general rule is to broil fish 10 minutes per inch of thickness.)

4 Transfer the fish to a warmed serving platter or individual plates. Spoon the Watercress-Watermelon Pickle Butter over the fish and garnish with watercress sprigs and the remaining lemon wedges.

Watercress-Watermelon Pickle Butter

3 tablespoons unsalted butter
2 tablespoons fresh lemon juice
1 tablespoon minced shallot
1 teaspoon cider vinegar
2 tablespoons finely chopped watercress
1½ tablespoons finely chopped, drained watermelon pickle
Dash of cayenne pepper

1 In a small saucepan, melt the butter over low heat. Stir in the lemon juice, shallots and vinegar and stir until the shallots are translucent, about 30 seconds; do not let brown.

2 Stir in the watercress and watermelon pickle and stir until warmed through. Stir in the cayenne.

Orange-Glazed Muffins

MAKES 12 MUFFINS

1¾ cups all-purpose flour
6 tablespoons sugar
2½ teaspoons baking powder
½ teaspoon salt
1 egg, lightly beaten
¾ cup milk
5½ tablespoons unsalted butter, melted
¼ cup fresh orange juice

1 Preheat the oven to 400°. Lightly grease twelve 2½-inch muffin cups.

2 In a large mixing bowl, combine the flour, 2 tablespoons of the sugar, the baking powder and salt. Add the egg, milk and butter and mix lightly, until the dry ingredients are just moistened; the batter will be slightly lumpy.

3 Fill each muffin cup about two-thirds full and bake for about 20 minutes, or until the muffins are golden and the tops spring back when touched.

4 Meanwhile, combine the orange juice with the remaining 4 tablespoons sugar in a small saucepan and simmer over low heat for about 5 minutes, stirring frequently.

5 Spoon the warm orange glaze over the hot muffins in their pan. Allow to cool slightly. Remove the muffins from the pan and serve warm.

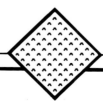

Brunch Fit for a Rajah

**Eggs in Curry
Sauce with Three Bell Peppers***

Mango Chutney

Pulao with Golden Raisins and Cashews*

Cucumber and Watercress Raita*

**Beverage Suggestion: Fruity white wine, such as
California Moscato Cannelli**

◆

Raspberry Sorbet

*RECIPE INCLUDED

This menu is for a summer brunch as bright and fragrant as a rajah's garden. The flavors sparkle, the textures are varied and the colors are a feast for the eyes.

Thankfully though, it doesn't take the rajah's palace staff or endless hours to prepare. In fact, it takes very little work—less than an hour of preparation from start to finish.

Prepare the base for the curry sauce in advance, if you wish, but reserve the cream and bell peppers to stir in at the last moment. The raita can also be made an hour or so ahead.

Start preparing the eggs and pulao about 30 minutes before serving. The eggs should still be hot when added to the warm curry sauce.

A sweet fruity chutney is the perfect partner for these curried eggs. Any good bottled chutney such as Major Grey's will do, or you can make your own fresh fruit chutney.

THE GAME PLAN

- Start the pulao and put the eggs on to cook.
- Meanwhile, make the raita, cover and refrigerate.
- Make the curry sauce.
- Drain and peel the eggs and add them to the warm sauce just before serving.
- **If Time Allows:** A few hours ahead of time, you can make the raita, cover and chill and make the curry sauce, reserving the cream and bell peppers to stir in as the sauce warms just before serving time.

Four Servings

Eggs in Curry Sauce with Three Bell Peppers

8 eggs
2 tablespoons unsalted butter
2 medium onions, finely chopped
1½ tablespoons all-purpose flour
1½ teaspoons Madras curry powder
½ cup Sauternes or other sweet white wine
1 Golden Delicious apple—peeled, cored and chopped
¼ cup heavy cream
½ cup diced bell pepper—preferably a mixture of red, green and black
Salt

1 Place the eggs in a large saucepan, add enough cold water to cover by 1 inch and bring just to a boil over moderately high heat. Remove from the heat, cover and let stand for 15 to 20 minutes.

2 Meanwhile, in a medium saucepan, melt the butter over low heat. Add the onion and sauté until softened but not browned.

3 Stir in the flour and curry powder. Gradually stir in the wine and 1½ cups of water. Add the apple and simmer over low heat for about 10 minutes.

4 Stir in the cream and bell peppers, season with salt to taste and cook 1 minute more.

5 Drain and peel the eggs and add to the curry sauce. Heat the eggs in the sauce for 1 or 2 minutes. Serve hot.

Cucumber and Watercress Raita

1 cup plain yogurt
½ cup peeled, seeded and coarsely diced cucumber
½ teaspoon sugar
⅛ teaspoon cayenne pepper
½ cup coarsely chopped watercress

In a small bowl, combine the yogurt, cucumber, sugar and cayenne pepper and blend well. Refrigerate, covered, until chilled. Turn into a serving bowl, sprinkle with the watercress and serve.

Pulao with Golden Raisins and Roasted Cashews

1 cup chicken broth
1 cup converted rice
1 tablespoon unsalted butter
½ teaspoon salt
⅓ cup golden raisins
½ cup salted, roasted cashew pieces
2 scallions, finely sliced

1 In a large saucepan, combine the broth and 1½ cups of water and bring to a boil.

2 Stir in the rice, butter and salt. Bring back to a boil over high heat, stir once, cover and cook over low heat for 12 to 15 minutes.

3 Stir in the raisins and cook 5 minutes more.

4 Fluff the rice with a fork and turn into a warmed serving bowl or platter. Sprinkle with the cashews and scallions and serve hot.

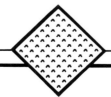

Quick Warm-Up Breakfast

Winter Fruit with Honey and Lemon*

◆

Irish Oatmeal Brûlée*

Canadian Bacon on Buttered Whole-Grain Toast*

Irish Breakfast Tea or Coffee

*RECIPE INCLUDED

What could be more warming than a bowl of hot Irish oatmeal with a rich, bubbling brown sugar glaze?

Irish oatmeal is known and loved by many for its full, nutty flavor, and although the traditional type takes time to cook, there are now some excellent instant versions available, such as the one made by McCann's.

My "brûlée" method makes this hearty cold-weather fare even richer when topped with a little heavy cream and dark brown sugar and popped under the broiler to brown briefly.

The sweet-tart mixture of honey and lemon juice is delicious drizzled over pears and bananas or almost any other fruit that's available.

And for those with really big appetites, I suggest a piece of warm Canadian bacon between slices of nutritious whole-grain toast to round out this per-fect-for-chilly-winter-mornings meal.

THE GAME PLAN

- Preheat the broiler.
- Make the Winter Fruit with Honey and Lemon.
- Start cooking the oatmeal.
- Meanwhile, start cooking the Canadian bacon.
- Toast the bread.
- Ladle the oatmeal into individual bowls, top with the cream and brown sugar and place in the hot broiler.
- Finish assembling the Canadian bacon sandwiches. Serve hot with the oatmeal and the fruit.
- **If Time Allows:** Prepare the fruit and drizzle it with the honey and lemon ahead of time.

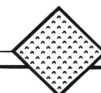

Four to Six Servings

Irish Oatmeal Brûlée

4 cups milk
1½ teaspoons salt
2 cups quick-cooking Irish
    oatmeal, such as McCann's
½ to ¾ cup heavy cream
6 tablespoons dark brown sugar

1 Preheat the broiler.

2 In a large saucepan, combine the milk, 2 cups of water and the salt and bring to a boil. Sprinkle the oatmeal slowly onto the surface of the liquid so that it does not stop boiling, and boil gently over moderate heat, stirring from time to time, for about 5 minutes.

3 Ladle the cooked oatmeal into individual heatproof bowls. Pour 1 or 2 tablespoons heavy cream around the edge of each bowl, and sprinkle the center with 1 to 1½ tablespoons of the brown sugar, to taste.

4 Place the bowls under the hot broiler and broil until the sugar melts and begins to bubble, 30 to 60 seconds. Serve hot.

Winter Fruit with Honey and Lemon

3 tablespoons honey
⅓ cup fresh lemon juice
3 medium firm-ripe pears—
    peeled, cored and sliced
3 bananas, sliced
Small clusters of red seedless
    grapes, for garnish

1 In a small bowl, combine the honey and lemon juice and blend together well.

2 Arrange the pears and bananas attractively in individual bowls. Drizzle the honey-lemon mixture over the fruit and hang a small cluster of grapes on the rim of each bowl.

Canadian Bacon on Buttered Whole-Grain Toast

5 tablespoons unsalted butter,
    softened
6 slices of Canadian bacon
12 thin slices whole-grain bread

1 Preheat the broiler. In a large skillet, melt 1 tablespoon of the butter. Add the Canadian bacon and sauté over moderately low heat for 1 to 2 minutes, until heated through and lightly browned. Drain the bacon on paper towels.

2 Place the bread slices in one layer on a large baking sheet and broil until lightly toasted.

3 Remove from the broiler, turn the slices over and spread the untoasted sides with the remaining 4 tablespoons butter.

4 Return the bread to the broiler and broil until the edges are lightly browned.

5 Remove the toast from the broiler and place a slice of the Canadian bacon on each of six slices of the toast. Top with the remaining six toast slices. Trim the crusts and serve.

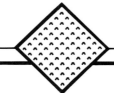

Impromptu and Festive Brunch

Brandy Old-Fashioneds*

◆

Pain Perdu*

Cider Syrup*

Sausage Patties with Fresh Ginger*

**Orange Salad
with Green Grapes and Grand
Marnier***

◆

Coffee

Thin Chocolate Mints

*RECIPE INCLUDED

Some weekends there's just no telling who will drop by or when. So it's good to have a few festive but easy brunch menus on hand that work well for two to 12 and make this kind of entertaining almost carefree.

This menu has just such magic. The main dish is plump, warm and very comforting Pain Perdu, the grandmother of French toast. It is served with a lavish splash of fragrant, hot cider syrup and is accompanied by patties of aromatic, homemade sausage, spiced with fresh ginger. Any of these recipes can be doubled, or even tripled, with ease, and each takes little more than 15 minutes to prepare. Adding to the cheer are Brandy Old-Fashioneds and a salad of oranges, grapes and watercress, laced with Grand Marnier.

THE GAME PLAN

- Make the salad.
- Form the sausage patties and assemble all the ingredients for the Pain Perdu.
- Start cooking the sausage and simmering the cider syrup while serving the Brandy Old-Fashioneds.
- Make the Pain Perdu and serve immediately with the sausage, cider syrup and salad.
- ○ **If Time Allows:** Mix the sausage and form the patties in advance. Make the cider syrup and reheat before serving. Assemble the salad, reserving the Grand Marnier to sprinkle over at the last moment.

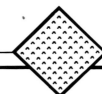

Four Servings

Brandy Old-Fashioneds

1 teaspoon sugar
6 ounces (¾ cup) brandy
Angostura bitters
Ice
4 thin slices of orange, for garnish

In each of four old-fashioned glasses, stir ¼ teaspoon of the sugar and 1½ ounces of the brandy until the sugar dissolves. Add 2 to 3 dashes of bitters to each glass, fill each with ice and stir. Garnish each glass with a slice of orange.

Orange Salad with Green Grapes and Grand Marnier

1 bunch of watercress
4 navel oranges, peeled and cut crosswise into ¼-inch slices
¼ cup Grand Marnier
1 pound seedless green grapes, cut into small clusters

Make a bed of watercress on a serving platter. Arrange the orange slices on top and sprinkle with the Grand Marnier. Garnish the platter with the clusters of grapes. Serve at room temperature or refrigerate, covered, until chilled.

Pain Perdu

¾ cup milk
1½ teaspoons sugar
1 teaspoon vanilla extract
2 eggs, beaten
2 tablespoons unsalted butter
2 tablespoons vegetable oil
8 slices (about 1 inch thick) stale Italian or French bread or brioche
Confectioners' sugar (optional)
Cider Syrup

1 In a shallow dish, mix the milk, sugar and vanilla. Place the eggs in another shallow dish.

2 In a large skillet, melt 1 tablespoon of the butter in 1 tablespoon of the oil over moderate heat. Dip 4 of the bread slices first in the milk mixture and then in the egg. Add to the skillet and sauté, turning once, until lightly browned on both sides, about 3 minutes. Repeat with the remaining ingredients.

3 Serve hot, sprinkled with confectioners' sugar and accompanied with hot Cider Syrup.

Cider Syrup

MAKES 1 CUP

2½ cups fresh apple cider
1 cinnamon stick or 1 tablespoon Calvados

Put the cider and cinnamon in a small saucepan. Bring to a boil and continue to boil until reduced to 1 cup, about 15 minutes. Remove the cinnamon before serving. The syrup will be quite thin. Serve hot.

Sausage Patties with Fresh Ginger

1 pound ground pork
1 teaspoon salt
½ teaspoon freshly ground pepper
1 tablespoon chopped fresh ginger
½ teaspoon crumbled sage
2 tablespoons chopped fresh parsley

1 Mix all the ingredients together until blended. Form into 8 small patties, about 2 inches in diameter.

2 In an ungreased cast iron or heavy nonstick skillet, brown the sausage patties over moderately high heat, about 2 minutes on each side. Reduce the heat to moderately low and cook, turning once, until there is no trace of pink in the center, about 15 minutes. Drain on paper towels.

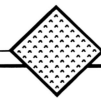

Special Occasion Breakfast

**Strawberries
Marinated in Port and Red
Currant Sauce***

◆

Oysters Broiled in Blankets*

Sautéed Tomato Slices

Jam Muffins with Sweet Butter*

◆

Queen Mary's or English Breakfast Tea

*RECIPE INCLUDED

Plump, fresh oysters wrapped in "blankets" of crisp, smoky bacon, known to some as "angels on horseback," are a traditional savory course in England and are often served as an appetizer in this country.

I've found, however, that they also make excellent breakfast and brunch fare when served on buttered toast. They are best, of course, when very fresh, just-shucked oysters are used. Take care not to overcook them as the oysters will become tough.

Tomato slices, lightly seasoned and sautéed in butter are a colorful accompaniment to the oysters. The Strawberries Marinated in Port and Red Currant Sauce and the warm Jam Muffins provide the sweet contrast that the savory oysters and bacon need at breakfast.

THE GAME PLAN

- Preheat the oven to 400°. Prepare the muffin batter and bake.
- While the muffins bake, prepare the berries and their sauce, toss together and chill. Assemble all the ingredients for the broiled oysters.
- When the muffins are done, turn the oven up to broil and partially cook the bacon slices.
- Roll the oysters in the parsley and scallions, wrap in the bacon slices and stick in the broiler.
- Sauté the tomatoes and serve immediately with the oysters, muffins and berries.
- **If Time Allows:** Make the muffins in advance and warm before serving.

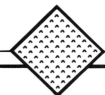

Four Servings

Strawberries Marinated in Port and Red Currant Sauce

1½ tablespoons port
3 tablespoons red currant jelly
1½ pints strawberries, hulled and halved

1 In a small saucepan, combine the port and jelly and warm over moderately low heat, stirring, until the jelly is melted. Let cool slightly.

2 Place the strawberries in a mixing bowl with the port-currant sauce, toss and chill until serving time.

Oysters Broiled in Blankets

12 slices bacon, halved crosswise
¼ cup minced fresh parsley
2 tablespoons minced scallion
Dash of hot pepper sauce
2 dozen fresh oysters, shucked and patted dry
8 slices firm-textured white bread—toasted, buttered and crusts removed
Lemon slices, for garnish
Sprigs of watercress, for garnish

1 Preheat the broiler. Place the bacon slices in one layer on a disposable broiler pan or a baking sheet lined with aluminum foil and broil 6 inches from the heat source until half cooked, about 3 minutes. Drain the fat from the pan and pat the bacon dry with paper towels.

2 In a small bowl, combine the parsley, scallion and hot sauce and mix together well. Roll each oyster in the parsley-scallion mixture, wrap in a bacon slice and secure with a wooden toothpick.

3 Place the oysters on one layer in the broiler pan and broil, turning once with tongs, until the bacon is evenly browned and slightly crisp, 3 to 4 minutes. Do not overcook; the oysters should be just heated through and should remain plump and juicy.

4 Place the buttered toast on individual serving plates, top each with three oysters and garnish with the lemon slices and watercress sprigs. Serve immediately.

Jam Muffins with Sweet Butter

MAKES 12 MUFFINS

1¾ cups all-purpose flour
2 tablespoons sugar
2½ teaspoons baking powder
½ teaspoon salt
1 egg, lightly beaten
¾ cup milk
⅓ cup unsalted butter, melted
4 teaspoons good quality raspberry, blackberry or Damson plum jam

1 Preheat the oven to 400°. Lightly grease twelve 2½-inch muffin cups.

2 In a large mixing bowl, combine the flour, sugar, baking powder and salt. Add the egg, milk and butter and mix lightly, until the dry ingredients are just moistened; the batter will be slightly lumpy.

3 Fill each muffin cup about two-thirds full with batter. Make a small indent in each and spoon a heaping ¼ teaspoon of the jam into the center of each muffin. Bake for 25 minutes or until the muffins are golden brown and the tops spring back when touched. Serve hot with a generous amount of sweet butter.

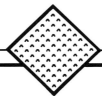

Soup and Salad Fall Brunch

Mulled Cider

Spanish Chick-Pea and Tomato Soup*

Zucchini-Cheese Salad*

Boston Brown Bread

Toasted Whole Wheat English Muffins

◆

**Vanilla Ice Cream with Chestnuts
and Brandy***

*RECIPE INCLUDED

Whatever your favorite fall activity—from football to leaf-gazing—this warming family brunch or supper menu offers a perfect way to celebrate.

Spanish Chick-Pea and Tomato Soup is thick, rich and comforting. The salad is rich with nuts, cheese and the crunch of zucchini. Dessert is delightfully smooth. The total effect is a delicious sense of well-being.

If you are preparing the entire menu, get the soup going first, then start the salad. Boston brown bread is available in cans—just follow the heating instructions on the label and serve with lots of sweet butter. Whole wheat English muffins are now available in many stores. Slather them with butter and pop them under the broiler until lightly browned. The dessert can be readied at the last minute.

THE GAME PLAN

- Start making the soup.
- Meanwhile, prepare the salad ingredients and the dressing; toss and arrange the salad on plates.
- Warm the brown bread and make the mulled cider.
- Toast the muffins just before the soup is ready to serve.
- Warm the chestnuts and brandy just before serving the dessert.
- **If Time Allows:** The salad dressing can be made ahead and tossed with the cheese and zucchini before serving. The soup can be made ahead, but reserve the green pepper to add to the soup when reheated.

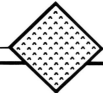

Four to Six Servings

Zucchini-Cheese Salad

¾ cup vegetable oil
¼ cup white wine vinegar
1 teaspoon dried mint
½ teaspoon dried basil
¼ teaspoon salt
⅛ teaspoon coarsely ground
  pepper
1 pound Muenster cheese, cut into
  1-by-¼-inch julienne strips
1 pound zucchini, cut into ¾-by-
  ⅛-inch julienne strips
1 small head of leaf lettuce
1 cup (4 ounces) shelled walnuts
1 tomato, cut into 8 wedges
2 ounces alfalfa sprouts (optional)

1 Whisk the vegetable oil, vinegar, mint, basil, salt and pepper
in a small bowl until blended.

2 In a medium bowl, toss the
cheese and zucchini with the
dressing. Line a salad bowl or
plates with the leaf lettuce.
Mound the cheese and zucchini
on top of the lettuce, sprinkle with
the walnuts and decorate with
the tomato wedges and alfalfa
sprouts, if desired.

Spanish Chick-Pea and Tomato Soup

3 tablespoons olive oil
2 medium onions, chopped
1 can (16 ounces) chick-peas,
  rinsed and drained
2½ cups chicken broth
2 garlic cloves
2 cups chopped, peeled fresh
  tomatoes, or 1 can (17 ounces)
  Italian tomatoes, drained and
  coarsely chopped
½ teaspoon cumin
¼ teaspoon thyme
½ cup chopped green bell
  pepper
Salt
4 scallions, chopped, for garnish
⅓ cup chopped fresh parsley, for
  garnish
Juice of ½ lemon
Hot pepper sauce

1 In a large heavy saucepan
or kettle, heat the oil. Add the
onions and sauté over moderate
heat until softened.

2 Set aside ½ cup of the chick-
peas. Place the remaining chick-
peas in a blender or food processor along with 1 cup of the broth
and the garlic and process until
pureed.

3 Stir this puree, the remaining
1½ cups broth, the tomatoes,
cumin and thyme into the saucepan and bring to a boil over
moderately high heat. Reduce the
heat to low, cover and simmer for
5 minutes.

4 Add the green pepper and
the reserved ½ cup of chick-peas
and cook 5 minutes longer. Season to taste with salt and serve
hot in individual bowls garnished
with scallions, parsley and a few
drops of lemon juice and hot
pepper sauce.

Vanilla Ice Cream with Chestnuts and Brandy

1 jar (10 or 11 ounces) chestnuts in
  syrup
2 tablespoons brandy
1 quart vanilla ice cream

Heat the chestnuts with their
syrup plus the brandy in a small
saucepan over moderate heat
until the chestnuts are warmed
through. Divide the ice cream
into equal portions; spoon the
chestnuts and brandied syrup
over the ice cream.

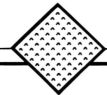

POULTRY

30-Minute Spring Dinner

Kirsch-Cassis Aperitif*

◆

Roasted Green Pepper Salad*

Chicken with Sun-Dried Tomatoes*

Toasted Croutons with Scallions and Parsley*

Beverage Suggestion: California Sauvignon Blanc, such as Carneros Creek

◆

Chocolate Ice Cream with Apricot Brandy

Macaroons or Amaretti Cookies

Espresso

*RECIPE INCLUDED

Although no longer a novelty, Italian sun-dried tomatoes *(pumate)* packed in olive oil are one of the most delicious and exciting new foods to reach our markets. Their warm concentrated flavor and lush texture add richness to many dishes, and despite the slightly expensive price, a few go a long way. The flavorful oil can be used, too—I like to brush it over toasted slices of French bread and spread goat cheese on top. These tomatoes are an ideal complement to chicken, especially when their pungency is mellowed by the addition of cream.

This spring menu is full of hearty flavors, from Roasted Green Pepper Salad to Toasted Croutons with Scallions and Parsley. Chocolate ice cream with apricot brandy makes a rich dessert.

The entire meal can be prepared in half an hour, and suits family dinners as well as more formal occasions. Any clean, crisp white wine makes a happy match.

THE GAME PLAN

- Preheat the oven to 350°.
- Roast the peppers for the salad and while they're "sweating," make the vinaigrette.
- Put the croutons in for the first baking.
- Prepare and sauté the chicken.
- Start the sauce for the chicken.
- While the sauce is reducing, finish the croutons, peel the peppers and arrange the peppers and onion on a platter.
- Keep the chicken and croutons warm and hold off on dressing the salad until after you serve aperitifs.
- **If Time Allows:** The peppers can be roasted and peeled in advance.

Four Servings

Kirsch-Cassis Aperitif

4 ounces (½ cup) kirsch
4 ounces (½ cup) crème de cassis
Club soda
2 teaspoons fresh lemon juice
Orange bitters or Angostura
  bitters
4 orange slices, for garnish

Fill each of 4 large wine glasses halfway with ice cubes. Pour in 1 ounce each kirsch and cassis, then fill the glasses with club soda. Add ½ teaspoon lemon juice and 2 to 3 dashes of bitters per glass. Stir well. Garnish each glass with an orange slice.

Toasted Croutons with Scallions and Parsley

8 slices French bread, cut 1 inch
  thick
8 teaspoons unsalted butter, at
  room temperature
2 scallions (white and tender
  green), finely chopped
2 teaspoons finely chopped
  parsley

1 Preheat the oven to 350°. Spread both sides of each slice of bread with ½ teaspoon of the butter. Place the slices in a single layer on a foil-lined baking sheet. Bake for 6 minutes, or until toasted on top.

2 In a small bowl, toss the scallions and parsley together. Remove the croutons from the oven and turn them. Sprinkle the scallion-parsley mixture over the croutons. Return the croutons to the oven and bake for 4 minutes, or until golden brown on top.

Roasted Green Pepper Salad

3 large green bell peppers
4 thin slices of red onion,
  separated into rings
¼ cup olive oil
1½ tablespoons balsamic vinegar
⅛ teaspoon thyme
¼ teaspoon salt
⅛ teaspoon freshly ground black
  pepper

1 Roast the peppers over a gas flame or under a hot broiler as close to the heat as possible, turning frequently, until charred all over, about 6 minutes. Seal in a paper bag and let "sweat" for 5 to 10 minutes. When cool enough to handle, rub off the skin and rinse briefly under cold running water; pat dry. Remove the seeds and ribs and cut the peppers into julienne strips.

2 Arrange the peppers on a serving platter. Scatter the onion rings on top.

3 In a small bowl, whisk the oil, vinegar, thyme, salt and pepper until blended. Pour over the salad before serving.

Chicken with Sun-Dried Tomatoes

4 skinless, boneless chicken breast
  halves (about 1½ pounds)
3 tablespoons unsalted butter
½ teaspoon salt
¼ teaspoon freshly ground
  pepper
1 large shallot, minced
⅔ cup heavy cream
½ cup dry white wine
⅛ teaspoon marjoram
¼ cup coarsely chopped sun-
  dried tomatoes

1 Cut each chicken breast crosswise on the diagonal into 6 equal pieces.

2 In a heavy skillet, melt the butter over moderately high heat. When the foam begins to subside, add the chicken pieces. Sprinkle with the salt and pepper. Sauté over moderate heat, turning, until the chicken is just opaque throughout, 4 to 5 minutes.

3 Remove the chicken with a slotted spoon. Add the shallot to the skillet and sauté, stirring, until softened, about 1 minute.

4 Add the cream, wine, marjoram and sun-dried tomatoes. Bring to a boil over moderate heat and cook, uncovered, stirring occasionally, until the sauce is slightly thickened, about 5 minutes. Return the chicken to the skillet. Simmer gently, spooning the sauce over the chicken, until heated through, 2 to 3 minutes.

A Warming Meal-in-One-Pot

Croque-Monsieurs*

◆

Poached Breast of Chicken with Autumn Vegetables*

Pork and Liver Dumplings*

Green Caper Sauce*

Beverage Suggestion: Côtes-du-Rhône

◆

Fudgy Brownies

Coffee, Tea or Milk

*RECIPE INCLUDED

This menu is good, basic fare with a decidedly French accent. Begin with grilled ham and cheese sandwiches, called *croque-monsieurs* in France. Cut into small shapes and elevated in taste with Gruyère cheese and prosciutto, these moist, crunchy morsels make popular finger food the whole family can nibble while the rest of the dinner is being prepared.

The main course is a fast translation from the classic French *poule-au-pot,* chicken and vegetables simmered together in one pot. The traditional recipe involves long preparation; ours takes little time. The large hen of the classic version has been transformed into chicken breasts, the usual forcemeat stuffing into small meat dumplings that can be simmered in the broth from the chicken and vegetables. Our Green Caper Sauce—to be passed separately—is more northern Italian in style, but adds a pleasant piquancy to the delicately flavored chicken. A gorgeous selection of autumn vegetables, cooked in the same pot with the chicken, rounds out the meal.

THE GAME PLAN

- Mix and form the dumplings.
- Make the caper sauce.
- Make the croque-monsieurs.
- Start making the chicken and vegetables. While they simmer, serve the croque-monsieurs with aperitifs.
- Remove the chicken and vegetables from the broth, add the dumplings and poach; serve all together accompanied by the caper sauce.
- **If Time Allows:** The caper sauce can be made ahead. The dumplings can also be mixed and formed in advance and refrigerated, covered, until ready to cook.

Four Servings

Croque-Monsieurs

8 thin slices firm-textured white bread, crusts removed
8 thin slices Gruyère cheese (about 4 ounces)
4 thin slices prosciutto
2 tablespoons unsalted butter

1 Make 4 sandwiches, filling each with a slice of cheese, a slice of prosciutto and another slice of cheese, trimming as necessary to fit the bread.

2 In a medium skillet, melt 1 tablespoon of the butter over moderately low heat. Add 2 of the sandwiches and grill, turning once, until the bread is golden brown on each side and the cheese is slightly melted, about 3 minutes. Repeat with the remaining butter and sandwiches.

3 Cut the sandwiches into small squares or triangles and serve as an hors d'oeuvre.

Poached Breast of Chicken with Autumn Vegetables

2 whole chicken breasts (about ¾ pound each)
4 small red potatoes (about 2 inches in diameter), peeled
4 medium carrots, peeled and quartered lengthwise
4 small turnips, peeled and halved
4 small white onions (about 1 inch in diameter), peeled
4 medium celery ribs, cut into 3-inch lengths

Bouquet garni: 6 sprigs of parsley, ½ teaspoon thyme, 4 peppercorns and 1 bay leaf tied in a double thickness of cheesecloth
½ teaspoon salt
Pork and Liver Dumplings

1 Place the chicken breasts in a large deep pot. Add enough water to cover by 1 inch. Bring to a boil over moderate heat; skim off the foam.

2 Add the potatoes, carrots, turnips, onions, celery, bouquet garni and salt; return to a boil. Reduce the heat to moderately low, cover the pot and simmer until the chicken is no longer pink and the vegetables are tender, about 25 minutes.

3 Remove the chicken with a slotted spoon and cover loosely with foil to keep warm. Add the dumplings to the broth and simmer, uncovered, until they float to the top, 3 to 5 minutes. Cover and cook for about 5 minutes longer, or until a dumpling cut in half is no longer pink in the center.

4 Meanwhile, peel the skin off the chicken breasts and pull the meat from the bone in one piece. Cut the chicken into thin slices. Arrange on a large platter and surround with the vegetables.

5 Remove the dumplings from the broth with a slotted spoon and serve hot with the chicken and vegetables.

Pork and Liver Dumplings

1 chicken liver, trimmed
½ pound ground pork
½ cup fresh bread crumbs
1 egg, beaten
3 tablespoons minced fresh parsley
1 tablespoon minced onion
2 garlic cloves, crushed through a press
¾ teaspoon salt
¼ teaspoon freshly ground pepper

1 Crush the liver to a paste with a mortar and pestle or mince with a sharp knife.

2 In a medium bowl, combine the liver with the remaining ingredients and mix well. Shape into 1-inch balls.

Green Caper Sauce

MAKES ABOUT 1 CUP

½ cup olive oil
3 tablespoons fresh lemon juice
½ cup drained capers, chopped (1½ jars, 3¼ ounces each)
¼ cup chopped green bell pepper
1 tablespoon chopped fresh chives
1 tablespoon chopped fresh parsley
Salt and freshly ground pepper to taste

In a small bowl, whisk the olive oil and lemon juice until well blended. Stir in the remaining ingredients.

Fourth of July Supper

White Wine Spritzers

◆

Iced Cucumber Soup with Shrimp*

Bluegrass-Style Fried Chicken*

Louisiana Spoon Bread*

Sliced Tomatoes with Lemon Juice, Oil and Fresh Basil

Beverage Suggestion: Sparkling Vouvray

◆

Peaches in Raspberry Sauce*

*RECIPE INCLUDED

It isn't July 4th without fireworks, red-white-and-blue bunting and brass bands. And it isn't a proper Independence Day without a gathering of friends to celebrate the joys of the day with a seasonal repast—one that places few demands on the cook's time, like this one: iced shrimp soup, fried chicken with cream gravy, spoon bread, tomatoes with aromatic fresh basil, peaches swimming in raspberry sauce, and a sparkling white wine.

If you are preparing the entire menu, first preheat the oven for the spoon bread; then slice the peaches and prepare the raspberry sauce; finally prepare the soup and the tomatoes with basil. Bake the spoon bread just before serving the soup course. Have the chicken ready, but cook it only after you have been refreshed with the wine, soup and good company. Combine the peaches and raspberry sauce just before serving.

THE GAME PLAN

- Preheat the oven to 400°.
- Prepare the peaches and make the raspberry sauce, but wait to spoon the sauce over the peaches until just before serving.
- Prepare the soup and chill, reserving the garnishes to sprinkle over at serving time. Assemble the tomato and basil salad.
- Assemble all the ingredients for the chicken and make the wine spritzers.
- Prepare the spoon bread and bake. Serve the spritzers.
- Serve the soup.
- Prepare the chicken and serve with the hot spoon bread and the tomatoes and basil.
- Spoon the sauce over the peaches and serve.
- **If Time Allows:** The soup can be made ahead and chilled until serving.

Iced Cucumber Soup with Shrimp

2 cups chicken stock or canned broth
1½ cups plain yogurt
2 medium cucumbers, peeled and sliced, plus ½ cup chopped cucumber
⅓ cup sliced onion plus ½ cup chopped onion
½ cup crushed ice
6 ounces cooked shrimp—shelled, deveined and chopped
½ cup chopped, green bell pepper
Hot pepper sauce
Freshly ground pepper

1 Place the stock, yogurt, sliced cucumbers, sliced onion and ice in a blender or processor and blend for a few seconds.

2 Divide the soup among four chilled soup bowls and garnish each with some of the shrimp, green pepper, chopped cucumber and chopped onion. Sprinkle each serving with a drop of hot sauce and a little pepper.

Louisiana Spoon Bread

1½ cups milk
¾ cup cornmeal
1¼ teaspoons salt
1 small garlic clove, crushed
2 tablespoons unsalted butter
1 teaspoon sugar

2 eggs, lightly beaten
1½ teaspoons baking powder
½ cup grated Cheddar

1 Preheat the oven to 400°. Bring the milk to a boil in a medium saucepan over moderate heat. Lower the heat and add the cornmeal slowly, stirring constantly with a wooden spoon. Add the salt and cook 1 minute. Remove from the heat.

2 Stir the garlic into the cornmeal mixture, along with the butter, sugar, eggs, baking powder and all but 2 tablespoons of the cheese.

3 Pour the batter into a greased 9-inch pie pan. Sprinkle with the reserved cheese and bake 25 minutes, or until golden.

Bluegrass-Style Fried Chicken

1½ pounds boneless chicken breasts
Salt and freshly ground pepper
2 teaspoons paprika
⅓ cup all-purpose flour
3 tablespoons unsalted butter
2 tablespoons vegetable oil
1 cup half-and-half
⅛ teaspoon nutmeg
Dash of cayenne
2 tablespoons finely chopped parsley, for garnish

1 Season the chicken breasts with salt and pepper to taste. Mix the paprika with the flour and evenly coat the chicken breasts with the mixture.

2 In a nonstick skillet, heat the butter in the oil until it begins to foam. Working in batches if necessary, add the chicken breasts and cook them over moderately high heat for 5 to 7 minutes on each side, or until just cooked through and evenly browned. Transfer the chicken to a heated serving platter.

3 Pour off the fat from the skillet and add the half-and-half. Place the skillet over moderate heat and bring the mixture almost to a boil—it will thicken slightly. Stir in the nutmeg, cayenne and salt to taste. Cook for 1 minute more, stirring constantly.

4 Surround the chicken with the gravy and sprinkle with the parsley.

Peaches in Raspberry Sauce

4 medium peaches
2 tablespoons fresh lemon juice
2 tablespoons light brown sugar
1 package (10 ounces) quick-frozen raspberries, thawed

1 Slice the peaches into a bowl. Squeeze a small amount of lemon juice over them to keep them from discoloring. Add the brown sugar and toss to coat the peaches.

2 Force the raspberries through a sieve into another bowl; discard the seeds. Spoon the puree over the peaches.

Special Occasion Dinner

Iced Vodka with Lemon Zest

Tender Celery Hearts Stuffed with St. André Cheese*

Ripe Green Olives

◆

**Sautéed Chicken Breasts with Madeira and
Spiced Cherries***

Wild Rice

Bibb Lettuce with Golden Cream Dressing*

◆

Vanilla Ice Cream with Hazelnuts and Curaçao*

Café Filtre

*RECIPE INCLUDED

One of the best things about chicken is its versatility. It can be plain or fancy, unadorned or sumptuously sauced. Here it's dressed up beautifully with spiced cherries, a Russian favorite, and a Madeira sauce. The dish makes an elegant contrast to two North American delights: wild rice, which is actually not rice but a tall aquatic grass that grows in the lakes of Minnesota, and Bibb lettuce, a sweet, tender limestone lettuce grown in Kentucky.

Ice cold vodka sprinkled with lemon zest is a pleasant aperitif with celery hearts stuffed with creamy St. André cheese. If you can't find St. André, use any other triple-creme cheese. Sautéed hazelnuts and Curacao make a quick, flavorful sauce to spoon hot over cold ice cream.

THE GAME PLAN

- Prepare and assemble the celery hearts.
- Make the spiced cherries and set aside.
- Prepare the greens for the salad and make the dressing, but wait to dress the salad just before serving.
- Start the wild rice.
- Assemble all the ingredients for the chicken.
- Serve the celery hearts, olives and iced vodka.
- Finish the chicken and serve with the salad and rice.
- Prepare the sauce for the ice cream just before serving.
- **If Time Allows:** The celery, spiced cherries and the salad dressing can be made in advance.

Four Servings

Tender Celery Hearts Stuffed with St. André Cheese

4 ounces St. André or other triple-crème cheese
2 teaspoons Sauternes or other sweet white wine
16 tender celery ribs, trimmed
Freshly ground pepper

In a small bowl, combine the cheese and Sauternes and beat with a fork until smooth. Stuff the mixture generously into the celery hearts. Grind a little fresh pepper over each and serve.

Sautéed Chicken Breasts with Madeira and Spiced Cherries

4 large skinless, boneless chicken breast halves (about 6 ounces each)
4 tablespoons unsalted butter
½ cup medium-sweet Madeira
Salt and freshly ground pepper
Spiced Cherries

1 Trim off the excess fat, remove the tendons and pound each chicken breast half lightly between waxed paper to flatten.

2 In a large skillet, melt the butter until foaming, but not browned. Add the chicken breasts and sauté over moderate heat for about 4 minutes. Turn and sauté 3 to 4 minutes longer, until lightly browned and just cooked through. Remove the chicken from the skillet and keep warm while preparing the sauce.

3 Pour off the excess fat from the skillet, add the Madeira and simmer, scraping up any browned bits that cling to the bottom of the pan, until reduced by one-fourth, about 2 minutes.

4 Arrange the chicken breasts on a warmed serving platter. Season with salt and pepper to taste and spoon the Madeira sauce over them. Surround the chicken with the Spiced Cherries and serve hot.

Spiced Cherries

1 can (16 ounces) unsweetened, pitted red cherries in liquid
2 tablespoons sugar
1 teaspoon fresh lime juice
½ teaspoon lime zest
¼ teaspoon ground ginger
⅛ teaspoon cinnamon
⅛ teaspoon ground cloves
2 teaspoons cornstarch

1 Drain the liquid from the cherries, reserving ¾ cup. Place the cherry liquid in a medium saucepan. Add the sugar, lime juice and zest, ginger, cinnamon and cloves. Dissolve the cornstarch in a small amount of the liquid and return to the saucepan. Bring to a boil over moderate heat, stirring constantly with a whisk until thickened.

2 Add the cherries and poach them in the sauce over low heat, stirring, for 10 minutes.

Bibb Lettuce with Golden Cream Dressing

1 egg yolk
⅓ cup heavy cream
1 teaspoon tarragon vinegar
¼ teaspoon salt
⅛ teaspoon freshly ground pepper
2 small heads of Bibb lettuce
2 tablespoons minced chives, for garnish

1 In a small mixing bowl, combine the egg yolk, cream, vinegar, salt and pepper, and whisk until slightly thickened.

2 Arrange the lettuce leaves on individual serving plates. Spoon the dressing over just before serving and sprinkle with the chives.

Vanilla Ice Cream with Hazelnuts and Curaçao

2 tablespoons unsalted butter
¼ cup coarsely chopped hazelnuts
Salt
½ cup Curaçao or other orange liqueur
1 pint vanilla ice cream

1 In a small skillet, melt the butter and sauté the hazelnuts until lightly browned. Season with salt to taste. Stir in ¼ cup of the Curaçao and simmer, stirring, for 5 to 10 seconds longer. Remove from the heat and stir in the remaining ¼ cup of Curaçao.

2 Spoon the ice cream into 4 dessert dishes, spoon the warm nut and Curaçao mixture over the top and serve.

Alfresco Lunch

Pink Tequilas*

Potted Shrimp*

**Toast Triangles or Strips of Cracked
Wheat Bread**

◆

**Chicken and Avocado Salad with
Bacon***

Beverage Suggestion: California Chardonnay

◆

**Peaches with Apricot Sauce and
Amaretti***

Iced Coffee

*RECIPE INCLUDED

Plump poached chicken breasts lend themselves beautifully to creative salad making. They can be cubed, sliced or slivered and mixed with almost limitless ingredients and seasonings.

This elegant chicken salad uses the contrasting tastes and textures of crisp bacon and silky avocado slices, along with a smooth and flavorful gorgonzola cheese.

Leftover cooked chicken can be used if you have it, or you can poach the chicken breasts a few hours in advance for quicker last-minute preparation. If so, the chicken doesn't need to be chilled. In fact, I prefer not to refrigerate cooked chicken, unless very hot weather requires it. Refrigeration toughens the meat and robs it of some flavor. Do chill the salad bowl or platter in advance, however.

THE GAME PLAN

- Make the Potted Shrimp.
- Poach the chicken breasts.
- Prepare the peaches and spoon the hot apricot sauce over them; but wait to sprinkle the Amaretti crumbs on until just before serving.
- Prepare all the remaining salad ingredients and the dressing.
- Make the Pink Tequilas and serve with the Potted Shrimp and toast triangles.
- Assemble the salad just before serving.
- **If Time Allows:** The Potted Shrimp can be made well in advance. The peaches can be prepared and topped with the sauce well ahead. The chicken breasts and bacon can also be cooked in advance.

Four Servings

Pink Tequilas

Ice cubes
4 tablespoons fresh lime juice
4 tablespoons grenadine syrup
6 ounces (¾ cup) light tequila
Club soda
4 twists of lime zest

Fill four 12-ounce wine goblets with ice. To each, add 1 tablespoon of the lime juice, 1 tablespoon of the grenadine and 1½ ounces of the tequila. Fill each with club soda and stir. Garnish each drink with a twist of lime.

Potted Shrimp

½ pound cooked shrimp—shelled, deveined and chopped
¼ cup unsalted butter, at room temperature
¼ teaspoon fresh lemon juice
Hot pepper sauce
¼ teaspoon salt
1½ tablespoons finely sliced scallion
Toast triangles or strips of cracked wheat bread

1 Combine the shrimp, butter and lemon juice in a food processor. Season with a few drops of hot pepper sauce and salt and process to a coarse-textured paste.

2 Stir in the scallion and spoon the mixture into a 2-cup ramekin. Chill for 1 hour. Serve with toast triangles or strips of cracked wheat bread.

Chicken and Avocado Salad with Bacon

Bouquet garni: 6 sprigs of parsley, ½ teaspoon thyme, 4 peppercorns and 1 bay leaf tied in cheesecloth
2 whole chicken breasts (about ¾ pound each)
6 strips of bacon
1 cup sour cream
2 ounces crumbled gorgonzola or other soft, blue-veined cheese (about 3 tablespoons)
1 tablespoon fresh lemon juice
¼ teaspoon salt
⅛ teaspoon freshly ground pepper
1 cup thinly sliced celery
Lettuce leaves, such as Boston, Bibb, romaine or leaf
4 hard-cooked eggs, quartered
2 ripe avocados—peeled, sliced and sprinkled with lemon juice
Pinch of cayenne pepper

1 Fill a large soup kettle about half full with water, add the bouquet garni, bring to a boil and simmer for 5 to 10 minutes. Add the chicken breasts, reduce the heat to moderately low and poach for about 15 minutes.

2 Meanwhile, preheat the broiler. Arrange the bacon strips on a broiler pan and broil about 6 inches from the heat until crisp, about 3 minutes on one side and another minute on the second side. Drain and let cool.

3 In a small mixing bowl, combine the sour cream and gorgonzola with the lemon juice, salt and pepper, and beat well.

4 Drain the chicken breasts and pat them dry. Remove and discard the skin, and pull the meat from the bone in one piece. Cut the meat into 1-inch cubes.

5 In a mixing bowl, combine the chicken and celery with half the dressing and toss well.

6 To assemble, arrange the lettuce leaves on a large salad platter. Place the chicken and celery mixture on top. Arrange the eggs and avocado slices around the edge. Spoon the remaining dressing over the top, crumble the bacon strips over and sprinkle with the cayenne.

Peaches with Apricot Sauce and Amaretti

4 large peaches
2 teaspoons fresh lemon juice
4 tablespoons pulpy apricot jam
4 tablespoons crumbled Amaretti cookies

1 Plunge the peaches in a large saucepan of rapidly boiling water for 30 seconds; rinse them in cold water and slip the skins off. Halve and pit the peaches and sprinkle with the lemon juice. Arrange the peaches, cut-side up, on a serving platter.

2 In a small saucepan, melt the jam with 1 tablespoon of water, stirring. Spoon some of the apricot sauce into the cavity of each peach half. Let cool.

3 Just before serving, sprinkle each peach half with 1 tablespoon of the Amaretti crumbs.

Chinese Comfort Food

Sweet and Sour Bourbon*

◆

Crisp Three-Vegetable Salad*

Chinese-Style Chicken and Noodles*

**Beverage Suggestion: Light California
Gewürztraminer**

◆

Miniature Grape Tarts*

Hot Jasmine Tea

*RECIPE INCLUDED

Chicken and noodles, no matter what its nationality, is one of the most comforting dishes in the world. I can think of no better way to end a hectic day than to relax with a Sweet and Sour Bourbon, a variation on a whiskey sour, then enjoy this quickly stirred up Chinese version of chicken and noodles. A slightly sweet, fresh vegetable salad makes a pleasant, crisp accompaniment to the noodles, and a plate of glistening little grape tarts is a pretty end to the meal with a pot of hot jasmine tea.

It's all comfortingly simple to prepare. Even the grape tarts take very little time if you use packaged pastry shells, preferably the unsweetened variety. Several imported brands are available in specialty food shops. The best I've found calls the shells "salad cups" for some unfathomable reason.

Fresh Chinese noodles are available in Oriental groceries and even in some supermarkets. They are usually quite long and need to be cut into manageable pieces. If Chinese noodles are not available, other fresh pastas can be used or good quality dried capellini or very thin spaghetti.

THE GAME PLAN

- Soak the mushrooms for the chicken and noodles.
- Meanwhile, make the grape tarts.
- Make the salad.
- Assemble and prepare all of the ingredients for the chicken and noodles.
- Make and serve the Sweet and Sour Bourbons.
- Cook the chicken and noodles and toss the two together; serve immediately.
- **If Time Allows:** The grape tarts and salad can be made ahead. The mushrooms can also be soaked in advance.

Six Servings

Sweet and Sour Bourbon

8 ounces (1 cup) bourbon
6 tablespoons fresh lemon juice
6 tablespoons orgeat (see Note)
Ice cubes
6 slices of orange, for garnish

Combine the bourbon, lemon juice and orgeat in a cocktail shaker with several cubes of ice and shake vigorously. Strain into six whiskey sour glasses and garnish each with an orange slice.

Note: Orgeat is a non-alcoholic, slightly almond-flavored syrup. If it's not available, substitute superfine sugar to taste.

Crisp Three-Vegetable Salad

⅓ cup rice vinegar
1 tablespoon Japanese soy sauce
2 teaspoons superfine sugar
Salt
1 bunch (about 12) radishes, thinly sliced
3 medium carrots, thinly sliced
3 tender celery ribs, thinly sliced
1 tablespoon minced fresh coriander

In a large mixing bowl, combine the vinegar, soy sauce and sugar, and season with salt to taste. Add the radishes, carrots and celery and toss. Sprinkle with the coriander. Serve at room temperature or slightly chilled.

Chinese-Style Chicken and Noodles

12 dried Chinese or shiitake mushrooms
5 tablespoons vegetable oil
¾ pound fresh Chinese noodles or ½ pound dried capellini
¾ pound skinless, boneless chicken breast, cut lengthwise into 3-by-¼-inch strips
4 or 5 scallions, cut into 1-inch lengths
1 can (8 ounces) bamboo shoots—rinsed, drained and sliced
⅛ teaspoon cayenne pepper
3 tablespoons soy sauce
Salt
2 teaspoons Oriental sesame oil, or to taste

1 Place the mushrooms in a small bowl, pour boiling water over them and let soak for 15 minutes. Drain the mushrooms, squeezing out excess water. Cut off and discard the stems and cut the caps into ¼-inch slices.

2 Bring a large pot of salted water to a boil and add 1 tablespoon of the oil.

3 Meanwhile, in a wok or a very large skillet, heat 3 tablespoons of the oil. Add the chicken, scallions and mushrooms and stir over moderately high heat for 30 seconds. Stir in the bamboo shoots and cook for 1 minute more.

4 Add the noodles to the pot of boiling water and cook until al dente, 1 to 3 minutes. Rinse the noodles under cold water and drain thoroughly.

5 Add the remaining tablespoon of oil to the skillet, add the noodles and sprinkle with the cayenne and soy sauce. Season with salt to taste and warm over moderately low heat until heated through. Sprinkle the sesame oil over the noodles, toss to mix well and serve hot.

Miniature Grape Tarts

2 tablespoons quince jelly or 1 tablespoon each apple and red currant jelly
6 ounces cream cheese
4 teaspoons port
4 teaspoons sugar
12 miniature pastry shells, about 1¾ inches in diameter, or 12 small unsweetened pastry barquettes
¾ cup seedless grapes, cut in half lengthwise

1 In a small saucepan, melt the jelly with ½ teaspoon water. Set aside.

2 In a small bowl, beat the cream cheese until soft. Beat in the port and sugar and blend well.

3 Spread a little of the cream cheese mixture on the bottom of each pastry shell or barquette. Arrange some of the grapes, cutside down, on each pastry shell. Brush the grapes on each tart with some of the melted jelly.

Mediterranean-Flavor Dinner

Mozzarella with Fresh Basil*

———————— ◆ ————————

Broiled Chicken Thighs Diavolo*

Zucchini and Tomatoes*

Italian Bread with Parsley and Scallion*

Beverage Suggestion: Vernaccia di San Gimignano or Pinot Grigio

———————— ◆ ————————

Peaches in White Wine*

Espresso

*RECIPE INCLUDED

A distinctly Mediterranean flavor dominates this menu, particularly appropriate for the summer months. With colorful groceries and gardens overflowing with fragrant fresh herbs, ripe fruits and vegetables, the ingredients are all at hand.

As an aperitif, you might begin with one of my hot-weather favorites—sweet vermouth and club soda poured over lots of ice in a tall glass, with a dash of bitters and a slice of orange. For a refreshing first course, Mozzarella with Fresh Basil celebrates one of summer's most aromatic herbs.

The main course, Broiled Chicken Thighs Diavolo, is seasoned with rosemary and made pleasingly piquant by the addition of hot red pepper and a splash of vinegar. Zucchini with Tomatoes and a buttery Italian Bread with Parsley and Scallion round out the menu.

As a dessert, nothing could be simpler than Peaches in White Wine, but the peaches must be ripe—juicy and sweet. If you are unsure of quality, substitute strawberries or nectarines. Use a dry white wine or a sweet, effervescent dessert wine, such as Asti Spumante.

THE GAME PLAN

- Make the marinade and let the chicken thighs marinate in it.
- Meanwhile, prepare and assemble the mozzarella with fresh basil.
- Prepare the Italian Bread with Parsley and Scallion up to the point of baking.
- Preheat the broiler. Put the marinated chicken thighs in to broil.
- Meanwhile, make the zucchini and tomatoes.
- When you turn the chicken thighs, put the bread on the bottom shelf of the oven to bake while the chicken finishes cooking.
- Pour the wine over the peaches just before serving them.
- **If Time Allows:** The chicken thighs can be marinated earlier in the day and the zucchini and tomatoes can be made in advance and reheated just before serving.

Four Servings

Mozzarella with Fresh Basil

8 ounces mozzarella cheese, preferably fresh, thinly sliced
4 teaspoons chopped fresh basil
4 teaspoons olive oil
Strips of green bell pepper and radish roses, for garnish
Freshly ground pepper

Arrange the cheese on individual serving plates, overlapping the slices slightly. Sprinkle 1 teaspoon of the basil and 1 teaspoon of the oil over each serving of cheese. Garnish with green pepper strips and radish roses, if desired. Pass a pepper mill and let each person season to taste.

Broiled Chicken Thighs Diavolo

¼ cup olive oil
¼ cup dry white wine
1 tablespoon white wine vinegar
1 teaspon salt
½ teaspoon crushed hot red pepper, or to taste
2 large garlic cloves, minced
1 teaspoon minced fresh rosemary or ½ teaspoon dried
8 large chicken thighs (about 2 pounds)
1 tablespoon chopped fresh parsley, for garnish

1 In a medium bowl, whisk the oil, wine, vinegar, salt, hot pepper, garlic and rosemary until blended. Add the chicken thighs to the marinade and turn to coat all over. Let marinate at room temperature for up to 1 hour, until you are ready to cook them.

2 Preheat the broiler. Arrange the chicken thighs, skinside down, in a single layer in a disposable broiling pan. Broil 4 to 5 inches from the heat for 7 minutes, basting frequently with the marinade. Turn and broil, basting frequently, until the skin is golden brown, 5 to 8 minutes longer. Transfer the chicken to a warm platter.

3 Skim the excess fat from the pan juices and pour the juices over the chicken. Garnish with the parsley, if desired.

Zucchini and Tomatoes

2 tablespoons unsalted butter
1 small onion, thinly sliced
1 pound small zucchini, cut into thin (about 2½-by-¼-by-⅛-inch) sticks
1 large tomato—peeled, seeded and coarsely chopped
½ teaspoon salt
Freshly ground pepper

1 In a large skillet, melt the butter over moderate heat. Add the onion, cover the pan and cook for about 2 minutes, until the onion begins to soften.

2 Add the zucchini and cook covered, stirring occasionally, until the zucchini is barely tender, about 3 minutes.

3 Add the tomato, cover and continue to cook until heated through, about 2 minutes. Season with the salt and pepper to taste.

Italian Bread with Parsley and Scallion

8 slices Italian bread, cut 1 inch thick
4 tablespoons unsalted butter
2½ tablespoons minced scallions
2 tablespoons minced fresh parsley

1 Preheat the oven to 400°. Place the bread slices on a baking sheet.

2 In a small saucepan, melt the butter over moderately low heat. Add the scallions and parsley and cook for about 1 minute, until wilted. Spoon the herb butter over the bread. Bake for about 8 minutes, until the edges of the bread are lightly browned.

Peaches in White Wine

4 peaches, peeled and sliced
2 cups white wine, chilled
Sugar

Divide the peach slices among 4 large wine glasses. Pour ½ cup wine over each serving. Allow to sit for 1 to 2 minutes. Pass a bowl of sugar separately for those desiring extra sweetness. Eat the peach slices with a spoon; then drink the wine.

Country Salad with Country Dressing

Light and Easy Supper

Lime Rickeys*

Red Radish Slices on Buttered Pumpernickel Squares

◆

Lemon-Roasted Breast of Chicken*

Gingered Rice*

Bibb Lettuce Chiffonade*

Beverage Suggestion: California Sauvignon Blanc, such as Preston Vineyards

◆

Fresh Goat Cheese

◆

Sliced Fresh Peaches with Heavy Cream or Crème Fraîche

Iced Coffee

*RECIPE INCLUDED

Whole chicken breasts, with skin and bone attached, roast remarkably well in a hot oven in a reasonably short time. The results—tender and juicy meat and crisp skin—approximate a whole roasted bird with no fussing or trussing involved. For more elegant service, the meat is carved off the bone of each half in one piece.

Pleasant accompaniments with the tarragon- and lemon-scented chicken are white rice, fragrant with fresh ginger, and a tender lettuce salad, tossed with lemony egg dressing.

Lime Rickeys with radish canapés whet the appetite. Fresh goat cheese rounds out this relatively light meal. Sliced sweet, juicy peaches doused with cream are a refreshing dessert.

THE GAME PLAN

- Preheat the oven to 450°. Prepare the chicken breasts and place in the oven to roast.

- Prepare the greens for the chiffonade and make the dressing, but wait to toss until just before serving.

- Put the rice on to steam.

- Make the Lime Rickeys and the radish-pumpernickel squares and serve them while the rice and chicken finish cooking.

- Slice the peaches for dessert just before serving.

○ **If Time Allows:** The dressing for the chiffonade can be made ahead.

Four Servings

Lime Rickeys

4 tablespoons fresh lime juice
(from 2 to 3 small limes)
2 tablespoons sugar
6 ounces (¾ cup) gin
Crushed ice
Club soda
Twists of lime zest, for garnish

1 Combine the lime juice, sugar and gin. Stir to dissolve the sugar.

2 Half fill 4 tall glasses with crushed ice. Divide the lime-gin mixture among them, then fill with an equal amount of club soda. Add the lime twists and serve.

Gingered Rice

2 tablespoons dry white wine
1½ tablespoons finely shredded
fresh ginger
1 teaspoon salt
1 tablespoon unsalted butter
1 cup rice

Place the wine, ginger, salt, butter and 2 cups of cold water in a small heavy saucepan. Bring to a boil over high heat, reduce the heat to low and stir in the rice. Cover and cook for 15 to 20 minutes, or until all the liquid is absorbed. Toss gently with a fork before serving.

Bibb Lettuce Chiffonade

1 tablespoon white wine vinegar
1 tablespoon fresh lemon juice
¼ cup olive oil
1 hard-cooked egg, finely
chopped
1 tablespoon minced chives
1 teaspoon minced fresh parsley
Pinch of sugar
⅛ teaspoon salt
Pinch of freshly ground pepper
3 small heads of Bibb lettuce, torn
into bite-size pieces

In a small jar, combine the vinegar, lemon juice, oil, egg, chives, parsley, sugar, salt and pepper; cover and shake well. Just before serving, pour the dressing over the lettuce and toss until coated.

Lemon-Roasted Breast of Chicken

2 whole chicken breasts, about 1
pound each
1 garlic clove, cut in half
1 lemon, cut in half
1 teaspoon tarragon
1 teaspoon salt

1 Preheat the oven to 450°. Rub both sides of each chicken breast with a cut side of the garlic and lemon. Loosen the breast skin with your fingers without tearing it and spread ½ teaspoon tarragon under the skin of each breast.

2 Place skin-side up on a rack in a small shallow roasting pan. Squeeze a little lemon juice from half the lemon over the chicken and sprinkle with the salt.

3 Roast for 40 minutes, until the chicken has just lost its pink near the center. Remove from the oven and let sit for 10 minutes.

4 To serve, cut the meat, with skin attached, off the bone in a single piece from each side of the breast.

International Flavors Dinner

Mushrooms Stuffed with Goat Cheese and Thyme*

◆

Baked Baby Chicken with Ginger*

Couscous with Scallions and Green Apple*

**Beverage Suggestion: California Sauvignon
Blanc such as Wente Bros.**

◆

**Chilled Orange Slices with
Grand Marnier-Flavored Whipped Cream**

Demitasse

*RECIPE INCLUDED

This menu is a veritable melting pot of international influences: a French accent in the appetizer, a hint of the Orient in the chicken with ginger and lime, echoes of North Africa in the couscous with scallions and green apple.

Keep this menu in mind for spring. The light and tart flavors make it welcome as the weather grows warmer, and as a bonus, the chicken is also delicious at room temperature on a bed of shredded lettuce.

Baby chickens, or poussins, are sweet and very tender. They are now being raised in many parts of the country and are frequently available in specialty butcher shops. However, if you can't find them, game hens will work nicely in this recipe.

Precooked couscous is available dried in boxes at most well-stocked supermarkets. It cooks very quickly and is an unusual alternative to rice.

THE GAME PLAN

- Preheat the oven. Assemble the stuffed mushrooms.
- Chill the oranges for dessert and whip the cream.
- Prepare the chickens for roasting, mix the basting butter and put the chickens and the stuffed mushrooms in to cook at the same time.
- Put the stock on to boil for the couscous.
- Stir the couscous into the stock and serve the mushrooms while the chicken and couscous finish cooking.
- Make the sauce for the chicken, toss the apple with the couscous and serve.
- Beat the egg whites and combine with the remaining froth ingredients, folding the whipped cream in at the end. Spoon the froth over the oranges, sprinkle with zest and serve.
- **If Time Allows:** The chicken can be roasted ahead of time and served at room temperature. The mushrooms can be stuffed and refrigerated, covered, until time to bake them.

Four Servings

Mushrooms Stuffed with Goat Cheese and Thyme

8 large mushrooms
1 tablespoon unsalted butter
1 small onion, finely chopped
3 tablespoons Montrachet or other mild goat cheese
½ teaspoon thyme
¼ teaspoon salt
Pinch of freshly ground pepper
3 tablespoons olive oil

1 Preheat the oven to 425°. Separate the mushroom stems from the caps. Finely chop the stems. Set the whole caps aside.

2 In a small skillet, melt the butter over low heat. Add the onion and cook, stirring occasionally, until softened and translucent, about 5 minutes. Add the mushroom stems and cook until all of the liquid has evaporated, about 3 minutes.

3 Add the cheese to the skillet and cook, stirring, until just melted, about 2 minutes. Season with the thyme, salt and pepper.

4 Brush the outside of the mushroom caps with the oil. Fill with the cheese mixture and place on a baking sheet. Drizzle any remaining oil on top.

5 Bake for 10 minutes, or until the stuffed mushrooms are lightly browned.

Couscous with Scallions and Green Apple

2 cups chicken broth
4 tablespoons unsalted butter
1 cup precooked medium-grain couscous
4 scallions, thinly sliced
1 large tart apple, peeled and finely diced
Salt

1 In a medium saucepan, combine the broth and butter. Bring to a boil. Remove from the heat and stir in the couscous and scallions. Cover and let stand until the broth is absorbed, about 5 minutes.

2 Add the apple and toss to mix. Season with salt to taste. Serve hot.

Baked Baby Chicken with Ginger

4 baby chickens (poussins) or game hens, about 1¼ pounds each, butterflied
2 garlic cloves, halved
¾ teaspoon coarse (kosher) salt
¼ teaspoon freshly ground pepper
4 tablespoons unsalted butter, melted
1 tablespoon fresh lime juice
1 tablespoon fresh ginger juice (see Note)
¼ teaspoon paprika

¾ cup dry white wine
Sprigs of watercress, for garnish

1 Preheat the oven to 425°. Wipe the chickens dry. Rub each all over with half a garlic clove. Sprinkle both sides with the salt and pepper. Brush each with ½ tablespoon of the melted butter. Place skin-side down on a rack over a roasting pan.

2 In a small bowl, combine the remaining 2 tablespoons butter, the lime juice, ½ tablespoon of the ginger juice and the paprika.

3 Roast the chickens for 10 minutes, basting twice with the flavored butter. Turn and roast for 20 minutes longer, basting twice, until the juices run clear when the chicken is pricked in the thigh. Remove to a serving platter and cover loosely with foil to keep warm.

4 Place the roasting pan on top of the stove. Pour in the wine and cook over moderate heat, scraping up any browned bits. Pour the sauce into a small saucepan. Boil until reduced to ½ cup, about 5 minutes. Remove from the heat and stir in the remaining ½ tablespoon ginger juice.

5 To serve, pour the sauce over the chicken. Garnish with the watercress.

Note: To make ginger juice, very finely mince fresh unpeeled ginger; place in a double thickness of cheesecloth and twist and squeeze to extract the juice.

Leisurely Summer Menu

Summer Wine*

**Deviled Eggs with Calamata Olives and
Cayenne Walnuts***

◆

**Chicken Breasts with Cucumber, Basil and
Cream***

**Tomatoes with Mustard and Brown
Sugar Dressing***

French Bread

◆

Sugared Peaches

Iced or Hot Coffee

*RECIPE INCLUDED

Fresh basil, cucumbers and cream are the crisp, cool ingredients that combine with poached chicken breasts in this menu to make a composed lunch or dinner salad as refreshing as a spring breeze. Ripe tomatoes with a tart-sweet mustard and brown sugar dressing add another touch of color. My deviled eggs with bits of Calamata olives and cayenne-laced walnut pieces are an appetite-whetting hors d'oeuvre. And for dessert, I serve ripe peaches sweetened with a little sugar. An ample pitcher of chilled Summer Wine and lots of crusty French bread are all that's needed to complete this leisurely menu.

The whole meal can be put together in little more than the time it takes you to slice some cucumbers and poach the chicken breasts.

——————— THE GAME PLAN ———————

- Make the deviled eggs and start poaching the chicken breasts.

- Meanwhile, make the dressing for the chicken and the tomato slices with mustard and brown sugar dressing.

- Make the Summer Wine and serve with the deviled eggs.

- Prepare the basil and cucumber cream mixture, spoon over the chicken, garnish with the radishes and serve with the tomatoes and French bread.

○ **If Time Allows:** The deviled eggs and the dressings for the chicken and the tomatoes can be made ahead. You can also make the Summer Wine in advance, reserving the cucumber and lemon slices and sparkling water to add at the last moment.

Four Servings

Summer Wine

1 bottle (750 ml) dry white wine
1 cup Marsala wine
¼ cup brandy
¼ cup superfine sugar
Ice
½ medium cucumber, thinly sliced
3 slices of lemon
1 bottle (8 ounces) sparkling
   mineral water, seltzer or club
   soda

Pour the white wine, Marsala, brandy and sugar in a large glass pitcher or punch bowl. Add several ice cubes and stir until the sugar is dissolved. Stir in the cucumber and lemon slices. Add the sparkling water, stir and serve.

Deviled Eggs with Calamata Olives and Cayenne Walnuts

1 teaspoon unsalted butter
3 tablespoons coarsely chopped
   walnuts
Pinch of cayenne pepper
4 hard-cooked eggs
3 tablespoons mayonnaise
2 tablespoons chopped Calamata
   or other brine-cured olives
Watercress or parsley sprigs, for
   garnish

1 In small skillet, melt the butter. Add the walnuts and sauté over moderately low heat until heated through, about 2 minutes. Sprinkle the nuts with the cayenne, toss and set aside to cool.

2 Peel the eggs and cut them in half lengthwise. Place the yolks in a small bowl, add the mayonnaise and mash together until smooth. Stir in the olives.

3 Spoon the yolk mixture into the cavities of the egg whites and sprinkle some of the sautéed walnuts over the top of each egg half, pressing the nuts down gently to keep them in place. Garnish each egg half with a sprig of watercress or parsley.

Tomatoes with Mustard and Brown Sugar Dressing

¼ cup vegetable oil
1 tablespoon cider vinegar
2 teaspoons dark brown sugar
1½ teaspoons Dijon-style mustard
Salt
3 medium tomatoes, sliced
4 scallions, chopped, for garnish

1 In a small mixing bowl, combine the oil, vinegar, sugar and mustard. Season to taste with salt and beat together well.

2 Arrange the tomato slices on a serving platter. Spoon the dressing over them. Sprinkle with the scallions and serve.

Chicken Breasts with Cucumber, Basil and Cream

Bouquet garni: 6 sprigs of
   parsley, ½ teaspoon thyme,
4 peppercorns and 1 bay leaf
   tied in a double thickness of
   cheesecloth
2 whole chicken breasts (about ¾
   pound each)
¼ cup olive oil
1 tablespoon fresh lemon or lime
   juice
¾ teaspoon salt
⅛ teaspoon freshly ground white
   pepper
6 tablespoons heavy cream
1½ cucumbers—peeled, seeded
   and cut into ⅛-inch slices
   (about 2½ cups)
1½ tablespoons chopped fresh
   basil
4 radishes, sliced

1 Fill a large soup kettle about half full with water, add the bouquet garni, bring to a boil and simmer for 5 or 10 minutes. Add the chicken breasts, reduce the heat to moderately low and poach at a bare simmer for about 15 minutes.

2 Meanwhile, in a small mixing bowl, combine the oil, lemon juice, ½ teaspoon of the salt, the pepper and 3 tablespoons of the cream and blend well.

3 Drain the chicken breasts and pat them dry. Remove and discard the skin, and pull the meat from the bone in one piece. Slice each breast half lengthwise into 3 or 4 pieces and arrange them on a large platter. Spoon the dressing over the chicken.

4 In a small bowl, toss the cucumbers and basil with the remaining 3 tablespoons cream and ¼ teaspoon salt and spoon around the chicken. Sprinkle the radishes evenly over the top of the chicken and serve.

Southern-Style Chicken Dinner

Mississippi Chicken Strips*

Green Bean Succotash*

Hoppin' John*

**Tomato, Cucumber and Bermuda Onion
Salad**

Hot Cornbread or Corn Sticks

**Beverage Suggestion: Vouvray or California
Chenin Blanc**

◆

Hot Sourmash Whiskey Sundaes*

*RECIPE INCLUDED

Some of my growing up took place just north of the Mason-Dixon line. My mother's family lived "across the river" and on Sundays and other occasions, we would often cross over for dinner with our Southern relatives.

This menu is in the style of dinners across the river. Chicken, succotash and Hoppin' John were favorites. The latter, which is rice with black-eyed peas, was traditionally served on New Year's Day to insure good luck through the year, and it is said to have derived its name from the custom of having the children of the house hop around the table once before eating the dish. We always had a salad of sliced tomatoes, cucumbers and Bermuda onions sprinkled with cider vinegar, salt and pepper with down home meals like this one. And there was usually hot cornbread or corn sticks if someone had the time and felt like fussing with it.

THE GAME PLAN

- Sauté the pecans for the sundaes.
- Start the rice for the Hoppin' John.
- Start cooking the green beans.
- Combine the flour and seasonings for the chicken and shake the chicken pieces in it.
- Add the remaining ingredients to the green beans and cook.
- While the succotash and rice finish cooking, sauté the chicken strips. Serve all together hot.
- Make the sourmash sauce for the ice cream just before serving it.
- **If Time Allows:** The pecans can be sautéed, the spices for the chicken mixed and the succotash and Hoppin' John cooked in advance and reheated at serving time.

Four Servings

Mississippi Chicken Strips

½ cup all-purpose flour
½ teaspoon salt
½ teaspoon paprika
¼ teaspoon freshly ground
  pepper
¼ teaspoon thyme
¼ teaspoon onion powder
¼ teaspoon garlic powder
⅛ teaspoon crumbled sage
1½ pounds skinless, boneless
  chicken breast halves, cut into
  2½-by-¾-inch strips
About ½ cup vegetable oil

1 Combine the flour, salt, paprika, pepper, thyme, onion powder, garlic powder and sage in a paper or plastic bag and shake to blend. Add the chicken strips and shake them in the spices to coat well.

2 In a large skillet, heat ¼ cup of the oil until hot but not smoking. Add the chicken strips in a single layer, working in batches if necessary, leaving ample space between each strip. Sauté over moderately high heat until crisp and golden brown, about 3 minutes. Turn and sauté 1 minute longer. Transfer the chicken to paper towels to drain while sautéing the remaining pieces, adding more oil as needed. Serve hot.

Green Bean Succotash

1 pound green beans, cut into
  1-inch lengths
1 cup corn kernels (scraped from
  3 medium ears)
⅓ cup milk
1½ tablespoons unsalted butter
¼ teaspoon salt
Freshly ground pepper

1 Bring 2 cups of water to a boil in a medium saucepan. Add the beans and cook until crisp-tender, 2 to 3 minutes.

2 Drain the beans, rinse under cold water to refresh and return them to the saucepan. Add the corn, milk, butter and salt and season with pepper to taste. Simmer, uncovered, until the corn is cooked, 5 to 7 minutes. Serve hot.

Hoppin' John

1 tablespoon unsalted butter
1 teaspoon salt
½ teaspoon hot pepper sauce
1 cup converted rice
1 can (16 ounces) black-eyed peas
  with pork, drained
¼ teaspoon freshly ground
  pepper

1 In a large saucepan, bring 2 cups of water to a boil. Stir in the butter, salt, hot sauce and rice. Bring back to a boil, reduce the heat to low, cover, and cook until the rice is done, 17 to 20 minutes.

2 Stir the black-eyed peas and pepper into the rice and simmer over very low heat until the beans are warmed through.

Hot Sourmash Whiskey Sundaes

¼ cup chopped pecans
1 tablespoon plus 1 teaspoon
  unsalted butter
¼ cup honey
1 tablespoon dark brown sugar
2½ tablespoons sourmash,
  bourbon or rye
1 pint vanilla ice cream

1 In a small skillet, sauté the pecans in 1 teaspoon of the butter until lightly browned, about 2 minutes. Set aside.

2 In a small saucepan, combine the honey and sugar with ¼ cup of water and bring to a boil. Boil for about 2 minutes.

3 Remove the saucepan from the heat and stir in the remaining 1 tablespoon butter until melted, then stir in the whiskey.

4 Place a generous scoop of ice cream in each of 4 dessert dishes. Top each portion with 1 to 2 tablespoons of the hot sauce and sprinkle 1 tablespoon of the pecans over each.

Summer Picnic Basket

Prosciutto-Wrapped Breadsticks*

Shrimp and Assorted Vegetables with Green Sauce*

Eggs Vinaigrette with Celery and Olives*

Broiled Cornish Game Hens*

Italian Bread

Beverage Suggestion: Valpolicella, such as Bolla

◆

Nectarines

Brownies

*RECIPE INCLUDED

Summer is picnic season, and this festive array of food is particularly appropriate for outdoor dining. The bright flavors, simple preparation and variety of appetizers included also make this menu appealing for any kind of informal, spur-of-the-moment entertaining.

If you're picnicking, all the food can be put out together, and guests can help themselves. For home dining, you may prefer to break the meal into courses. Begin with a dazzling mix of tasty nibbles. Paper-thin prosciutto wrapped around crunchy breadsticks and a colorful platter of pink shrimp with a selection of your favorite crisp vegetables are easy-to-enjoy finger foods. The eggs, in a zesty vinaigrette enlivened with bits of stuffed olive, celery and scallion, require a small plate and fork.

After all these preliminaries, the only accompaniment you'll need to the Cornish game hens is some good Italian bread and a light, chilled red wine, such as Valpolicella. For dessert, bring along a basket of ripe nectarines and a batch of brownies.

THE GAME PLAN

- Season the hens, prepare the basting sauce, broil the hens and let them cool.
- Meanwhile, butter the breadsticks and wrap each in prosciutto.
- Prepare the eggs vinaigrette.
- Prepare the green sauce, shell the shrimp and cut up the vegetables.
- Seal all separately in plastic wrap or containers and chill until ready to transport in a cold chest or picnic basket.
- **If Time Allows:** Prepare all elements of this menu except the proscuitto-wrapped breadsticks the night before and reserve the vinaigrette to pour over the eggs just before packing them for the picnic. If dining at home, prepare the appetizers in advance and serve them in two courses or all at once while the hens are broiling. Serve the hens hot or at room temperature.

Six Servings

Prosciutto-Wrapped Breadsticks

2 tablespoons unsalted butter, at room temperatue
12 thin breadsticks, 3 or 4 inches long (break longer sticks in half if necessary)
6 slices prosciutto, halved crosswise

Butter the breadsticks and wrap a piece of prosciutto around each. Wrap well in plastic wrap until serving time.

Eggs Vinaigrette with Celery and Olives

6 hard-cooked eggs, halved lengthwise
½ cup chopped celery
¼ cup chopped pimiento-stuffed green olives
3 scallions, thinly sliced
2 tablespoons plus 1 teaspoon red wine vinegar
1 garlic clove, crushed through a press
½ teaspoon Dijon-style mustard
¼ teaspoon salt
¼ teaspoon freshly ground pepper
⅓ cup olive oil

1 Place the eggs cut-side down in a serving dish. Sprinkle with the celery, olives and scallions.

2 In a small bowl, whisk together the vinegar, garlic, mustard, salt and pepper. Gradually beat in the oil. Spoon the dressing over the eggs.

Shrimp and Assorted Vegetables with Green Sauce

½ cup mayonnaise
½ cup sour cream
¼ cup chopped spinach
2 tablespoons chopped scallions
2 teaspoons fresh lemon juice
½ teaspoon tarragon
¼ teaspoon hot pepper sauce
Salt
Assorted raw vegetables, such as broccoli, cauliflower, radishes, carrots, celery, zucchini, scallions
1¼ pounds medium or large cooked shrimp, shelled and deveined

1 In a small bowl, combine the mayonnaise, sour cream, spinach, scallions, lemon juice, tarragon, hot sauce and salt to taste. Stir to blend well.

2 Cut up the vegetables as you would for crudités: divide broccoli and cauliflower into florets; cut carrots, zucchini and celery into sticks. Arrange the shrimp and vegetables attractively on a platter. Serve the dipping sauce on the side.

Broiled Cornish Game Hens

3 Cornish game hens (about 1¼ pounds each), split in half
Salt and freshly ground pepper
4 tablespoons unsalted butter
⅓ cup strong coffee
¼ cup thick steak sauce, such as A-1
1 tablespoon unsweetened cocoa powder

1 Wipe the hens dry. Sprinkle with salt and pepper. Place skin-side down on a greased broiler rack.

2 In a small pan, combine the butter, coffee, steak sauce and cocoa. Cook over moderate heat, stirring frequently, until the butter is melted and the basting sauce is smooth.

3 Brush the hens with the basting sauce. Broil about 6 inches from the heat, basting frequently, for 15 minutes. Turn the hens. Brush well with sauce. Broil, basting frequently, for 15 to 20 minutes, until the juices run clear. Serve hot, at room temperature or chilled.

Note: These Cornish hens may be grilled over charcoal about 4 to 5 inches from the heat. Turn and baste frequently. Placing a loose tent of aluminum foil over the hens while grilling speeds up the cooking time and helps keep the meat moist.

Cool Country Fare

Iced Spiced Tea*

Country Salad with Country Dressing*

Cornmeal-Buttermilk Biscuits*

◆

**Chilled Watermelon
Served with Lemon Wedges and
Powdered Sugar**

Store-Bought Pecan Sandies

*RECIPE INCLUDED

Although gourmet stores are booming in large towns and cities, many of us still like to escape by retreating to more remote locales where often one catchall general store serves as grocery, hardware and drug store—and even gas station—all in one. Shopping can be basic at best, culinary decisions limited to the elemental. This menu is designed for the primitive pantry. No specialty ingredients are called for; exactness is not essential.

Your produce shopping list will include one or two lemons, an orange, a bunch of scallions, two tomatoes (homegrown, if possible), some parsley, if it is available, a watermelon—or any other seasonal fruit—and a head of lettuce: iceberg will do quite nicely, thank you. From the deli corner, smoked ham and turkey. Flour, cornmeal, baking powder and dry spices I assume to be on the pantry shelf. Eggs, milk and cream should be easily had.

THE GAME PLAN

- Preheat the oven to 425°. Prepare the biscuit dough and bake.
- Make the tea.
- Make the salad dressing.
- Assemble the salad and serve with the hot biscuits and the tea.
- **If Time Allows:** The tea and the dressing can be made ahead.

Four Servings

Iced Spiced Tea

4 tea bags or 1 tablespoon black
   or orange-pekoe tea
1 cinnamon stick
12 whole cloves
½ lemon
1 orange
4 cups boiling water
3 tablespoons sugar, or to taste
Thin slices of lemon, for garnish

1 Place the tea, cinnamon and cloves in a heatproof pitcher or a saucepan. Squeeze the juice of the half-lemon and the orange over the tea. Add the rinds.

2 Pour on the boiling water and let steep for at least 5 minutes. Strain into another pitcher and add the sugar while the tea is still warm, stirring to dissolve the sugar. Serve in tall glasses over ice. Garnish with lemon slices.

Country Salad

¾ pound thinly sliced smoked
   ham, slivered
½ pound thinly sliced cooked
   turkey or chicken, slivered
2 tomatoes—peeled, seeded and
   cut into thin strips
⅓ cup sliced scallions
2½ tablespoons chopped dill
   pickle
6 cups shredded lettuce
Country Dressing (recipe follows)
Lettuce leaves, for garnish

1 hard-cooked egg, finely
   chopped
1 tablespoon minced fresh parsley
Freshly ground pepper

1 In a large bowl, combine the ham, turkey, tomatoes, scallions, pickle and shredded lettuce. Toss lightly to mix.

2 Add the dressing and fold gently to coat evenly. Serve the salad on a bed of lettuce leaves. Sprinkle the chopped egg, parsley, if you have it, and freshly ground pepper to taste over the top.

Country Dressing

½ teaspoon powdered mustard
½ cup heavy cream
2½ tablespoons fresh lemon juice
¼ teaspoon salt
Several dashes of hot pepper
   sauce
⅓ cup mayonnaise

In a small bowl, stir the mustard with 2 teaspoons of the cream until smooth and blended. Stir in the remaining cream, the lemon juice, salt and hot sauce. Add the mayonnaise and beat until smooth.

Cornmeal-Buttermilk Biscuits

MAKES ABOUT 8 BISCUITS

1½ cups sifted unbleached flour
1 tablespoon baking powder
1 teaspoon sugar
½ teaspoon salt
⅛ teaspoon cayenne pepper
½ cup yellow cornmeal
6 tablespoons lightly salted butter,
   cut into small pieces
½ cup buttermilk

1 Preheat the oven to 425°. Sift together the flour, baking powder, sugar, salt and cayenne into a medium bowl. Stir in the cornmeal.

2 Cut in the butter until the mixture resembles coarse meal. Gently stir in ½ cup of buttermilk. The dough should be moist but not sticky; if it is too dry, add additional buttermilk 2 teaspoons at a time.

3 Turn out the dough onto a lightly floured work surface. Knead 2 or 3 times. Roll out the dough ¾ inch thick. With a 2-inch cutter or glass, cut the dough into rounds, or cut into diamond shapes with a sharp knife.

4 Bake on a greased baking sheet for 12 to 15 minutes, until lightly browned.

MEAT

Steak for a Celebration Dinner

Champagne

◆

Shell Steaks with Caper Butter*

Broiled Mushroom Caps*

Steamed Red Potatoes with Cream and Nutmeg*

Braised Endive*

**Beverage Suggestion: California Zinfandel,
Gattinara from Italy or Portuguese Periquita**

◆

Raspberry Cream with Chocolate Curls*

Coffee Spiked with Amaretto

*RECIPE INCLUDED

If you've ever been called upon to produce an elegant celebration dinner at the spur of the moment, you'll appreciate this menu. The whole festive meal can be whipped up in less than an hour and guests will certainly suspect you put in more effort and planning than is needed here.

Capers and a little Dijon mustard add an elegant extra touch to the shell steaks, as do the broiled mushroom caps that are served on the side. Braised Belgian endive is an unusual accompaniment that demands no fuss. Small red potatoes are dressed up with a light coating of warm cream and sprinkled with nutmeg. A luscious raspberry cream garnished with chocolate curls is an excellent finale.

To drink—serve champagne for aperitifs to set the celebratory mood, followed by a red wine with the dinner. Since the sauce for the steaks is authoritatively seasoned, choose a gutsy red—a California Zinfandel, a Gattinara from Italy or a Portuguese Periquita. With dessert serve coffee spiked with Amaretto.

THE GAME PLAN

- Prepare the raspberry puree and whip the cream for the dessert and chill separately until just before serving.

- Start preparing the endive.

- Put the potatoes on to steam.

- Preheat the broiler. Assemble the mushrooms and put them in to broil.

- Meanwhile, cook the steaks.

- Just before the steaks are ready to serve, quarter the potatoes and toss with the nutmeg cream. Serve hot with the steaks, mushroom caps and endive.

- Just before serving dessert, fold the raspberries and whipped cream together and shave the chocolate curls over the top of the Raspberry Cream.

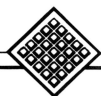

Six Servings

Broiled Mushroom Caps

12 large mushrooms, stemmed
¼ cup olive oil
¾ teaspoon thyme
Salt and freshly ground pepper
6 lemon wedges, for garnish
Watercress sprigs, for garnish

1 Preheat the broiler. Arrange the mushroom caps, hollow-sides up, in a baking dish and pour 1 teaspoon of the oil into each. Sprinkle a big pinch of thyme and salt and pepper to taste into each cap.

2 Broil the caps for 8 to 10 minutes, or until they have begun to render their liquid and they are a deep brown.

3 Transfer to a warmed plate. Garnish with lemon wedges and watercress and serve hot.

Steamed Red Potatoes with Cream and Nutmeg

12 small to medium red potatoes, unpeeled
½ cup heavy cream
⅛ teaspoon nutmeg
Salt and freshly ground pepper

1 Steam the potatoes until tender, about 20 minutes.

2 In a small saucepan, heat the cream and nutmeg over low heat, stirring occasionally. Keep the cream hot.

3 Cut the potatoes into quarters and toss with the hot cream. Season with salt and pepper to taste and serve hot.

Braised Endive

6 tablespoons unsalted butter
6 heads of Belgian endive, halved
⅔ cup chicken broth
Juice of 1 lemon
2 teaspoons dark brown sugar
Salt and freshly ground pepper
2 tablespoons chopped parsley

1 In a large saucepan, melt the butter over moderately high heat until it foams. Add the endive halves, cut-side down. Cook until the outer leaves begin to turn translucent, 3 to 4 minutes.

2 Add the chicken broth, lemon juice, sugar and salt and pepper to taste. Cover and cook over moderate heat for 10 minutes. Uncover, increase the heat slightly and cook until the liquid is almost evaporated and the endive is lightly browned, 6 to 8 minutes. Transfer to a platter and garnish with the parsley.

Shell Steaks with Caper Butter

1 tablespoon olive oil
6 shell steaks, cut 1 inch thick
Salt and freshly ground pepper
8 tablespoons unsalted butter, cut into pieces
4 scallions, sliced
1 tablespoon Dijon-style mustard
1 tablespoon drained capers, coarsely chopped
¼ cup chopped flat-leaf parsley

1 In a large heavy skillet, warm the oil over moderately high heat until hot but not smoking. Add the steaks, increase the heat to high and sear until lightly browned on one side, about 1½ minutes. Lower the heat to moderate, turn the steaks and cook for 1 to 2 minutes for rare or 2 to 3 minutes for medium-rare. Salt and pepper the steak to taste. Transfer to a warm platter.

2 Add the butter to the pan, stirring and scraping over moderate heat until the butter melts. When it foams, add the scallions and cook, stirring, until they wilt, about 30 seconds. Stir in the mustard and capers, then the parsley and any juices that have accumulated on the platter. Place each steak on a plate and spoon the sauce over them. Serve hot.

Raspberry Cream with Chocolate Curls

1 package (10 ounces) frozen raspberries, thawed and drained
1½ cups heavy cream
1 ounce of semisweet chocolate

1 Force the raspberries through a fairly fine mesh sieve. Beat the heavy cream until it forms soft peaks. Fold the raspberry puree into the whipped cream. Spoon into a serving bowl or individual serving dishes.

2 Shave curls from the chocolate with a vegetable peeler or sharp paring knife. Sprinkle the curls over the cream.

Old-Fashioned Sunday Dinner

Pork Chops with Apples and Bourbon*

Broiled Sweet Potatoes*

Sugared Onion Slices with Walnuts*

**Watercress and Orange Salad with Dining
Car Dressing***

Beverage Suggestion: Rosé d'Anjou or Liebfraumilch

◆

French Vanilla Ice Cream with Honey

Coffee

*RECIPE INCLUDED

Sunday dinners always used to be family affairs with good old-fashioned comforting foods such as the thick, sage-scented pork chops cooked with apples and bourbon in this menu. The only break with that homey tradition here is that the pork is cooked quickly rather than being roasted slowly.

Two broiled vegetables—buttery sweet potatoes and thick slices of onion sprinkled with brown sugar and chopped walnuts—are the perfect accompaniments to this Sunday dinner menu.

Even the dressing for a colorful watercress and orange salad is nostalgic—a reminder of the days when some of the best of simple American cooking was served up on train dining cars by waiters in stiffly starched white jackets. Dining car salads were always a special treat to me.

For dessert, drizzle a little honey over a good, rich French vanilla ice cream. For added punch, stir a little rum into the honey.

THE GAME PLAN

- Put the sweet potatoes on to boil.
- Assemble the salad and make the dressing, but wait to spoon the dressing and dates over until just before serving.
- Preheat the broiler. Start sautéing the pork chops.
- Meanwhile, prepare the onions and put them in to broil for 5 minutes.
- Drain the sweet potatoes and prepare them for broiling.
- Turn the onions, add the remaining ingredients and return them to the hot broiler along with the potatoes.
- Finish making the pork chops and their sauce and serve with the onions, potatoes and salad.
- **If Time Allows:** The dressing or the salad can be made in advance and the sweet potatoes can be boiled ahead of time.

Four Servings

Broiled Sweet Potatoes

4 small sweet potatoes, about 4
  inches long
2 tablespoons unsalted butter
½ teaspoon savory
Salt and freshly ground pepper

1 Place the potatoes in a large
pan of boiling water and cook,
covered, for 20 to 25 minutes.

2 Preheat the broiler. Drain the
potatoes and cut each in half
lengthwise. Spread ¾ teaspoon
of the butter over the cut side of
each potato half and season
each with a pinch of the savory
and salt and pepper to taste.

3 Place on a broiler pan lined
with aluminum foil and broil for
about 5 minutes, until lightly
browned. Serve hot, accompanied by extra butter, if desired.

Sugared Onion Slices with Walnuts

6 center slices (¾ to 1 inch thick)
  of yellow onion
4 tablespoons unsalted butter,
  melted
Salt
1 tablespoon brown sugar
2 tablespoons chopped walnuts

1 Preheat the broiler. Brush the
onion slices with about half of the
melted butter, place them on a
broiler pan lined with aluminum
foil and broil for 5 minutes.

2 Turn the onion slices with a
spatula. Season with salt to taste
and sprinkle ½ teaspoon of
brown sugar and 1 teaspoon
chopped walnuts over each slice.
Drizzle the remaining butter over
the onions and broil for 3 more
minutes, until the sugar is melted
and the onions are crisp-tender.
Serve hot.

Watercress and Orange Salad with Dining Car Dressing

1 large bunch of watercress
2 large oranges, peeled and
  sliced
¼ cup vegetable oil
1 tablespoon cider vinegar
½ teaspoon paprika
½ teaspoon sugar
¼ teaspoon Worcestershire sauce
⅛ teaspoon powdered mustard
⅛ teaspoon freshly ground
  pepper
1½ tablespoons chopped dates

1 Arrange the watercress on a
large platter or on four individual
serving plates. Place the orange
slices on the watercress.

2 In a small bowl, combine the
oil, vinegar, paprika, sugar,
Worcestershire sauce, mustard
and pepper and whisk until thoroughly blended.

3 Pour the dressing over the
salad and sprinkle the dates
evenly on top.

Pork Chops with Apples and Bourbon

4 boneless loin pork chops, cut 1
  inch thick and trimmed of fat
1 garlic clove, halved lengthwise
Pinch of sage
Salt and freshly ground pepper
2 tablespoons unsalted butter
1 teaspoon fresh lemon juice
½ cup chopped onion
1 medium apple, preferably
  Granny Smith or Golden
  Delicious, peeled and diced
⅓ cup bourbon

1 Pat the pork chops dry. Rub
each on both sides with the cut
sides of the garlic clove. Season
with the sage and salt and pepper to taste.

2 In a large skillet, heat the
butter until it sizzles. Add the pork
and sauté over moderately high
heat until the chops are golden
brown on both sides and cooked
through, 10 to 14 minutes. Remove from the pan, sprinkle with
the lemon juice and keep warm.

3 Add the onion (and more
butter, if necessary) to the skillet
and sauté over moderate heat
for 1 minute. Stir in the apple and
sauté 1 minute longer. Add the
bourbon, and cook, stirring, for 1
minute. Spoon the onion, apple
and bourbon sauce over the pork
chops and serve.

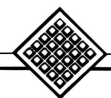

Light and Spicy Dinner

Spiced Lamb Chops with Sansho Pepper and Scallions*

Red Potatoes with Lime Juice and Green Chiles*

◆

Cucumber, Kiwi and Bibb Lettuce Salad*

Beverage Suggestion: California Zinfandel, such as Sebastiani

◆

Strawberries with Cream and Cointreau*

Demitasse

*RECIPE INCLUDED

Each of the dishes in this menu sparkles with an unusual combination of flavors. The lamb chops are spiced with *sansho*, the fragrant Japanese pepper made from the pods of prickly ash. Lime juice and zingy green chiles accentuate the flavor of the red potatoes. A refreshing assortment of cucumbers, kiwi fruit and Bibb lettuce gives new dimension to a simple green salad. For dessert, strawberries are topped with whipped cream that has been spiked with a dash of Cointreau.

Busy cooks will also appreciate the way this meal fits neatly into their schedules. While the lamb is marinating, prepare the salad and the dessert. Sauté the lamb and steam the potatoes simultaneously. Or prepare the dessert and salad ahead of time and assemble them just before dinner.

To make the dessert ahead, crush the strawberries, place them in the wine glasses and set in the refrigerator to chill. Whip the cream without the Cointreau and refrigerate in a sieve set over a bowl (this way, when the cream "weeps," the water will drain off and the whipped cream will be even thicker). Whip in the Cointreau at the last moment or simply splash over the berries.

THE GAME PLAN

- Make the marinade for the lamb, add the chops and let them marinate.

- Prepare the berries and whip the cream for the dessert, reserving the Cointreau to add just before serving; chill the two separately.

- Make the dressing and assemble the salad, but wait to toss together until just before serving.

- Put the potatoes on to steam and sauté the lamb; just before serving, toss the potatoes with the remaining ingredients.

- Whip the Cointreau into the cream just before serving dessert and spoon over the berries.

○ **If Time Allows:** The lamb can be marinated ahead. The berries and cream can be prepared and chilled in advance, and the dressing and salad can be made in advance and chilled until time to toss together.

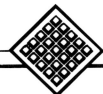

Four Servings

Spiced Lamb Chops with Sansho Pepper and Scallions

2 tablespoons sake
2 tablespoons Oriental sesame oil
2 tablespoons vegetable oil
2½ teaspoons rice wine vinegar
1 garlic clove, crushed through a press
½ teaspoon salt
¼ teaspoon sansho pepper or ground Szechuan pepper
8 loin lamb chops, trimmed of fat
1 tablespoon soy sauce
2 scallions, thinly sliced

1 In a large shallow dish, combine the sake, 1 tablespoon of the sesame oil, 1 tablespoon of the vegetable oil, 1 teaspoon of the rice vinegar, the garlic, salt and *sansho* pepper. Add the lamb chops, turn to coat and marinate at room temperature, turning once, for 20 minutes. Remove and pat dry.

2 In a large heavy skillet, warm the remaining 1 tablespoon vegetable oil over high heat until shimmering. Working in two batches, add 4 lamb chops and sauté, turning once, until browned and slightly resistant to the touch, about 4 minutes on each side. Remove to a plate and cover loosely with foil to keep warm. Sauté the remaining 4 lamb chops.

3 Meanwhile, in a small bowl, combine the remaining 1 tablespoon sesame oil, 1½ teaspoons rice vinegar and the soy sauce to make a glaze. Return the lamb chops to the pan. Pour the glaze on top and cook, stirring, until the chops are well coated and warmed through, about 2 minutes. Divide among warmed plates and sprinkle the scallions on top.

Red Potatoes with Lime Juice and Green Chiles

6 medium, red potatoes, quartered
2 tablespoons unsalted butter
1 tablespoon fresh lime juice
1 small hot green chile, minced
½ teaspoon salt

1 Steam the potatoes until fork-tender, about 15 minutes.

2 In a small saucepan, melt the butter over low heat. Stir in the lime juice and chile. Add the potatoes and salt and toss gently until well coated.

Cucumber, Kiwi and Bibb Lettuce Salad

¼ cup vegetable oil
1 tablespoon fresh lemon juice
½ teaspoon sugar
½ teaspoon paprika
1 European seedless cucumber, thinly sliced
3 kiwis, peeled and thinly sliced
1 head of Bibb lettuce, torn into bite-size pieces
Freshly ground pepper

1 In a small bowl, whisk together the oil, lemon juice, sugar and paprika.

2 Place the cucumber, kiwis and lettuce in a serving bowl. Add the dressing and toss to coat. Grind pepper on top to taste.

Strawberries with Cream and Cointreau

1½ pints fresh strawberries, hulled
⅓ cup sugar
1 cup heavy cream, chilled
2 tablespoons Cointreau or other orange liqueur

1 Divide half the strawberries among 4 wine glasses. Place the remaining strawberries and the sugar in a bowl and crush together. Spoon over the whole strawberries.

2 Beat the cream until it stands in soft peaks. Beat in the Cointreau. Spoon over the berries.

Variations on a British Favorite

Garnished Smoked Salmon*

◆

**Pan-Fried Steaks with Shallots
and Mushrooms***

**Individual Yorkshire Puddings
with Rosemary***

Broiled Tomatoes on a Bed of Watercress

**Beverage Suggestion: California Petite Sirah,
such as Parducci or Joseph Phelps**

◆

Ginger Sundae*

Coffee or Tea

*RECIPE INCLUDED

This menu captures the aroma and flavor of time-honored English special occasion food by taking a few small liberties with tradition: Yorkshire pudding, always a hands-down favorite, is delicious served with quick-cooking rib steaks. If you have beef drippings left over from a roast, substitute them for the peanut oil to add extra flavor.

For an easy accompaniment, sprinkle tomato halves with salt, pepper and thyme; top them with butter and broil until lightly browned. Serve them on a bed of watercress. A finale of ice cream topped with spicy ginger syrup is certain to please.

And, it's particularly nice to know that in under an hour you can create a feast that has the hearty elegance of a Victorian celebration.

THE GAME PLAN

- Make the Garnished Smoked Salmon.
- Assemble all the ingredients for the steaks and the broiled tomatoes.
- Preheat the oven to 450°. Oil the muffin tins and put them in the oven. Prepare the batter for the Yorkshire pudding, pour into the hot muffin tins and bake.
- Meanwhile, serve the salmon with aperitifs.
- Start the steaks about 10 minutes before the Yorkshire puddings are finished baking.
- Remove the Yorkshire puddings from the oven, turn to broil and put the tomatoes in to broil.
- Prepare the sundaes just before serving.
- ○ **If Time Allows:** The salmon can be assembled in advance and covered until serving time.

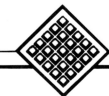

Six Servings

Garnished Smoked Salmon

1 to 2 tablespoons unsalted butter, softened
6 slices cracked wheat or sprouted whole wheat bread
½ pound smoked salmon, thinly sliced
2 hard-cooked eggs, finely chopped
½ cup finely chopped sweet yellow onion (½ large onion)
½ cup finely chopped fresh parsley
1 lemon, cut into small wedges
Coarsely ground pepper

1 Butter the bread and trim off the crusts.

2 Arrange the salmon slices (about 2 thin slices per person) on each plate and surround them with a tablespoon each of chopped egg, onion, parsley plus a lemon wedge. Cut the buttered bread into triangles and pass separately, along with a pepper mill if you wish.

Pan-Fried Steaks with Shallots and Mushrooms

¼ cup vegetable oil
6 boneless rib steaks, about 1 inch thick, trimmed of excess fat
6 tablespoons unsalted butter
18 mushroom caps (from about 1 pound of mushrooms)
2 tablespoons chopped shallots
¼ cup beef broth
¾ cup dry white wine

Pinch of salt
½ teaspoon freshly ground pepper
Chopped fresh parsley, for garnish

1 Divide the oil between two large heavy skillets and place over high heat. When the oil is smoking, add 3 steaks to each skillet and sauté, turning once, for 2 minutes on each side. Reduce the heat to moderate and cook for 2 minutes longer on each side for rare, 3 for medium-rare or longer if desired. Remove to a heated platter or plates and cover with foil to keep warm.

2 Pour off the fat from the skillets and add 2 tablespoons of the butter to each; melt over moderately high heat. When the butter is sizzling, divide the mushroom caps between the pans and sauté, tossing, until tender and nicely browned, about 4 minutes. Spoon the mushrooms over the steaks.

3 Add another tablespoon of butter to each skillet and divide the shallots between the pans. Sauté until softened, about 30 seconds. Add half the broth, wine, salt and pepper to each skillet. Boil for about 3 minutes, scraping up the browned bits from the bottom of the pans, until the liquid is reduced by half.

4 Pour the sauce over steaks and mushrooms and sprinkle with parsley.

Individual Yorkshire Puddings with Rosemary

¼ cup peanut oil
1 cup all-purpose flour
1 cup milk
2 eggs, beaten
1 teaspoon crumbled rosemary
½ teaspoon salt

1 Preheat the oven to 450°. Put 1 teaspoon of the oil into each of the 12 cups of a 3-inch muffin tin and put in the oven as it preheats.

2 Sift the flour into a large bowl, make a well and add the milk, eggs, rosemary and salt; beat until smooth.

3 Fill the hot, almost-smoking muffin cups about one-third full of batter. Immediately place in the oven and bake for 15 minutes, or until the sides are set and lightly browned. Reduce the oven temperature to 375° and bake for 10 to 15 minutes longer, until deep brown. Serve hot.

Ginger Sundae

1½ pints vanilla ice cream
6 teaspoons finely chopped preserved stem ginger
6 tablespoons syrup from the preserved ginger
¾ cup heavy cream, whipped
1½ tablespoons brandy (optional)

Scoop the ice cream into 6 dessert dishes. Sprinkle 1 teaspoon of the ginger and 1 tablespoon of the syrup over each serving. Top with the whipped cream, flavored with the brandy.

Veal Scallops with a Special Touch

Veal Scallops with Port and Green Peppercorn Sauce*

Broiled Baby Zucchini with Rosemary*

Julienned Carrots with Lemon Zest*

Beverage Suggestion: Light Oregon or Washington Riesling

◆

**Coffee Ice Cream with Maple-Rum Cream
Sauce***

*RECIPE INCLUDED

Every busy cook's recipe repertoire includes dish-es that have a little special sparkle for entertain-ing. This is one of my favorites in the "quick, for company" category.

The veal scallops are made with a little port and fresh green peppercorns. If you wish, thinly sliced turkey breast cutlets can be substituted for the veal to make a more economical meal. Miniature or baby zucchini and other tiny vegetables are now being cultivated and can be found in specialty pro-duce markets around the country. They are sweet, tender and make for a very pretty presentation. Young, small-size vegetables work equally well. The carrots are very simple, with only a sprinkling of tangy lemon zest to add a special touch.

THE GAME PLAN

- Prepare the maple-rum cream, cover and refrigerate until serving.
- Put the carrots on to cook.
- Preheat the broiler. Prepare the zucchini and place in the broiler.
- Start sautéing the veal.
- Turn the zucchini and return it to the broiler.
- Toss the carrots in the butter and seasonings and keep warm.
- Transfer the veal to a serving platter, make the sauce and serve with the carrots and zucchini.
- Spoon the maple-rum cream over the ice cream and sprinkle with the walnuts just before serving.
- **If Time Allows:** The maple-rum cream can be made in advance, covered and chilled until serving time. Stir the cream just before spooning over the ice cream.

Four Servings

Veal Scallops with Port and Green Peppercorn Sauce*

8 veal scallops, about 1 pound
¼ cup all-purpose flour
2 tablespoons unsalted butter
2 tablespoons vegetable oil
Salt
½ cup port
1 tablespoon drained green
  peppercorns

1 Lightly pound the veal scallops between sheets of waxed paper to flatten. Dredge the veal in the flour; shake off any excess flour.

2 In a large skillet, melt 1 tablespoon of the butter in 1 tablespoon of the oil (see Note). Add half the veal scallops, or as many as will fit in the skillet without crowding and sauté over moderately high heat for 1 to 2 minutes on each side, until lightly browned. Transfer to a warmed serving platter, season with salt to taste and keep warm. Add the remaining butter and oil and repeat with the remaining veal scallops.

3 Drain the fat from the skillet. Add the port and simmer over high heat, scraping up any brown bits that cling to the pan, until reduced by half, about 1 minute. Stir in the peppercorns. Pour the sauce over the veal and serve.

Note: To save time, two skillets can be used to sauté all of the veal at once. Divide the butter and oil between the two skillets and deglaze only one pan to make the sauce.

Broiled Baby Zucchini with Rosemary

8 miniature or 4 young zucchini,
  halved lengthwise
1½ tablespoons unsalted butter,
  melted
½ teaspoon crumbled rosemary
¼ teaspoon salt
Freshly ground pepper
1 teaspoon fresh lemon juice

1 Preheat the broiler. Brush the zucchini with the melted butter and place them, cut-side down, on a broiler pan lined with aluminum foil. Broil for 4 minutes.

2 Turn the zucchini, season with the rosemary, salt and pepper to taste. Broil for 2 to 5 minutes longer, until crisp-tender. Squeeze a few drops of lemon juice over each zucchini half and serve hot.

Julienned Carrots with Lemon Zest

¾ pound carrots, cut into thick
  julienne strips
2 tablespoons unsalted butter
Salt
2 teaspoons fresh lemon juice
½ teaspoon grated lemon zest
Pinch of cayenne pepper

1 In a large skillet, simmer the carrots in ¼ inch of water until crisp-tender, 5 to 10 minutes.

2 Drain the carrots and return them to the skillet. Add the butter, season with salt to taste and shake over moderate heat until the butter is melted and the carrots coated. Sprinkle with the lemon juice, zest and cayenne and toss over moderate heat for a few more seconds. Serve hot.

Coffee Ice Cream with Maple-Rum Cream Sauce

½ cup heavy cream
2 tablespoons dark rum
3 ounces maple sugar candy,
  diced or crumbled, or 3
  tablespoons maple syrup
1 pint coffee ice cream
4 teaspoons chopped walnuts

1 In a small mixing bowl, whip the cream. Fold in the rum and maple sugar candy.

2 Spoon the ice cream into four dishes. Divide the maple-rum cream among the dishes and sprinkle each serving with 1 teaspoon of the chopped walnuts.

A Rustic Winter Meal

Italian Sweet Vermouth

Radishes with Butter and Coarse Salt

◆

Sausages in White Wine*

No-Fuss Risotto*

Baked Tomatoes with Mustard and Brown Sugar*

Beverage Suggestion: Chardonnay

◆

Fresh Cheese with Herbs* or Chèvre

Ripe Pears and Walnuts

Coffee and Slivovitz

*RECIPE INCLUDED

Dreary winter months seem to cry out for the comforts of hearty country fare, to be enjoyed in the company of a few good friends. The following menu for a rustic feast can be readied and served in less than an hour. Bright fruits and vegetables set off the aromatic richness of sausages in wine with risotto.

Start off with goblets of Italian sweet vermouth over ice with a splash of sparkling mineral water or soda and a twist of lemon peel, accompanied by radishes served with a crock of sweet butter and a small bowl of coarse salt. Then bring on a platter of piping hot sausages ringed with risotto and garnished with juicy baked tomatoes. A rich Chardonnay goes well with these and the cheese, pears and nuts that follow. Serve the herbed fresh cheese or a young French goat cheese, such as Montrachet. Let your guests crack their own walnuts at the table. Top all this off with coffee and slivovitz.

THE GAME PLAN

- Preheat the oven to 350°. Start the sausages.

- Meanwhile, prepare the tomatoes and place in the oven. Put the sausages in the oven with the tomatoes.

- Start the risotto. (This will rest well for 10 minutes or so after cooking if kept covered.)

- Make the fresh cheese with herbs.

- To serve, ring the risotto around the edge of a platter. Arrange the sausages in the center and the tomatoes around the edge.

- **If Time Allows:** The fresh cheese can be made ahead and refrigerated until serving. The sausages can be cooked a few hours in advance and heated up before serving.

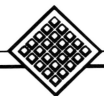

Six Servings

Fresh Cheese with Herbs

8 ounces cream cheese
3 tablespoons sour cream
2 tablespoons heavy cream
1 garlic clove, minced
3 scallions, coarsley chopped
¾ cup fresh parsley, coarsely
  chopped
½ teaspoon salt
¼ teaspoon freshly ground
  pepper
½ teaspoon thyme

1 In a mixing bowl, whip the cream cheese until light. Add the sour cream, heavy cream, garlic, scallions, parsley, salt and pepper. Beat until well mixed.

2 Put the cheese in a serving bowl just large enough to hold it and sprinkle with the thyme.

Sausages in White Wine

1 tablespoon unsalted butter
2½ pounds link pork sausages
½ cup dry white wine, preferably
  white Burgundy or Chardonnay
¾ cup chopped fresh parsley, for
  garnish

1 Preheat the oven to 350°. In a noncorrodible ovenproof skillet with a lid, melt the butter.

2 Add the sausages and sauté them over moderately high heat for 5 minutes. Drain off the fat and continue to cook over moderately high heat until they are well browned, 5 to 10 minutes more. (Do not drain any more fat.)

3 Add the wine, cover the pan, place in the oven and bake for 15 to 20 minutes. Remove the pan from the oven and set aside until ready to serve.

4 Arrange the sausages on a platter in the center of a ring of risotto. Spoon the wine sauce over the sausages and sprinkle with the parsley.

Baked Tomatoes with Mustard and Brown Sugar

6 small tomatoes
1½ teaspoons salt
2 tablespoons Dijon-style mustard
2 tablespoons brown sugar
2 tablespoons unsalted butter

1 Preheat the oven to 350°. Cut a thin slice from the top of each tomato, discarding the tops. Using a spoon or a knife, remove some of the tomato flesh to make an indentation about 1 inch deep.

2 Sprinkle each tomato with ¼ teaspoon of the salt. Spread each with 1 teaspoon of the mustard, top with 1 teaspoon of the brown sugar and 1 teaspoon of the butter.

3 Place the tomatoes in a buttered, ovenproof dish and bake for 20 to 30 minutes, depending on the ripeness of the tomatoes. To serve, arrange the tomatoes on the risotto.

No-Fuss Risotto

1½ tablespoons unsalted butter
1 medium onion, chopped
1 cup Arborio rice
2½ cups chicken broth
2 ounces prosciutto (or other
  ham), cut into julienne strips
2 tablespoons freshly grated
  Parmesan cheese

1 In a medium saucepan, melt the butter over low heat. Stir in the onion and cook gently, stirring, for 2 minutes. Add the rice and, continuing to stir, cook until the rice grains are translucent, about 3 minutes.

2 Add the chicken stock, increase the heat to moderately high and bring to a boil. Lower the heat again, cover the pan tightly and cook the risotto for 20 minutes, or until all the liquid is absorbed. Toss the prosciutto and cheese into the rice.

3 To serve, make a ring of the rice on a large heated platter and arrange the sausages in the center and place the baked tomatoes around the outside.

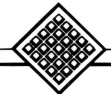

Dinner Party for Four

Smoked Salmon and Cucumber Salad*

Beverage Suggestion: Fumé Blanc, such as Robert Mondavi

◆

Lamb Chops with Wild Mushroom Sauce*

Zucchini with Freshly Grated Parmesan Cheese*

Beverage Suggestion: Red Bordeaux, such as Lafon-Rochet

◆

Raspberry Brûlée*

Café Filtre

*RECIPE INCLUDED

The classic elements of a celebratory meal are all present in this menu: smoked salmon, lamb chops in a sauce rich with wild mushrooms, luxurious crème brûlée with raspberries.

The ingredients are admittedly more expensive than usual, but the taste is worth it. Cèpes are available in most specialty food stores. Dried cèpes must be soaked in hot water until soft.

Certain elements of the recipes can be prepared in advance. The cucumbers can be sliced and the cream sauce prepared for the appetizer; do not combine the two until 15 minutes before serving, or the sauce will become watery. The cèpes can be soaked anytime that day; drain after 30 minutes, though, or the flavor will be in the liquid and not in the cèpes. The zucchini can be presliced and refrigerated. The crème brûlée can be put together before dinner and quickly broiled just before serving. None of the dishes takes more than 15 minutes to cook.

THE GAME PLAN

- Soak the cèpes.
- Make the cucumber salad and chill.
- Assemble the raspberry brûlées (except for the brown sugar) and chill until broiling.
- Assemble and prepare all of the ingredients for the lamb chops and the zucchini.
- Assemble the smoked salmon and cucumber salad and serve.
- Start sautéing the lamb and make the zucchini; serve both hot.
- Preheat the broiler. Sprinkle the raspberry brulées with the sugar and broil; serve hot.
- **If Time Allows:** Many items in this menu can be made in advance: soak the cèpes, drain after 30 minutes and set aside; prepare the cucumber salad, cover and refrigerate, and make the raspberry brûlées, reserving the sugar to add just before broiling.

Four Servings

Lamb Chops with Wild Mushroom Sauce

½ ounce dried cèpes
3 tablespoons unsalted butter
1 tablespoon olive oil
8 loin lamb chops, cut 1 inch thick
1 tablespoon minced shallots
⅓ cup dry Madeira
1 teaspoon fresh lemon juice
½ teaspoon salt
¼ teaspoon pepper

1 Cover the cèpes with hot water and soak until soft, about 30 minutes; drain.

2 Meanwhile, in each of 2 large heavy skillets, melt ½ tablespoon of the butter in ½ tablespoon of the olive oil. When the foam subsides, add the lamb chops. Sauté over moderately high heat, turning once, until lightly browned, 4 to 5 minutes on each side. Remove to a heated platter and cover.

3 Pour off any excess fat from one of the pans. Add the shallots and drained cèpes and sauté over moderate heat until the shallots are softened but not browned, about 1 minute.

4 Add the Madeira, raise the heat to high and cook, scraping any browned bits, until reduced by half, about 1 minute. Return any accumulated meat juices to the pan; add the lemon juice, salt and pepper and heat through.

5 Remove the skillet from the heat. Swirl in the remaining 2 tablespoons butter, 1 tablespoon at a time. Pour over the lamb.

Smoked Salmon and Cucumber Salad

2 medium cucumbers
¼ cup heavy cream
2 teaspoons grated onion
1 tablespoon minced fresh dill
4 thin slices of square Danish pumpernickel bread
1 tablespoon unsalted butter, at room temperature
8 thin slices of smoked salmon (4 to 6 ounces)
¼ teaspoon freshly ground pepper
4 lemon wedges

1 Peel the cucumbers and slice in half lengthwise. Scoop out and discard the seeds. Slice crosswise into thin crescents.

2 In a medium bowl, combine the cream, onion and dill. Add the cucumber and toss to coat. Refrigerate until well chilled, about 15 minutes.

3 Remove the crust from the pumpernickel. Lightly butter each slice. Cut each slice diagonally into 4 triangles.

4 Arrange 2 slices of the salmon on each serving plate. Sprinkle lightly with the pepper. Using a slotted spoon, drain a serving of cucumber from the sauce and place next to the salmon. Garnish each plate with a lemon wedge and 4 triangles of pumpernickel.

Zucchini with Freshly Grated Parmesan Cheese

1½ pounds medium zucchini
1½ tablespoons unsalted butter
Pinch of freshly ground nutmeg
Salt
2 tablespoons grated Parmesan

1 Cut the zucchini lengthwise into ¼-inch-thick slices and then crosswise into thin matchsticks.

2 In a large skillet, melt the butter over moderate heat. Add the zucchini and sauté, tossing frequently, until crisp-tender, about 3 minutes. Season with the nutmeg and salt to taste.

3 Place in a warmed serving bowl. Sprinkle on the Parmesan.

Raspberry Brûlée

2 packages (10 ounces each) frozen raspberries in syrup, thawed and drained
1 cup crème fraîche or ¼ cup heavy cream whipped into ½ cup sour cream
¼ cup brown sugar

1 Divide the berries among 4 heatproof ramekins or custard cups of ¾- to 1-cup capacity. Cover with the crème fraîche and chill.

2 Adjust the broiler rack to 4 inches from the heat and preheat the broiler. Sprinkle each ramekin with 1 tablespoon of the sugar. Broil until the sugar just melts, about 2 minutes. Serve immediately or chill until serving time.

Creating a Family Favorite

Plat de Crudités*

Vinaigrette with Anchovies*

◆

Dilled Veal Balls with Sour Cream and Caper Sauce*

Buttered Noodles

Beverage Suggestion: California Sauvignon Blanc

◆

Boysenberry or Raspberry Sherbet Cassis*

Walnut Cookies*

*RECIPE INCLUDED

Simple and unassuming, this dinner is made for easy conversation and good cheer. The vegetable is served first, in the form of a *plat de crudités,* an assortment of colorful raw ingredients arranged artfully on a tray. It can be presented at table or with drinks in front of the fire, with dipping sauce or dressed as a salad. Dark pumpernickel or French bread will help soak up the lemony vinaigrette with anchovies.

Dilled veal balls, flecked with scallion, in a tangy sour cream and caper sauce, are sure to be a family favorite. Serve them over buttered noodles for a substantial supper.

For dessert, try one of the finer sherbets (or sorbets) currently on the market. Boysenberry or raspberry is excellent, with a generous splash of crème de cassis to make it extra special. I've added a recipe for some quick and delicious walnut cookies as well, but if you are in a pinch for time, good-quality store-bought cookies will do nicely.

THE GAME PLAN

- Preheat the oven to 375°. Prepare the walnut cookies and bake.
- Prepare the crudités and the vinaigrette.
- Mix and form the veal balls.
- Put the noodles on to boil; start sautéing the veal balls.
- Serve the crudités with aperitifs.
- Finish the veal balls and the sauce. Drain and butter the noodles and serve with the veal balls.
- Pour the cassis over the sherbet just before serving with the walnut cookies.
- **If Time Allows:** All of the vegetables for the crudités (except the tomatoes and mushrooms) can be cut up ahead of time and refrigerated in a container of ice water. The cookies can be baked the day before and the vinaigrette made ahead. The veal balls and sauce can be made earlier and reheated.

Six Servings

Plat de Crudités

Cucumber, peeled and thinly
  sliced
Carrot sticks
Cauliflower, separated into florets
Fennel or celery sticks
Tomatoes, cut into eighths
Green bell peppers, cut into rings
Broccoli, separated into florets
Radishes
Mushrooms, halved if large
Black olives, such as Calamata,
  Alfonso or Niçoise
Vinaigrette with Anchovies

Arrange any selection of the
above vegetables decoratively
on a platter. Sprinkle with the Vinaigrette with Anchovies (or with
lemon juice, olive oil and
chopped parsley) or serve the
vinaigrette as a dipping sauce.

Vinaigrette with Anchovies

MAKES ABOUT ½ CUP

⅓ cup olive oil
1 tablespoon red wine vinegar
1 tablespoon fresh lemon juice
2 teaspoons minced onion
1 teaspoon minced chives or
  scallion green
1 teaspoon chopped fresh parsley
3 flat anchovy fillets, chopped
2 to 4 dashes hot pepper sauce,
  to taste

Whisk all the ingredients until
mixed.

Dilled Veal Balls with Sour Cream and Caper Sauce

1½ pounds ground veal
1 cup fresh bread crumbs
1 egg, lightly beaten
4 scallions, chopped
1 tablespoon chopped fresh dill or
  1 teaspoon dried
1½ teaspoons salt
½ teaspoon freshly ground
  pepper
3 to 4 tablespoons unsalted butter
1 tablespoon all-purpose flour
1¼ cups sour cream
2 tablespoons drained capers,
  chopped
1 tablespoon juice from the caper
  bottle
¼ teaspoon nutmeg
Chopped fresh dill or parsley

1 In a medium bowl, mix the
veal, bread crumbs, egg, scallions, dill, salt and pepper. Form
into 1-inch balls.

2 In a large skillet, melt 3 tablespoons of the butter over
moderately high heat. Add the
veal balls and sauté, turning occasionally, until they are brown
all over and cooked through,
about 7 minutes. Remove the
veal balls and keep warm.

3 If there is less than 1 tablespoon of drippings in the skillet,
add the remaining 1 tablespoon
butter and heat until melted. Add
the flour and cook, stirring, over
moderately low heat for about 3
minutes to make a roux. Stir in the
sour cream until smooth. Add the

capers, caper juice and nutmeg.
Heat until warmed through but
do not allow to boil.

4 Add the veal balls to the
sauce and turn to coat. Serve
over buttered noodles and garnish with the dill or parsley.

Boysenberry or Raspberry Sherbet Cassis

1½ pints boysenberry or
  raspberry sherbet
¾ cup crème de cassis

Scoop ½ cup of sherbet into
each of 6 bowls. Pour 2 tablespoons of cassis over each.

Walnut Cookies

½ cup solid vegetable shortening
¾ cup packed light brown sugar
1 egg, lightly beaten
1¼ cups all-purpose flour
½ teaspoon baking soda
½ teaspoon salt
1 teaspoon vanilla extract
½ cup chopped walnuts

1 Preheat the oven to 375°.
Cream the shortening and brown
sugar until blended. Add the egg,
flour, baking soda, salt, vanilla
and 1 teaspoon of hot water. Mix
well. Stir in the walnuts.

2 Drop by heaping teaspoon-
fuls, about 1½ inches apart, onto
a greased cookie sheet. Bake for
about 12 minutes, or until the
cookies are golden and crisp.

Dinner for a Chilly Evening

Pumpkin Bisque*

◆

Medallions of Pork with Pommard Sauce*

Poached Pears*

Beverage Suggestion: Pommard, such as Louis Latour

◆

Chèvre and/or Reblochon

French Bread

◆

Café Brûlot*

Chocolate Cookies

*RECIPE INCLUDED

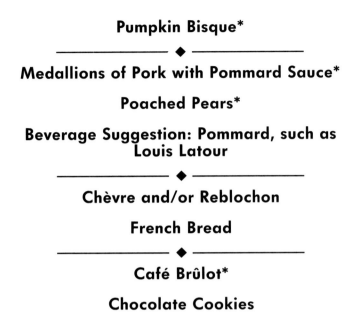

Steaming bowls of pumpkin bisque fragrant with spices, tender medallions of pork in a rich red-wine sauce, with poached pears, a good French cheese and a dramatic finale—flaming Café Brûlot. In concert, they can conquer the gloom of the chilliest winter evening. And all can be prepared in just a simmer and a sizzle.

When making the entire menu, it is usually easiest to do the peeling, slicing, chopping and measuring for all the recipes first; then combine the ingredients and cook just before serving time—each dish takes under 15 minutes to cook.

For those who enjoy a truly dramatic touch, lower the lights after dinner and flambé the Cognac, sugar and spices for the Café Brûlot at table—in a silver bowl, which is traditional, or in a chafing dish.

THE GAME PLAN

- Start the pumpkin bisque.
- While it simmers, assemble all of the ingredients for the pork and for the Café Brûlot.
- Place the pear slices in a skillet with the remaining ingredients, but wait to start simmering them until you start cooking the pork.
- Serve the bisque.
- Start preparing the pork and put the pears on to simmer; serve them hot, together.
- Prepare the Café Brûlot at the table just before serving.
- **If Time Allows:** The bisque can be prepared in advance and reheated just before serving.

Four Servings

Pumpkin Bisque

1½ tablespoons unsalted butter
1 small onion, chopped
1 cup (8 ounces) pumpkin puree
   or canned pumpkin
1¾ cups chicken broth
½ teaspoon cinnamon
¼ teaspoon nutmeg
1 cup heavy cream
Salt and freshly ground pepper
2 scallions, thinly sliced, for
   garnish

1 In a medium saucepan, melt the butter over moderate heat. Add the onion and sauté until softened and translucent, about 3 minutes. Add the pumpkin, chicken broth, 2 cups of water and the cinnamon and nutmeg. Bring to a boil, reduce the heat and simmer for 5 minutes.

2 Reduce the heat to low and add the cream. Gently heat the bisque until hot. Season to taste with salt and pepper. Sprinkle with the scallions before serving.

Medallions of Pork with Pommard Sauce

8 boneless loin pork chops, cut ¼
   inch thick and trimmed of fat
3 tablespoons unsalted butter
2 shallots, finely chopped
1 cup beef stock or canned broth
½ cup Pommard or other red
   Burgundy

½ teaspoon thyme
½ teaspoon sugar
2 tablespoons chopped fresh
   chives
Watercress, for garnish
Poached Pears

1 Pound the pork chops between waxed paper until they are about ⅛ inch thick. In a large skillet, melt 2 tablespoons of the butter over moderate heat. Add the pork (in 2 batches) and cook for 1½ minutes on each side, or until no trace of pink remains, being careful not to overcook. Remove from the pan and cover to keep warm.

2 Add the remaining 1 tablespoon butter and the shallots to the skillet and sauté for 1 minute. Add the beef stock, increase the heat to high and boil for 1 minute longer, scraping up any brown bits that cling to the pan. Add the wine, thyme and sugar and simmer for 3 minutes.

3 Arrange the pork on a platter or individual plates. Spoon the sauce over the chops and sprinkle with the chives. Serve with watercress and the Poached Pears.

Poached Pears

4 pears—peeled, cored and cut in
   ½-inch slices
1 tablespoon sugar
2 strips of lemon zest, each about
   ½ by 2 inches

Place the pear slices in a large skillet with the sugar, lemon zest and ½ cup of water. Bring to a boil over moderate heat. Reduce the heat, cover and simmer, stirring gently once or twice, for 3 to 4 minutes, until the pears are tender but still slightly firm.

Café Brûlot

¼ cup brandy
10 small sugar cubes or 2
   tablespoons granulated sugar
2 slivers of orange zest, about 2
   inches long
2 slivers of lemon zest, about 2
   inches long
1 tablespoon whole cloves
1 cinnamon stick, broken into
   small pieces
2 cups hot, freshly brewed strong
   coffee or espresso

1 Combine the brandy, sugar, orange zest, lemon zest, cloves and cinnamon in a saucepan or a chafing dish and heat for about 30 seconds, or until warm. Turn off the heat and carefully ignite with a match. Let flame for about 1 minute. (If using a silver bowl, heat and ignite the brandy in a pan and then pour into the bowl.)

2 Pour in the hot coffee and stir well to dissolve the sugar. To serve, ladle into demitasse cups.

Spring Lamb Dinner

Asparagus with Beurre Fondue*

◆

Roast Rack of Lamb*

Baby Carrots with Dill*

Salad of Belgian Endive, Apple and Walnuts*

French Bread

Beverage Suggestion: Beaujolais Villages

◆

Pineapple with Sherbet, Strawberries and Rum*

*RECIPE INCLUDED

Throughout the ages, two spring delicacies have traditionally graced the celebrants' table: one, a roasted spring lamb; the other, the first asparagus of the year (in France a wish is made on the first bite).

This menu focuses on these springtime splendors. Asparagus spears served as a first course are followed by the fastest and one of the best roasts I know of: a rack of lamb—accompanied by dilled baby carrots and a crisp, unusual salad. The menu *does* take slightly longer than two-shakes-of-a-lamb's-tail to prepare—but not much more.

Here are some suggestions for those preparing the entire menu. Be certain to preheat the oven well in advance. The lamb needs a very hot oven. Prepare and serve the asparagus while the lamb and carrots are cooking. Relax and enjoy the asparagus before returning to the kitchen for the brief final preparations of the main course.

THE GAME PLAN

- Preheat the oven to 450°.
- Prepare the pineapple for the dessert.
- Season the lamb and place it in the oven.
- Make the salad and chill until serving.
- Put the asparagus on to cook and make the beurre fondue.
- Start cooking the carrots.
- Serve the asparagus and the beurre fondue while the carrots and lamb finish cooking.
- Deglaze the lamb roasting pan; drain the carrots and toss with the remaining ingredients and serve the lamb, carrots and salad together.
- Finish making the dessert just before serving.
- ○ **If Time Allows:** The dessert can be made in advance up to the point of adding the rum and frozen until serving time. The salad dressing can also be made ahead.

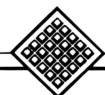

Four Servings

Asparagus with Beurre Fondue

2 pounds asparagus
2 cups salted boiling water
5 tablespoons unsalted butter
1 tablespoon heavy cream
Pinch of cayenne pepper
Salt

1 Snap off the tough ends of the asparagus and discard. Tie the asparagus in a bundle and stand them upright in a tall pot. Add 2 cups of salted boiling water to the pot and cover. Cook until tender, 5 to 15 minutes, depending on the thickness.

2 Meanwhile, in a small saucepan, melt the butter over low heat. Stir in the cream, cayenne and salt to taste.

3 When the asparagus are done, drain and serve hot with the beurre fondue.

Roast Rack of Lamb

2 racks of spring lamb, trimmed (about 1½ pounds each)
1 teaspoon thyme
Salt and freshly ground pepper
1 teaspoon vegetable oil
½ cup dry white wine

1 Preheat the oven to 450°. Season the lamb with the thyme and salt and pepper to taste. Place in a roasting pan and sprinkle the oil over the meat. Roast for 30 to 40 minutes, ac-

cording to taste (rack of lamb is best when quite pink). The lamb should be rare after 30 minutes, medium after 35 minutes and well done after 40 minutes.

2 Transfer the roasted lamb to a serving platter. Discard all but 1 tablespoon of the drippings from the pan. Deglaze the pan with the white wine. Pour the juices over the lamb, carve and serve.

Salad of Belgian Endive, Apple and Walnuts

¼ cup vegetable oil
1 tablespoon wine vinegar
2 teaspoons Dijon-style mustard
Salt and freshly ground pepper
4 heads of Belgian endive
1 Golden Delicious apple, cored and chopped
½ cup walnut pieces
1 bunch of watercress

1 In a small bowl, combine the oil, vinegar, mustard and salt and pepper to taste and beat well with a fork.

2 Separate the endive into leaves. Toss the apple, endive, walnuts and watercress with the dressing.

Baby Carrots with Dill

¾ pound baby carrots
2 cups boiling water
2 tablespoons unsalted butter
½ teaspoon salt
Fresh dill to taste

1 In a large skillet, cook the baby carrots in the boiling water until tender, 10 to 15 minutes. Drain well and return to the pan.

2 Add the butter and salt and shake over moderate heat until the butter is melted and the carrots are well coated.

3 Just before serving, snip some fresh dill over the carrots.

Pineapple with Sherbet, Strawberries and Rum

1 ripe pineapple
Sugar, to taste
1 pint orange sherbet
1 pint lemon sherbet
Dark rum, to taste
Strawberries, for garnish

1 Cut the pineapple in half, top to bottom, leaves and all. Scoop out the fruit, discarding the tough center core. Chop the fruit and sweeten with the sugar.

2 Fill the pineapple shells halfway to the top with orange sherbet and top with half the sweetened chopped pineapple. Add mounds of lemon sherbet and the rest of the chopped pineapple.

3 Sprinkle with rum, decorate with strawberries and serve.

All-American Summer Menu

Gin and Tonics

Crisped Flatbread Parmesan*

◆

Skillet Ham with Speedy Creole Tomato Sauce*

Corn on the Cob with Cumin Butter*

Cucumbers in Cream with Basil*

Dinner Rolls

Beverage Suggestion: Chablis, Zinfandel or Premium Beer

◆

Fresh Blueberry Tumble*

*RECIPE INCLUDED

Summer is the season for meals with fresh, appetite-arousing flavors and dishes that are quick and easy and get the cook out of the kitchen fast.

This refreshing menu features the foods of summer—corn on the cob, crisp cucumbers, basil and blueberries, as well as a fresh tomato sauce over thick slices of ham. It's effortless to make and is excellent for a casual Sunday supper on the patio.

Start with cooling gin and tonics and toasted flatbread with Parmesan cheese.

Serve a Chablis, Zinfandel or cold premium beer with the meal.

THE GAME PLAN

- Put the water for the corn on to boil.
- Preheat the oven and assemble the flatbread.
- Assemble and prepare the dessert ingredients and put them in separate bowls. Refrigerate the sour cream.
- Start making the tomato sauce.
- Put the corn in to cook; make the cumin butter.
- Make the salad. Toast the flatbread.
- Make the gin and tonics and serve with the toasted flatbread.
- Sauté the ham fillets and serve hot with the tomato sauce, corn and salad.
- **If Time Allows:** The dessert ingredients can be assembled in advance. The tomato sauce can be made ahead and reheated.

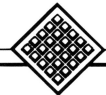

Four Servings

Crisped Flatbread Parmesan

12 Norwegian flatbread rectangles
2 tablespoons unsalted butter, melted
½ cup freshly grated Parmesan cheese

1 Preheat the oven to 350°. Arrange the flatbread in a single layer on a baking sheet.

2 Brush some melted butter over each piece of flatbread. Sprinkle each piece liberally with Parmesan.

3 Toast in the oven for 5 minutes. Serve warm or at room temperature.

Cucumbers in Cream with Basil

2 medium cucumbers—peeled, seeded and sliced
½ cup fresh basil leaves, coarsely chopped
¼ cup heavy cream
Salt to taste
Pinch of cayenne pepper

In a mixing bowl, combine all of the ingredients, toss together, transfer to a serving bowl and serve. (Don't bother with salad plates: this salad acts as a condiment, the flavors and textures mingling beautifully with those of the ham and tomato sauce.)

Skillet Ham with Speedy Creole Tomato Sauce

4 tablespoons unsalted butter
4 garlic cloves, minced
4 medium tomatoes—peeled, seeded and coarsely chopped
Pinch of cayenne pepper
4 ham "fillets" (½ pound each; see Note) or a 1- to 1½-pound ham steak
2 thinly sliced scallions, for garnish

1 In a small skillet, melt 3 tablespoons of the butter over very low heat; do not allow to brown.

2 Add the garlic and stir briefly. Add the chopped tomatoes and cayenne. Cook over low heat, stirring occasionally, until the tomatoes are slightly "melted" and the sauce is piping hot, 10 to 12 minutes.

3 In a heavy skillet large enough to comfortably accommodate the meat, melt the remaining 1 tablespoon butter. Brown the ham lightly on both sides. Cook only until heated through—a few minutes depending on the thickness of the meat.

4 Arrange the heated ham on a platter, surround with the hot tomato sauce, and sprinkle the scallions on top.

Note: These commercially packaged ham "fillets" look like large slices of Canadian bacon.

Corn on the Cob with Cumin Butter

1 tablespoon salt
1 tablespoon sugar
8 ears of corn, husked
3 tablespoons unsalted butter
1 tablespoon ground cumin
4 wedges of lime, for garnish

1 Bring a 4-quart pot of water to a boil. Add the salt, sugar and corn. Cook uncovered for 2 minutes. Cover the pot tightly, remove from the heat and let sit for 5 to 15 minutes (the corn will stop cooking after 5 minutes and simply remain hot).

2 Meanwhile, melt the butter over low heat and stir in the cumin. Steep at least 5 minutes and then pour into a small bowl.

3 Drain the corn and serve with cumin butter and a pastry brush for painting the corn at the table. Pass wedges of lime to squeeze over the corn.

Fresh Blueberry Tumble

12 gingersnaps
1 pint blueberries
1 cup yogurt or sour cream
4 tablespoons wildflower or orange-blossom honey

Crumble the gingersnaps into bits the size of coarse gravel. Pass the blueberries, yogurt, honey and gingersnap "gravel" in separate bowls and let guests help themselves to some of each.

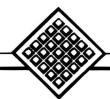

Easy Holiday Dinner

Rhine Wine Punch*

Crabmeat Canapés Balcomb*

◆

Veal Scallops with Black Mushrooms*

Wild Rice

Beverage Suggestion: California Pinot Noir, such as Beaulieu

Bibb Lettuce Salad with Vinaigrette Dressing

◆

Chocolate Ice Cream with Kahlúa

Quick Nut Drop Cookies*

Café Filtre and Brandy

*RECIPE INCLUDED

Cooking lovely, lavish dinners during the holiday season when you're busy shopping, wrapping presents and socializing can be difficult. So keeping in mind that most hectic time of the year, I've designed a menu that can be quickly prepared and that will lend a touch of festive elegance to your holiday celebrations.

To start, there's a full-flavored wine punch and delicate crabmeat canapés. For the main course, sautéed veal scallops in a creamy black mushroom sauce, served with wild rice. Chocolate ice cream with Kahlúa and crunchy nut cookies double for dessert. A fitting accompaniment for the strong coffee would be a glass of mellow brandy, preferably sipped at leisure in front of a glowing fire.

THE GAME PLAN

- Preheat the oven to 375°. Prepare the cookie batter and bake. Start the wild rice.

- Make the crabmeat, reserving the scallions to sprinkle over just before serving; chill.

- Soak the mushrooms. Prepare the salad greens and make the vinaigrette.

- Make the punch and serve with the canapés.

- Make the veal and serve with the wild rice.

- Drizzle Kahlúa over the ice cream and serve.

○ **If Time Allows:** The cookies and crabmeat mixture can be made ahead. The mushrooms can be soaked in advance, but drain them after 15 minutes.

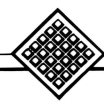

Four Servings

Rhine Wine Punch

12 whole strawberries, hulled
2 teaspoons sugar
2 cups Rhine wine, such as Johannisberg Riesling
2 ounces (¼ cup) kirsch
Club soda

1 In a small bowl, lightly bruise the strawberries. Toss with the sugar.

2 Pour ½ cup of the wine and 1 tablespoon of the kirsch into each of four large goblets half-filled with ice. Top with the soda and garnish with the berries.

Crabmeat Canapés Balcomb

6 ounces lump crabmeat (preferably fresh), picked over to remove any bits of cartilage
2 hard-cooked eggs, finely chopped
¼ cup finely chopped celery
¼ cup mayonnaise
2 tablespoons fresh lemon juice
½ teaspoon piquant sauce, such as A-1, Sauce Robert or Diable
⅛ teaspoon hot pepper sauce
2 tablespoons finely chopped scallions
Triangles of toast or melba toast

In a medium bowl, combine the crabmeat with the eggs, celery, mayonnaise, lemon juice, piquant sauce and hot sauce. Mix until well blended. Refrigerate, covered, until ready to serve. Just before serving, sprinkle the crabmeat with the scallions. Serve accompanied with the toast.

Veal Scallops with Black Mushrooms

8 large dried *shiitake* mushrooms (about ½ ounce)
8 tablespoons (1 stick) unsalted butter
1½ pounds (10 to 12) veal scallops
Salt and freshly ground pepper
2 tablespoons Cognac or brandy
1 cup heavy cream

1 In a small bowl, soak the mushrooms in very hot water until softened, about 15 minutes. Drain well; squeeze to remove as much liquid as possible. Cut off and discard the stems. Cut the caps into thin slivers.

2 In a large heavy skillet, melt 4 tablespoons of the butter over high heat. When the butter foams, add half of the veal scallops in a single layer and sauté, turning once, until lightly browned, 2 to 3 minutes on each side. Transfer to a warm platter. Season with salt and pepper to taste. Sauté the remaining scallops in the remaining butter in the same manner and transfer them to the platter.

3 Add the slivered mushrooms to the skillet and sauté over moderately high heat for 1 minute. Add the Cognac and stir, scraping up any browned bits from the bottom of the skillet. Add the cream and bring to a boil. Continue to boil for 1 to 2 minutes, until the sauce is slightly thickened. Return the scallops to the skillet and toss to coat them with the sauce.

Quick Nut Drop Cookies

MAKES ABOUT 2 DOZEN

½ cup (1 stick) unsalted butter, at room temperature
¼ cup plus 2 tablespoons granulated sugar
¼ cup plus 2 tablespoons dark brown sugar
1 egg
1 teaspoon vanilla extract
1¼ cups all-purpose flour
½ teaspoon baking soda
½ teaspoon salt
¾ cup coarsely chopped pecans or walnuts

1 Preheat the oven to 375°. In a medium bowl, beat the butter with the granulated sugar and brown sugar until light and fluffy. Beat in the egg and vanilla until blended.

2 Sift together the flour, baking soda and salt. Add the nuts. Gradually add this dry mixture to the butter mixture, stirring just until blended.

3 Drop rounded teaspoons of the dough, 2 inches apart, onto two greased cookie sheets.

4 Bake in the middle of the oven for 12 minutes, until golden. Transfer to a rack and let cool before serving.

Quick Elegance for Four

Tahini Dip* with Pita Triangles, Broccoli Florets and Cucumber Spears

◆

Medallions of Lamb with Walnuts and Orange Zest*

Stir-Fried Green and Red Peppers*

Bulgur with Scallions*

Beverage Suggestion: Cabernet Sauvignon

◆

Sultan's Yogurt*

Turkish Coffee

*RECIPE INCLUDED

The pièce de résistance of this menu is a recipe for medallions of lamb. Medallions, also known as *noisettes* or *mignonettes* in French, are lean, tender rounds of meat cut from the rib or loin. If you do not have a butcher who will prepare them for you, buy double rib or loin lamb chops and remove the meaty center from the bone. Trim off any fat and tie with string to help the medallions hold their shape when they are cooked. When prepared with shallots, walnuts, wine and orange zest, they are elegant and delicious.

The delicate, toasted flavor of bulgur wheat provides a perfect complement to the lamb. When cooking the entire menu, prepare the dessert first and chill it; garnish just before serving. Although the bulgur takes only about 20 minutes to cook, it rests well for an equal amount of time, so you may choose to start it before serving pre-dinner drinks and the hors d'oeuvre. Sauté the lamb and the peppers just before serving.

————— THE GAME PLAN —————

- Make the Sultan's Yogurt, reserving the grape clusters and additional honey to add just before serving. Chill.

- Make the tahini dip; prepare the pita triangles and the vegetables.

- Assemble all of the ingredients for the lamb and the stir-fried peppers.

- Start making the bulgur.

- While the bulgur simmers, serve the tahini dip and accompaniments with aperitifs.

- Start sautéing the lamb and stir-fry the peppers; serve both hot with the bulgur.

- Garnish the Sultan's Yogurt and make the Turkish coffee just before serving dessert.

○ **If Time Allows:** The Sultan's Yogurt and the tahini dip can be made ahead.

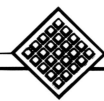

Four Servings

Tahini Dip

½ cup tahini (Middle Eastern sesame paste)
2 tablespoons fresh lemon juice
1 or 2 garlic cloves, crushed through a press
¼ teaspoon oregano
⅛ teaspoon ground cumin
Salt
Sprigs of parsley, for garnish

1 In a small bowl, stir together the tahini, lemon juice, garlic, oregano, cumin and enough water (about ⅓ cup) to make the mixture the consistency of thick sour cream. Add salt to taste.

2 Before serving, spoon the dip into a small serving bowl and decorate with parsley sprigs. Serve at room temperature with triangles of toasted pita bread, plus broccoli florets and cucumber spears for dipping.

Stir-Fried Green and Red Peppers

1 tablespoon vegetable oil
2 green and 2 red medium bell peppers (about 1¼ pounds), cut into ⅛-by-1-inch julienne strips
1 teaspoon fresh lemon juice
Salt

Heat a wok or large heavy skillet for 30 seconds over moderately high heat; add the oil. When the oil is hot, in about 30 seconds, add the peppers. Stir-fry the peppers for about 1 minute, or until they are tender but still slightly crunchy. Season with the lemon juice and salt to taste.

Medallions of Lamb with Walnuts and Orange Zest

3 tablespoons unsalted butter
8 medallions of lamb (about 3 ounces each), cut 1 inch thick from the rib or loin
Salt and freshly ground pepper
1 tablespoon chopped shallots
½ cup (about 2 ounces) chopped black or English walnuts
¼ cup Madeira
¼ cup dry red wine
1 tablespoon grated orange zest, for garnish

1 In a large heavy skillet, melt the butter over moderate heat until it sizzles. When the foam begins to subside, add the medallions and sauté, turning once, to the desired degree of doneness: 3 minutes on each side for rare, 4 minutes for medium-rare and 5 for well done. Season with salt and pepper to taste and transfer to a heated serving platter.

2 Add the shallots to the skillet and sauté over moderate heat until softened but not browned, about 1 minute. Stir the walnuts into the shallot butter and spoon the mixture over the lamb. Return the skillet to the stove.

3 Increase the heat to moderately high and pour in the Madeira and red wine, scraping up the brown bits that cling to the bottom of the pan. Boil until the sauce is reduced by half. Pour over the lamb, garnish with the orange zest, and serve hot.

Bulgur with Scallions

1 tablespoon unsalted butter
1½ cups bulgur
1 teaspoon salt
2 or 3 scallions, thinly sliced, for garnish

In a medium saucepan, melt the butter over moderate heat. Add the bulgur and sauté, stirring, for 2 minutes, until the bulgur has a toasty fragrance. Stir in 3 cups of water and the salt; increase the heat to high and bring to a boil. Immediately reduce the heat to low; cover the saucepan and simmer for 15 minutes, or until all the water has been absorbed. Fluff the bulgur lightly with a fork and garnish with the scallions.

Sultan's Yogurt

2 cups plain yogurt
3 tablespoons honey, or more to taste
½ cup golden raisins
1 cup (about 6 ounces) green seedless grapes
Small grape clusters, for garnish
Honey, for drizzling

1 In a small bowl, mix the yogurt and honey until blended. Stir in the raisins and grapes. Spoon the mixture into four large goblets or dessert bowls. Cover and refrigerate until chilled.

2 Before serving, garnish each serving with a grape cluster. Drizzle additional honey over the top, if desired.

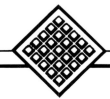

Hearty Fall Dinner

Lentil and Tomato Salad*

◆

Pork Scallops with Rosemary*

Mashed Butternut Squash

Crusty Italian Bread

Beverage Suggestion: Chianti, such as Antinori

◆

Cucumbers in Tarragon Vinegar*

◆

Gorgonzola and Ripe Pears

Espresso

*RECIPE INCLUDED

Here is a quick menu that features some of the heartier foods associated with fall—lentils and pork—but prepares them in a light fashion.

Lentils, cooked just al dente, are tossed with fresh ripe tomatoes, onion, scallions and a vinaigrette to make a very pleasant salad. Serve on a bed of lettuce as a first course, or arrange on a platter with some salami, prosciutto, roasted peppers and cheese to compose an easy antipasto.

Pork scallops, the meaty eye of the loin chop pounded thin, are sautéed very briefly over high heat so that they remain tender and juicy. Coated with a tangy white wine sauce fragrant with rosemary, they need only a simple accompaniment; mashed butternut squash would be a nice choice.

Cucumbers in tarragon vinegar serve as a light and refreshing palate-cleanser before a dessert of ripe pears and a fine Gorgonzola cheese. Drink a simple red wine throughout the meal and finish with small cups of strong black espresso.

THE GAME PLAN

- Start cooking the squash. At the same time, put the lentils on to cook.
- Slice and salt the cucumbers and let drain. Bone, trim and pound the pork scallops.
- Drain the lentils, toss with remaining ingredients, reserving half the parsley to add just before serving, and let cool.
- Mash the squash and keep warm.
- Serve the lentil salad.
- Cook the pork and serve with the squash.
- Toss the cucumbers with the remaining ingredients and serve.
- **If Time Allows:** The lentil salad can be made ahead and chilled until serving time.

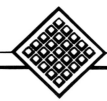

Four Servings

Pork Scallops with Rosemary

8 center-cut loin pork chops (about 2 pounds), cut ½ inch thick
Freshly ground pepper
3½ tablespoons unsalted butter
1 tablespoon vegetable oil
1 teaspoon rosemary, crushed
Salt
½ cup dry white wine

1 With a sharp knife, remove the meaty "eye" of the pork chop from the bone; trim off any excess fat.

2 Sprinkle the pieces of pork with pepper to taste, and pound the pieces between sheets of waxed paper until about ⅛ inch thick.

3 In a large skillet, melt 1½ tablespoons of the butter in the oil over high heat. When the butter foams, add the pork and sauté over moderately high heat on one side for 3 minutes, until nicely browned. Turn, sprinkle with the rosemary and salt to taste. Cook about 3 minutes longer, until browned on the second side.

4 Transfer the pork scallops to a heated platter. Pour the wine into the skillet and boil, scraping up any browned bits from the bottom of the pan, until reduced by half. Swirl in the remaining 2 tablespoons butter, 1 tablespoon at a time. Pour over the pork and serve hot.

Cucumbers in Tarragon Vinegar

1 European seedless cucumber or 2 medium cucumbers
¼ teaspoon salt
1 tablespoon olive oil
2 teaspoons tarragon vinegar

1 Score the cucumber lengthwise with a fork and slice into thin rounds. If using regular cucumbers, cut in half lengthwise, scrape out the seeds and cut into thin crescents.

2 Place the cucumber slices in a colander and toss with the salt. Let drain for 15 minutes.

3 In a serving bowl, toss the cucumbers with the oil and the vinegar.

Lentil and Tomato Salad

⅔ cup lentils, rinsed and picked over
1 small onion stuck with 2 whole cloves
1 bay leaf
½ teaspoon salt
2 medium tomatoes, seeded and coarsely chopped
⅓ cup chopped scallions
⅓ cup chopped fresh parsley
3 tablespoons olive oil
2 teaspoons fresh lemon juice
2 teaspoons red wine vinegar
Freshly ground pepper

1 In a medium saucepan, place the lentils, onion, bay leaf, salt and 2 cups of water. Bring to a boil, then reduce to a simmer; cover and cook until the lentils are just tender, about 25 minutes. Drain the lentils; discard the onion and bay leaf.

2 In a large noncorrodible bowl, gently toss the lentils with the tomatoes, scallions, half of the parsley, the olive oil, lemon juice and vinegar. Season with salt and pepper to taste. Serve at room temperature or chilled; garnish with the remaining parsley.

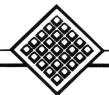

Fresh Herb-Scented Summer Dinner

Red Wine with Soda and an Orange Slice

Anchovy Toast*

— ◆ —

Grilled Flank Steak with Dill*

Tomatoes Provençale*

Zucchini with Fresh Basil*

French Bread

Beverage Suggestion: Zinfandel

— ◆ —

Fresh Apricots and Shelled Almonds

Butterscotch-Pecan Squares*

Espresso with Cinnamon Sticks

*RECIPE INCLUDED

Summer's bounty provides inspiration for this menu. The dishes are simple to prepare and very quick, especially if you do some preliminary preparation, such as chopping and slicing the ingredients for the tomatoes, cutting the zucchini and snipping the dill for the flank steak. Then ready the anchovy toast, fix some drinks and sit down and enjoy yourself until you and your dining companions choose to move on to more serious eating. Final preparation of the meal takes no more than 15 to 20 minutes. For dessert, bring out a bowl of golden apricots and some almonds. Follow them with butterscotch-pecan squares and espresso or a French roast *café filtre* with cinnamon stick stirrers.

THE GAME PLAN

- Preheat the oven to 350°. Prepare and bake the butterscotch-pecan squares.
- Meanwhile, make the tomatoes, assemble the ingredients for the zucchini and steak.
- Prepare the anchovy toast and put it in to broil when the dessert is done.
- Serve the hot anchovy toast with the aperitifs.
- Broil the steak and make the zucchini.
- Carve the flank steak and serve with the zucchini and the tomatoes.
- ○ **If Time Allows:** The dressing for the tomatoes and the dessert can be made ahead.

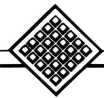

Four Servings

Anchovy Toast

1 can (2 ounces) anchovy fillets
2 garlic cloves, crushed
2 tablespoons olive oil
¼ teaspoon vinegar
12 slices of French bread, cut ½ inch thick

1 Preheat the broiler. Drain the anchovies and soak them in water for about 5 minutes to remove some of the salt. Drain and mash them in a bowl with the garlic, oil and vinegar.

2 Toast the French bread on one side. Spread the anchovy mixture over the untoasted sides and toast for 1 or 2 minutes; serve hot.

Grilled Flank Steak with Dill

1 flank steak, about 1½ pounds
Salt and freshly ground pepper
1 tablespoon unsalted butter
1½ tablespoons chopped fresh dill
¼ lemon
Hot pepper sauce

1 Preheat the broiler. Rub the steak with salt and pepper to taste and broil about 4 inches from the heat for 4 to 5 minutes on each side.

2 Transfer to a warm platter and dot with the butter, sprinkle with the dill, squeeze the lemon over and add a dash or two of pepper sauce. Carve on the diagonal into thin slices and serve.

Zucchini with Fresh Basil

1½ tablespoons unsalted butter
1½ pounds small zucchini, cut into ½-by-1½-inch julienne strips
1½ tablespoons minced fresh basil, dill or tarragon, or 1 teaspoon dried
Salt

In a skillet, melt the butter, add the zucchini and toss to coat. Cover and cook over moderate heat until the zucchini is nearly soft, about 10 minutes. Stir in the herbs and salt to taste. Serve hot.

Tomatoes Provençale

2 large tomatoes, peeled and halved crosswise
¼ cup coarsely chopped watercress
¼ cup thinly sliced celery
4 teaspoons chopped fresh parsley
½ cup olive oil
2 tablespoons fresh lemon juice
2 garlic cloves, minced
Salt and freshly ground pepper
1½ teaspoons grated orange zest
8 Calamata olives

1 Scoop a shallow indentation in each tomato half and gently squeeze out the seeds. Place the tomatoes on a serving platter, cut-side up. Sprinkle the watercress, celery and parsley over the tomatoes.

2 In a small bowl, whisk the oil, lemon juice, garlic and salt and pepper to taste until blended. Spoon the dressing over the tomatoes. Sprinkle with the orange zest and garnish each tomato half with 2 Calamata olives.

Butterscotch-Pecan Squares

MAKES 16 SQUARES

4 tablespoons unsalted butter, melted
1 cup firmly packed dark brown sugar
1 egg, beaten
1 teaspoon vanilla extract
1 cup all-purpose flour
1 teaspoon baking powder
¼ teaspoon salt
1 cup (4 ounces) chopped pecans

1 Preheat the oven to 350°. Butter an 8-inch square baking pan. In a medium bowl, beat the butter and brown sugar until blended. Mix in the egg and vanilla.

2 Sift together the flour, baking powder and salt. Add to the brown sugar mixture and stir until the batter is smooth; mix in the nuts.

3 Pour the batter into the baking pan and spread evenly. Bake for 20 minutes, or until the cake begins to pull away from the sides of the pan. Let cool in the pan before cutting into 2-inch squares.

Candlelight Dinner for Six

Hearts of Palm Vinaigrette*

◆

Lamb Chops Bar-le-Duc*

Green Beans with Lime Juice*

Wild Rice with Scallions*

Beverage Suggestion: Red Burgundy or Rioja, such as Marqués de Cáceres

◆

Mocha-Macaroon Dessert*

Demitasse

*RECIPE INCLUDED

This elegant three-course dinner can be prepared in under an hour and places few demands on the chef. So dress up, if you feel like it, light the candles and dine superbly with family or friends.

Some notes on the ingredients: Lamb chops Bar-le-Duc is named for a town in the Lorraine province of France, which is famous for its excellent red currant jams. If you use a jam from that district, the results will be outstanding, but any good-quality red currant jelly will do. The dessert calls for almond macaroons or amaretti cookies. Macaroons are usually available at good bakeries; amaretti, in wonderfully attractive tins, can be found in many food shops. Hearts of palm are available (in cans) at most well-stocked groceries.

THE GAME PLAN

- Start cooking the wild rice.
- Meanwhile, assemble the salad and prepare the vinaigrette, but wait to dress the salad until just before serving.
- Prepare the macaroons and whip the cream for the dessert.
- Put the lamb chops on to broil. Start the green beans.
- While they cook, make the toast and the sauce for the chops.
- Toss the remaining ingredients with the green beans and serve with the lamb chops, wild rice and salad.
- Just before serving, assemble the dessert.
- **If Time Allows:** The salad dressing can be made and the macaroons for dessert prepared a few hours in advance.

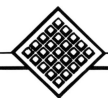

Six Servings

Hearts of Palm Vinaigrette

Small head of romaine
1 can (14 ounces) hearts of palm, about 6 pieces
1 hard-cooked egg, chopped
¼ cup white wine vinegar
1 tablespoon lemon juice
¾ cup olive oil
1 tablespoon capers, drained
½ teaspoon salt
¼ teaspoon powdered mustard
Freshly ground pepper, to taste

Arrange the romaine leaves on 6 salad plates. Slice the hearts of palm in half lengthwise and divide them among the plates. Combine the remaining ingredients in a jar with a tight-fitting cover and shake until well blended, or whisk together in a small bowl. Spoon the dressing over the hearts of palm.

Lamb Chops Bar-le-Duc

6 loin lamb chops, cut 1½ inches thick and trimmed of excess fat
6 slices of firm-textured white bread, toasted and crusts removed
¼ cup plus 1 tablespoon red currant jelly
2½ tablespoons medium-dry sherry
3 slivers of orange zest
Salt and freshly ground pepper

1 Preheat the broiler. Broil the lamb chops about 4 inches from the heat on one side for 10 minutes. Turn and cook them for 5 minutes on the second side. The chops will be pink in the center. If you prefer them more well done, cook longer on the second side.

2 While the chops are broiling, spread each slice of toast with ½ teaspoon of the jelly. Place the remaining ¼ cup of jelly, the sherry and orange zest in a small saucepan and cook over moderate heat for 2 to 3 minutes, stirring occasionally, until the jelly is melted and the sauce is hot.

3 When the lamb chops are done, season them with salt and pepper to taste. Place a chop on each slice of toast and spoon about a tablespoon of sauce over each serving.

Green Beans with Lime Juice

1½ pounds fresh green beans
2 tablespoons unsalted butter, melted
Juice of ½ lime (about 1 tablespoon)
Salt and freshly ground pepper

Steam the green beans until barely tender, 5 to 7 minutes. Toss them with the melted butter and lime juice. Season to taste with salt and pepper.

Wild Rice with Scallions

1½ cups (8 ounces) wild rice
3 scallions (white and tender green), thinly sliced
1 tablespoon unsalted butter
2¾ cups chicken broth
1 teaspoon salt

1 Wash the wild rice in several changes of water; drain well.

2 In a medium saucepan, sauté the scallions in the butter over moderate heat until softened, 1 or 2 minutes. Add the wild rice, chicken broth and salt and bring to a boil. Reduce the heat to low, cover the pan tightly and simmer gently for about 45 minutes, until the rice is tender and the broth has been absorbed.

Mocha-Macaroon Dessert

½ pound almond macaroons or amaretti cookies
⅓ cup dark rum
1 pint coffee ice cream, softened slightly
1 cup heavy cream, whipped
¼ cup slivered almonds

1 Crumble 2 of the macaroons and set them aside. Soak the remaining macaroons in the rum, turning them until they are moistened all over and have absorbed the liquid. Line a 2-quart serving bowl with the macaroons.

2 Just before serving, scoop the ice cream over the macaroons. Cover with the whipped cream and sprinkle the almonds and crumbled macaroons on top.

Pepper, Olive and Onion Salad

Watermelon Pickles Broiled in Bacon

PAGE 159

Dressing Up a Casual Classic

Veal Dumplings with Capellini and Fresh Tomato Sauce*

Arugula and Romaine Salad*

Italian Cracked Wheat Bread

Beverage Suggestion: Valpolicella

◆

Fresh Strawberry and Ricotta Barquettes*

Coffee

*RECIPE INCLUDED

An all-time family favorite, spaghetti and meatballs, is transformed here into a light and fresh pasta dish with veal dumplings and a quick tomato sauce over thin capellini. The only accompaniments needed for this informal family repast are a crisp green salad and lots of crusty bread. I like to serve a peppery arugula and romaine salad and Italian cracked wheat bread.

For dessert, fresh strawberries are diced and heaped into pastry barquettes filled with a tangy sweet mixture of ricotta cheese and honey. If you can't find packaged barquettes, you can simply scoop the ricotta and honey into individual dessert bowls and top with the diced berries.

THE GAME PLAN

- Make the strawberry barquettes.
- Make the fresh tomato sauce.
- While the sauce simmers, form and poach the dumplings; add them to the tomato sauce.
- Prepare the salad greens and make the dressing, but wait to add the dressing until just before serving.
- Cook the capellini.
- Drain the capellini and serve with the veal dumplings and tomato sauce and the salad.
- **If Time Allows:** The strawberry and ricotta barquettes can be made in advance. The veal dumplings can be mixed, formed and poached in advance and the tomato sauce can be made ahead and reheated with the dumplings just before serving.

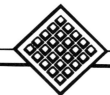

Four to Six Servings

Arugula and Romaine Salad

1 garlic clove, split lengthwise
1 small bunch of arugula
4 cups shredded romaine leaves
¼ cup olive oil
1 tablespoon red wine vinegar
¼ teaspoon Dijon-style mustard
Coarse (kosher) salt

1 Rub a salad bowl thoroughly with the cut sides of the garlic clove. Combine the arugula and romaine in the salad bowl.

2 In a small bowl, whisk the oil, vinegar, mustard and salt to taste together until well blended. Pour over the salad and toss lightly just before serving.

Fresh Tomato Sauce

4 tablespoons unsalted butter
6 tomatoes—peeled, seeded and cut into ⅛-inch dice—or 1 can (28 ounces) Italian plum tomatoes, drained and chopped
2 garlic cloves, minced
Salt
2 tablespoons shredded fresh basil leaves

In a large saucepan, melt the butter over low heat. Add the tomatoes and garlic and simmer, stirring occasionally, over low heat until thickened, 10 to 15 minutes. Season with salt to taste and stir in the basil.

Veal Dumplings with Capellini and Fresh Tomato Sauce

1 pound ground veal
1 cup fresh bread crumbs
½ cup scallions (white and tender green), finely chopped
½ cup chopped fresh parsley
2 garlic cloves, chopped
1 egg, lightly beaten
1¼ teaspoons salt
½ teaspoon freshly ground pepper
Fresh Tomato Sauce
½ pound capellini
2 tablespoons unsalted butter
1 cup freshly grated Parmesan cheese

1 In a large mixing bowl, combine the veal, bread crumbs, scallions, parsley, garlic, egg, salt and pepper and mix together thoroughly. Form into 1-inch balls.

2 Drop the veal dumplings into a large saucepan of boiling water and boil until they float to the surface, 3 to 5 minutes. Remove with a slotted spoon.

3 In a large saucepan, simmer the tomato sauce and the dumplings over low heat for 10 to 15 minutes, stirring occasionally.

4 Meanwhile, cook the capellini in a large pot of rapidly boiling water until tender. Drain and toss with the butter and place on a warmed serving platter. Spoon the dumplings and tomato sauce over the capellini and serve. Pass the grated Parmesan cheese at the table.

Fresh Strawberry and Ricotta Barquettes

½ cup ricotta cheese
2 tablespoons honey
8 unsweetened pastry barquettes, about 4 inches long (see Note)
1 pint fresh strawberries, 8 small whole berries reserved, remaining berries hulled and diced

In a small bowl, combine the ricotta and the honey and blend well. Fill each barquette about half full with the ricotta mixture, spreading it evenly over the pastry. Divide the diced strawberries among the barquettes, sprinkling them thickly and evenly over the cheese mixture. Decorate each tart with 1 small berry.

Note: Unsweetened pastry barquettes are available boxed in the specialty section of most well stocked supermarkets.

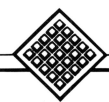

Cozy Dinner for Two

Mushroom Salad*

◆

Beefsteak Bigarade*

Buttered Green Beans

White Rice with Chinese Black Beans*

**Beverage Suggestion: California Petite Sirah
or a Red Rhône Wine, such as Gigondas**

◆

Syllabub*

Black Grapes

Pirouette Cookies

*RECIPE INCLUDED

Here is a warm and pleasing cold weather dinner with a mix of subtle and spicy flavors. Orange-scented bigarade sauce was made famous by the great French chef Antoine Carême. This tangy sauce is often served with duck; my simple, adapted version is paired with beef—shell steaks that are pounded and quickly seared.

Sliced mushrooms in a red wine vinaigrette make a different salad, which can serve as a vegetable side dish or as a first course. Fluffy white rice is unusually seasoned with Chinese fermented black beans and tossed just before serving with chopped parsley and scallion. For a sweet creamy finale, try the frothy English dessert syllabub, which has long been a favorite in the American South.

This dinner menu has been designed for two. (A romantic notion: you might consider serving it on Valentine's Day.)

THE GAME PLAN

- Make the syllabub, reserving the allspice to sprinkle over before serving; cover and chill.
- Make the mushroom salad.
- Start cooking the rice.
- Prepare the steaks up to the point of cooking them.
- Serve the mushroom salad.
- Put the green beans on to cook.
- Sauté the steaks and make the sauce; toss the rice with the remaining ingredients and serve along with the buttered beans.
- ○ **If Time Allows:** The mushroom salad and the syllabub can be made ahead. If the cream and the wine of the syllabub separate, just whip briefly before serving to blend.

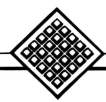

Two Servings

Beefsteak Bigarade

1 medium orange
2 trimmed shell or strip steaks, cut ½ inch thick, 5 to 6 ounces each
1 garlic clove, halved
¼ teaspoon salt
⅛ teaspoon freshly ground pepper
1 tablespoon unsalted butter
1 tablespoon olive oil
1 tablespoon minced shallot
2 tablespoons ruby port
1 teaspoon Cognac or brandy
½ teaspoon Dijon-style mustard
Watercress and thin slices of orange, for garnish

1 Remove the zest from one-quarter of the orange. Cut into thin slivers. Place in a small bowl and cover with ¾ cup boiling water. Drain and pat dry on paper towels. Halve the orange and squeeze ½ tablespoon of juice into a small bowl. Reserve the unsqueezed orange half.

2 Place each steak between 2 pieces of waxed paper and pound until about ¼ inch thick. Rub both sides with the cut garlic and the cut side of the reserved orange half. Season each with half of the salt and pepper.

3 In a large heavy skillet, melt the butter in the oil over moderately high heat until sizzling. Add the steaks and cook until lightly browned on the bottom, about 1½ minutes. Turn and cook on the second side until lightly browned and medium-rare, about 30 seconds. Remove from the skillet and cover loosely with foil to keep warm.

4 Over low heat, stir in the shallot, port, Cognac, mustard, reserved orange juice, slivered orange zest and 2 teaspoons of water until blended. Cook, scraping up any brown bits from the bottom of the skillet, until the sauce is slightly reduced, about 1 minute. Spoon the sauce over the steaks and serve garnished with the watercress and orange slices.

White Rice with Chinese Black Beans

½ cup rice
2 teaspoons unsalted butter
¼ teaspoon salt
1 tablespoon chopped fresh parsley
1 tablespoon chopped scallion
2 to 3 dashes hot pepper sauce, to taste
2 teaspoons fermented black beans, minced

1 Wash the rice and drain well. Place in a medium saucepan with 1 scant cup of water, the butter and the salt. Bring to a boil over high heat. Stir briefly, reduce the heat to low and tightly cover the saucepan. Cook for 18 to 20 minutes, until the rice has absorbed all of the liquid.

2 Add the parsley, scallion, hot pepper sauce and beans. Toss lightly to combine.

Mushroom Salad

½ pound mushrooms
3 tablespoons olive oil
1 tablespoon red wine vinegar, preferably balsamic
1 tablespoon chopped fresh parsley
½ tablespoon fresh lemon juice
¼ teaspoon salt
Freshly ground pepper

1 Wipe the mushrooms with a damp towel, trim and thinly slice.

2 In a medium bowl, whisk the oil, vinegar, parsley, lemon juice and salt until blended. Add the mushrooms and toss gently to coat evenly. Let marinate at room temperature, tossing occasionally, for 15 to 20 minutes for added flavor before serving. Pass the pepper at the table.

Syllabub

½ cup heavy cream
2 tablespoons milk
1 tablespoon Madeira
1 teaspoon Cognac or brandy
1 teaspoon confectioners' sugar
Dash of allspice

1 In a chilled medium bowl, beat the cream until soft peaks form. Beat in the milk, Madeira, Cognac, sugar and allspice; whip until thick and frothy.

2 To serve, spoon the syllabub into two large wine glasses. Cover and refrigerate until serving time. Sprinkle with more allspice just before serving.

With a Touch of Sherry

Sherry-Lime Mists*

Sautéed Almonds*

◆

Veal Scallops with Amontillado*

Saffron Rice with Pistachios*

Beverage Suggestion: Torres Viña Santa Diga, California Gamay or Beaujolais

◆

Bibb Lettuce and Mushroom Salad with Tarragon Dressing*

◆

Strawberries with Maple Syrup and Cream

Coffee or Tea

*RECIPE INCLUDED

Light food that requires little preparation is perfect for a soft spring or early summer evening. And this versatile menu, given a Spanish accent with sherry, almonds and saffron, can serve equally well as a family meal or a last-minute company dinner.

Begin by relaxing with a Sherry-Lime Mist, a surprisingly refreshing cocktail, and pass a bowl of golden sautéed almonds. Sherry is repeated in the main course, veal scallops with Amontillado. Amontillado is a nutty, fragrant sherry, but any good medium-dry variety can be used. Another alternative ingredient in this recipe is turkey, which substitutes beautifully for the veal, at much less expense. Saffron rice with pistachios provides a nice change and dresses up the meal.

For dessert, I've recommended a treat my whole family loves, strawberries with maple syrup and cream.

THE GAME PLAN

- Make the sautéed almonds.
- Prepare the greens and make the dressing for the salad, but wait to toss it at the table.
- Assemble all of the ingredients for the veal.
- Start the saffron rice with pistachios.
- Make the Sherry-Lime Mists and serve them with the sautéed almonds.
- Five minutes before the rice is finished, start cooking the veal and serve it hot with the rice.
- **If Time Allows:** The sautéed almonds can be made earlier in the day or the day before and stored in a covered jar. The dressing for the salad can also be made ahead.

Four Servings

Sherry-Lime Mists

Crushed ice
Medium or sweet sherry
1 lime

Fill 4 wine or large sherry glasses with crushed ice. Pour sherry over the ice. Cut the lime in half crosswise. Slice one half into 4 wedges; cut 4 paper-thin slices from the other half. Squeeze the juice from each wedge into a glass; stir. Float a slice of lime on top of each drink.

Sautéed Almonds

4 tablespoons unsalted butter
1½ cups or 1 can (7 ounces) blanched whole almonds
Salt

In a medium skillet, melt the butter over moderately low heat. Add the almonds and sauté, stirring frequently, until they are a light golden brown, 5 to 7 minutes. Remove from the heat and, while still warm, toss the nuts with salt to taste. Let cool before serving. Store in an airtight container.

Saffron Rice with Pistachios

1 tablespoon olive oil
1 tablespoon unsalted butter
1 small onion, finely chopped
1 cup rice
2 generous pinches of thread saffron, crumbled
1 cup chicken broth
2 tablespoons fresh lemon juice
½ teaspoon salt
¼ cup chopped natural-colored, unsalted pistachios

1 In a medium saucepan, heat the oil and butter. Add the onion and sauté over moderate heat until soft and translucent but not brown, about 3 minutes. Reduce the heat to low, add the rice and saffron and stir until the grains of rice are coated with oil. Add the broth, lemon juice, salt and 1¼ cups of water. Bring to a boil, reduce the heat to low and simmer, covered, for 20 minutes.

2 Mix half the pistachios into the rice and fluff with a fork. Sprinkle the remaining pistachios on top before serving.

Bibb Lettuce and Mushroom Salad with Tarragon Dressing

2 tablespoons tarragon vinegar
2 tablespoons olive oil
2 tablespoons heavy cream
¾ teaspoon sugar
¼ teaspoon salt
Pinch of cayenne pepper
3 heads of Bibb lettuce—leaves separated
¼ pound mushrooms, sliced
2 scallions, thinly sliced

1 In a small bowl, whisk together the vinegar, oil, cream, sugar, salt and cayenne until the sugar dissolves.

2 In a chilled salad bowl, combine the lettuce, mushrooms and scallions. Just before serving, pour on the dressing and toss.

Veal Scallops with Amontillado

1 pound veal or turkey scallops, pounded thin
⅓ cup all-purpose flour
½ cup milk
2 tablespoons olive oil
2 tablespoons unsalted butter
Salt and freshly ground pepper
½ cup medium-dry sherry, preferably Amontillado
1 tablespoon chopped fresh parsley, for garnish

1 Dredge the veal in the flour, dip in the milk and then again in the flour; shake off any excess.

2 In a large, heavy skillet, heat 1 tablespoon of the oil and 1 tablespoon of the butter. Add as many veal scallops as fit without crowding and sauté over moderately high heat for about 3 minutes on each side, until light brown. Transfer to a serving platter and season with salt and pepper to taste. Repeat with the remaining veal, oil and butter.

3 Add the sherry to the skillet and boil over high heat, scraping up any browned bits from the bottom of the pan, until reduced by half, about 1 minute. Pour the sauce over the veal and garnish with the parsley.

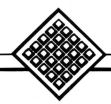

Eclectic Dinner for Friends

Chilled Vodka

Smoked Salmon Canapés with Capers and Horseradish Butter*

◆

Shashlik with Scallions and Spices*

Couscous with Chick-Peas*

Garlic-Red Pepper Sauce*

Cucumbers Vinaigrette*

Beverage Suggestion: Cold Beer, such as Anchor Steam

◆

Vanilla Ice Cream with Brandied Cherries

Turkish Coffee

*RECIPE INCLUDED

This eclectic dinner begins and ends rather elegantly and packs a garlicky wallop in between. Iced vodka poured into small glasses and smoked salmon hors d'oeuvre, enlivened with capers and horseradish butter, whet the appetite.

The flavorful food that follows is marvelous to share with good friends. It features shashlik—tender chunks of lamb, marinated briefly in garlic and spices, skewered with scallions and simply grilled—served on a bed of fragrant couscous and drizzled with a fiery sauce of garlic and hot red peppers. The couscous takes no time to prepare and can rest for 15 to 20 minutes before serving. A cooling side dish of cucumbers vinaigrette is the perfect accompaniment. Have plenty of cold beer on hand as well.

For dessert, I like to serve brandied cherries over the best vanilla ice cream available. Brandied cherries can be found in most specialty food shops.

THE GAME PLAN

- Make the marinade and marinate the lamb.
- Make the garlic-red pepper sauce, the salmon canapés and the cucumbers vinaigrette.
- Start the couscous. Preheat the broiler, and thread the meat and scallions onto skewers.
- Serve the vodka and salmon canapés and put the shashlik into the broiler.
- Serve the shashlik on top of the couscous with the garlic-pepper sauce and cucumbers.
- **If Time Allows:** The lamb can be marinated earlier in the day, and the garlic-red pepper sauce prepared well ahead. The cucumbers and salmon canapés can be prepared several hours before serving.

Six Servings

Smoked Salmon Canapés with Capers and Horseradish Butter

2 tablespoons unsalted butter, at room temperature
¾ teaspoon prepared white horseradish, drained
6 thin slices of square, Danish-style pumpernickel bread
6 ounces thinly sliced smoked salmon
Capers, for garnish

1 In a small bowl, blend the butter and horseradish. Spread each slice of pumpernickel with a thin layer of horseradish butter.

2 Place a layer of smoked salmon on the buttered bread. Cut each slice into 4 triangles or squares. Sprinkle a few capers on top of each canapé.

Shashlik with Scallions and Spices

½ cup olive oil
2 tablespoons red wine vinegar
2 tablespoons dry red wine
½ teaspoon salt
½ teaspoon freshly ground pepper
Generous pinch of nutmeg
Generous pinch of ground ginger
1 small garlic clove, crushed through a press
2½ pounds boneless lamb shoulder or leg, trimmed of excess fat and cut into 1½- to 2-inch cubes
18 scallions, cut into 1½-inch lengths

1 In a large noncorrodible bowl, combine the olive oil, vinegar, wine, salt, pepper, nutmeg, ginger and garlic; whisk until blended. Add the lamb cubes and toss well to coat. Let marinate at room temperature for 30 minutes, tossing occasionally.

2 Preheat the broiler 10 to 15 minutes before cooking time. Thread the lamb cubes onto 6 long metal skewers, alternating each piece of lamb with 2 or 3 pieces of scallion.

3 Broil 3 or 4 inches from the heat, turning occasionally, until the meat is browned outside and medium-rare inside, about 10 minutes.

Couscous with Chick-Peas

2 tablespoons unsalted butter
1 small onion, chopped
2 cups chicken broth
1 cup medium-grain couscous
½ cup chick-peas, canned or cooked
Chopped fresh coriander or parsley, for garnish

1 In a heavy medium saucepan, melt the butter over moderate heat. Add the onion and sauté until softened and translucent, about 4 minutes. Add the chicken broth and bring to a boil.

2 Slowly stir the couscous into the boiling liquid. Boil for 1 to 2 minutes. Remove from the heat and stir in the chick-peas.

3 Cover tightly and let stand until the couscous is tender, 10 to 20 minutes. Fluff the couscous with 2 forks before serving. Garnish with chopped fresh coriander or parsley if desired.

Garlic-Red Pepper Sauce

⅓ cup olive oil
1 tablespoon plus 1 teaspoon paprika
2 to 3 garlic cloves, crushed through a press
½ teaspoon salt
⅛ teaspoon cayenne pepper

In a small bowl, mix all the ingredients until thoroughly blended. Pass the sauce at the table, stirring well before using, as a condiment for both the shashlik and the couscous.

Cucumbers Vinaigrette

3 cucumbers
3 tablespoons balsamic vinegar
⅛ teaspoon salt
⅛ teaspoon freshly ground pepper

1 Peel the cucumbers; if they are unwaxed, remove only several strips of peel to make them more decorative. Slice very thin.

2 Toss the cucumbers with the vinegar, salt and pepper.

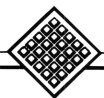

Hot Weather Menu

Gingered Melon*

◆

Beef Salad Vinaigrette*

Vermont Pan Bread*

Beverage Suggestion: Ice Cold Beer, such as New Amsterdam Amber

◆

Minted Earl Grey Iced Tea*

Chocolate Cookies

*RECIPE INCLUDED

This easy outdoor summer menu centers around a zesty composed salad. All the dishes can be prepared in advance or put together at the last moment, in less than 30 minutes.

If you make this meal ahead, slice the melon, extract the ginger juice and refrigerate both separately; season with the ginger and pepper just before serving for a sharp, refreshing flavor. Chop, wrap and refrigerate each ingredient for the beef salad vinaigrette so that the final assembly will go like clockwork. This way you have the option of grilling the beef beforehand or serving it slightly warm straight off the grill, which I think makes for tenderer meat. The pan bread is best served right from the oven, but measuring out the ingredients in advance can eliminate a last-minute rush.

Dessert can be as simple as you like. Chocolate cookies for example. Fresh fruit sprinkled with a little maple syrup and topped with sour cream or crème fraîche would also be good. Make lots of iced tea—it's the best summer cooler of all.

THE GAME PLAN

- Make the tea.
- Extract the ginger juice and slice the melon.
- Make the vinaigrette for the salad, and assemble and prepare all of the remaining salad ingredients except the beef.
- Preheat the oven to 425°. Make the pan bread batter and bake.
- Turn the oven to broil. Broil the beef and let it rest.
- Meanwhile, sprinkle the melon with the ginger juice and pepper, garnish and serve.
- Slice the beef, assemble the salad and serve with the warm bread and tea.
- If Time Allows: The ginger juice can be extracted and the melon sliced in advance. The vinaigrette can also be prepared and all the salad ingredients assembled, prepared and stored covered in the refrigerator, and the beef can be broiled ahead.

Six Servings

Beef Salad Vinaigrette

1 flank steak (about 2 pounds)
1 medium garlic clove, cut in half
⅓ cup plus 2 tablespoons olive oil
Salt and freshly ground pepper
1 head of oak leaf lettuce
1 small bunch of arugula
1 tablespoon capers, drained
1½ teaspoons finely chopped
   sweet gherkins
1 hard-cooked egg, minced
¼ cup minced fresh parsley
1 small red onion, cut into thin
   rings
3 tomatoes, sliced
1 European seedless cucumber,
   thinly sliced
1½ tablespoons red wine vinegar
1 tablespoon fresh lemon juice
¼ teaspoon powdered mustard

1 Preheat the broiler. Rub both sides of the steak with the garlic clove and brush with 2 tablespoons of olive oil. Broil the steak about 4 inches from the heat for 4 to 5 minutes on each side for medium-rare. Season with salt and pepper to taste. Let rest for about 5 minutes. Slice very thin crosswise on the diagonal.

2 Make a bed of the lettuce and arugula on a large platter. Arrange the sliced beef in the center of the leaves and sprinkle with the capers, gherkins, egg and parsley. Scatter the red onion rings over all. Surround with the tomatoes and cucumber.

3 In a small bowl, whisk together the remaining ⅓ cup oil, the vinegar, lemon juice, mustard, and salt and pepper to taste until blended. Spoon over the salad before serving.

Vermont Pan Bread

1¼ cups white cornmeal
¼ cup all-purpose flour
1¼ teaspoons baking powder
¾ teaspoon salt
1 cup milk
1 egg, beaten
2½ tablespoons solid white
   shortening
2 tablespoons unsalted butter, cut
   into small pieces
⅓ cup coarsely chopped pure
   maple sugar candy (about 2½
   ounces)

1 Preheat the oven to 425°. Sift the cornmeal, flour, baking powder and salt into a mixing bowl. Stir in the milk and egg.

2 Place the shortening in a large, heavy, ovenproof skillet (preferably cast iron) and heat in the oven for about 5 minutes, until the pan is hot and the shortening melted. Swirl to coat the skillet with the shortening. Immediately pour the melted shortening into the batter and mix well.

3 Pour the batter into the hot greased skillet. Dot with the butter and sprinkle evenly with the chopped maple sugar candy. Bake for 20 minutes, or until a knife inserted in the center comes out clean. Serve warm.

Gingered Melon

½ cup coarsely chopped,
   unpeeled fresh ginger (about
   1½ ounces)
1 cantaloupe, chilled
Freshly ground pepper
Sprigs of fresh mint, for garnish

1 Mince the ginger in a food processor. Scrape the pulp into a double thickness of dampened cheesecloth and twist to extract the juice.

2 Slice the cantaloupe into 6 wedges. With a thin sharp knife, slice the melon from the rind in one piece. Slice each melon wedge into bite-size pieces and rearrange them on the rind. Sprinkle the melon with the ginger juice and a grinding of the pepper. Alternatively, place the melon pieces in a bowl, toss with the ginger juice and pepper and spoon into cups. Garnish with mint sprigs. Serve chilled.

Minted Earl Grey Iced Tea

2 tablespoons Earl Grey tea or 6
   tea bags
½ teaspoon dried spearmint or 1
   mint tea bag
6 cups boiling water
Sugar
Thinly sliced lemon, for garnish

Place the tea and mint in a heatproof pitcher; add boiling water and steep for 10 to 15 minutes. Strain and add sugar to taste. Garnish with lemon slices, and serve over plenty of ice.

A Spirited Little Dinner

Dry Sherry

Tamari Almonds*

Green Olives

◆

Spirited Veal with Bourbon and Granny Smith Apples*

Croutons*

**Limestone Lettuce Salad with Walnut
Oil Dressing***

Beverage Suggestion: Rhine Wine or Champagne

◆

Chilled Green Grapes and Amaretti

Espresso

*RECIPE INCLUDED

The high spirits and fun that come from entertaining well and elegantly need not be sacrificed to a frantic winter schedule. This menu for four is both fast and festive. It is centered around veal dressed in an intriguing blend of fresh apples, bourbon and cream, wreathed with watercress and crisp buttered croutons. The ease of preparation and fragrance of this dish almost guarantee that the chef will emerge from the kitchen feeling cheerful, unhurried and ready to dine well.

To begin, serve a dry sherry for an aperitif with green olives and the Tamari Almonds, which can be made in advance or prepared just before serving.

A simple dessert, such as chilled grapes with amaretti cookies and espresso, is enough to finish off this delicious meal.

THE GAME PLAN

- Make the Tamari Almonds.
- Assemble and prepare all the ingredients for the veal and apples.
- Prepare the salad greens and make the dressing, but wait to toss at the table.
- Preheat the oven to 350°. Butter the bread for the croutons and place on a baking sheet.
- Serve the sherry, Tamari Almonds and olives.
- Put the croutons in the oven.
- Meanwhile, make the veal and serve it hot with the croutons and the salad.
- **If Time Allows:** The almonds can be made ahead.

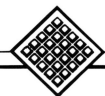

Four Servings

Tamari Almonds

1½ tablespoons unsalted butter
1½ cups whole blanched almonds
1½ tablespoons tamari (or
 Japanese soy sauce)
1 tablespoon sugar

1 In a heavy skillet, melt the butter, add the almonds and stir for about 1½ minutes over medium heat.

2 Sprinkle the tamari and sugar over the almonds and stir for 2 minutes, or until the almonds are coated and no liquid remains in the pan. Spread them over a plate or a sheet of waxed paper to dry.

Limestone Lettuce Salad with Walnut Oil Dressing

2 heads of limestone or Bibb
 lettuce
1½ tablespoons wine vinegar
¼ cup walnut oil
½ teaspoon salt
⅛ teaspoon freshly ground white
 pepper
1½ teaspoons minced fresh chives

1 Arrange the lettuce leaves on four individual salad plates.

2 In a small bowl, whisk together the vinegar, walnut oil, salt and pepper.

3 Dress the lettuce just before serving and sprinkle the chives on top.

Spirited Veal with Bourbon and Granny Smith Apples

½ lemon
4 veal scallops (about 1 pound),
 pounded thin
1 teaspoon coarse (kosher) salt
¼ teaspoon freshly ground
 pepper
4 tablespoons unsalted butter
1 Granny Smith apple, or any
 other tart cooking apple—
 peeled, cored and coarsely
 chopped
¼ cup bourbon
½ cup heavy cream
Watercress, for garnish
Croutons, for garnish

1 Squeeze the juice of lemon over the veal and then season with the salt and pepper.

2 In a large skillet, melt the butter over moderate heat. When the butter is very hot, add the veal and brown it quickly on both sides. Transfer the veal to a warm platter and keep warm. Add the chopped apple to the skillet. Sauté it for about 1½ minutes and move it to one side of the pan. Remove the pan from the heat and add the browned veal.

3 In a small saucepan, heat the bourbon and carefully ignite it. Pour the flaming bourbon over the veal and return the large skillet to moderate heat. When the flame of the bourbon has died out, pour in the heavy cream and stir constantly for about 2 minutes to thicken the sauce.

4 Transfer the veal to a heated platter. Top with the apples and the sauce. Surround the veal with the watercress and croutons.

Croutons

3 tablespoons unsalted butter, at
 room temperature
8 slices of French bread, cut 1
 inch thick

1 Preheat the oven to 350°. Butter both sides of each bread slice and place them on a foil-lined baking sheet.

2 Bake, turning the slices once, for 10 minutes. or until both sides are golden.

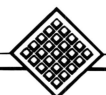

FISH & SHELLFISH

Weekend Lunch for Guests

Fillets of Sea Bass with Sun-Dried Tomatoes*

Green Bean Salad with Balsamic Vinaigrette*

Basil Biscuits*

Beverage Suggestion: Sancerre or Montrachet

◆

Brownies

Clementines or Tangerines

Café Filtre

*RECIPE INCLUDED

Sea bass, a delectable fish on its own, is made even more so here by a creamy sauce, bright and pungent with sun-dried tomatoes. This is an excellent dish for either a leisurely weekend lunch or a light dinner.

Hot biscuits flecked with fresh basil are a delicious and unusual accompaniment. If fresh basil is not available, omit it from the biscuit batter and blend a little store-bought pesto into whipped unsalted butter to lavish onto the hot split biscuits.

Sun-dried tomatoes can be purchased, usually packed in oil and herbs, in most specialty food shops. Or, you can make your own by halving Italian tomatoes, sprinkling them generously with coarse salt and drying them on a rack in a warm oven (about 125°) for 18 to 24 hours. Store them in a refrigerator in a jar filled with a good quality olive oil and herbs.

THE GAME PLAN

- Preheat the oven to 450°. Prepare the biscuits and bake. When they're done, reduce the oven temperature to 400° for the sea bass.

- Meanwhile, start preparing the sauce for the sea bass.

- Wrap the fillets in foil packets and place in the oven when the biscuits have finishing cooking.

- While the fish bakes, make the green bean salad.

- **If Time Allows:** The vinaigrette for the green beans can be made in advance and the sauce for the fish can be prepared ahead of time and reheated just before serving.

Four Servings

Fillets of Sea Bass with Sun-Dried Tomatoes

5½ teaspoons unsalted butter
1 large shallot, minced
½ cup bottled clam juice
½ cup dry white wine
2 tablespoons coarsely chopped, drained sun-dried tomatoes
1 cup heavy cream
4 fillets of sea bass, about 6 ounces each
Salt and freshly ground pepper

1 Preheat the oven to 400°. In a small saucepan, melt 1½ teaspoons of the butter, add the shallot and sauté over moderately low heat until softened. Stir in the clam juice and wine, bring to a boil and boil over high heat until reduced to ½ cup, about 5 minutes.

2 Stir in the sun-dried tomatoes. Add the cream and continue to boil over high heat, stirring constantly, until the sauce has reduced to ¾ cup, about 10 minutes. Keep the sauce warm over low heat.

3 Meanwhile, place each fillet on a piece of aluminum foil about 11 inches square. Dot each fillet with 1 teaspoon of the remaining butter and sprinkle lightly with salt and pepper. Fold the foil over and seal the edges to form a packet. Place the packets on a baking sheet and bake on the middle rack of the oven for 12 minutes.

4 Remove the fish from the foil and place on warmed serving plates. Pour the sauce over the fish and serve hot.

Green Bean Salad with Balsamic Vinaigrette

1 pound green beans
¼ cup olive oil
2 teaspoons balsamic vinegar
2 teaspoons fresh lemon juice
¼ teaspoon coarse (kosher) salt
Freshly ground pepper
3 radishes, thinly sliced
⅓ cup finely chopped red onion
2 tablespoons minced fresh parsley
1½ teaspoons drained capers

1 In a large saucepan of boiling water, cook the beans until crisp-tender, 6 to 8 minutes.

2 Meanwhile, in a small bowl, combine the oil, vinegar, lemon juice and salt; season with pepper to taste and blend well.

3 Drain the beans in a colander, rinse briefly under cold water to refresh, and pat dry on paper towels. Place them on a serving platter, sprinkle with the radishes, onion, parsley and capers. Spoon the dressing over the top and serve.

Basil Biscuits

MAKES ABOUT 10 BISCUITS

1 cup all-purpose flour
1½ teaspoons baking powder
¼ teaspoon salt
3 tablespoons cold unsalted butter, cut into cubes
2 tablespoons chopped fresh basil
1½ teaspoons minced shallot
⅓ cup milk

1 Preheat the oven to 450°. Into a large mixing bowl, sift together the flour, baking powder and salt. Using a pastry blender or two knives, cut the butter into the flour until the mixture resembles coarse meal.

2 Stir in the basil and shallot and mix well. Make a well in the center of the mixture, pour in the milk. Using a fork, quickly mix the dough. Knead for 30 seconds.

3 Turn the dough out onto a lightly floured work surface and quickly roll or pat it to a ½-inch thickness. Using a lightly floured 2-inch biscuit cutter, cut out the biscuits. Place on an ungreased baking sheet and bake for 12 to 15 minutes.

Effortless Dinner for Four

Vodka Martinis

Ginger and Bacon Canapés*

◆

Sea Scallops with Orange Butter*

Green Beans with Chervil*

French Bread

**Beverage Suggestion: California
Gewürztraminer**

◆

Café Royal*

Chocolates

*RECIPE INCLUDED

Gastronomic chronicler Waverley Root once said that he knew of no one who had a bad word to say about the scallop, with the exception of a young scallop shucker who, when interviewed by *The New Yorker*, commented "They don't have much personality."

The shucker may have had a point, but what the scallop lacks in personality, it certainly makes up for in taste and texture. It is one of the sweetest and most succulent of all shellfish. The sweetness combines well with port, orange juice and cubes of orange in the main dish here, one of my favorites for entertaining. It is amazingly simple to prepare and the results are quite impressive.

The scallops should be cooked until just opaque and heated through, so you should have everything else in the menu ready to serve before starting to sauté. Crisp-tender green beans tossed with chervil are a fresh, easy-to-make accompaniment to the scallops. Serve with French bread and a chilled white wine.

THE GAME PLAN

- Make the canapés.
- Put the beans on to cook.
- Meanwhile, assemble and prepare all the ingredients for the scallops.
- Drain the beans and toss with the seasonings; keep warm while cooking the scallops.
- Sauté the scallops and make the sauce. Serve hot with the beans and French bread.
- Just before serving dessert, prepare the Café Royal and serve hot.
- **If Time Allows:** The canapés can be made ahead and the beans can be cooked in advance and reheated gently before tossing them with the remaining ingredients.

Four Servings

Ginger and Bacon Canapés

6 teaspoons cream cheese, softened
1 teaspoon diced, drained preserved ginger
4 to 5 strips bacon—cooked until crisp, drained and crumbled
12 melba toast rounds

In a small bowl, combine the cream cheese, ginger and bacon and blend together thoroughly. Spread the cheese mixture onto the toast rounds and serve.

Green Beans with Chervil

1 pound fresh green beans
1 teaspoon fresh lemon juice
½ teaspoon chervil
⅛ teaspoon white pepper
¼ teaspoon salt

1 In a large saucepan of boiling water, cook the beans until crisp-tender, 6 to 8 minutes. Drain well and return the beans to the saucepan.

2 Add the lemon juice, chervil, pepper and salt. Toss until the beans are coated. Set aside and keep warm.

Sea Scallops with Orange Butter

1½ pounds sea scallops
4 tablespoons unsalted butter
¼ teaspoon salt
1 tablespoon chopped scallion
3 tablespoons port
¼ cup fresh orange juice
¼ cup heavy cream
1 large orange, peeled and cut into cubes about the size of the scallops

1 Cut off the small tough muscle on the side of each scallop. If the scallops are large, slice in half crosswise.

2 In a large skillet, melt the butter until it foams. Add the scallops and sauté over moderately high heat for about 1½ minutes on each side, until they are just opaque.

3 Remove the skillet from the heat and transfer the scallops to a colander set over a bowl to catch the juices. Sprinkle the scallops with the salt and keep warm while preparing the sauce.

4 Return the skillet to the heat, add the scallion, port, orange juice and the juices from the scallops. Reduce over high heat for 3 minutes. Stir in the cream and reduce for 2 minutes more, until slightly thickened.

5 Arrange the scallops and orange cubes in the middle of a warmed serving platter. Pour the sauce over the top and serve hot.

Note: For an elegant presentation, arrange the scallops and oranges in the center of a large platter, arrange the green beans around the edge and pour the hot sauce over the scallops and oranges.

Café Royal

1½ cups strong, freshly brewed French-roast coffee
4 lumps of sugar
4 thin strips of lemon zest, about 2 inches long
4 tablespoons brandy

1 Fill four demitasse cups two-thirds full with the hot coffee. Drop a lump of sugar into each cup and top each with a strip of lemon zest.

2 Pour 1 tablespoon of brandy slowly into each cup so that it floats on top of the coffee.

3 Carefully ignite the brandy in each cup with a long match and let it flame for one to two seconds, so that only a little of the brandy burns away. Put out the flames and serve immediately while still very hot.

Simple Fall Lunch

**Herring in Mustard-Cream with Apples
and Onions***

Parslied New Potatoes in Their Skins*

Sweet Cucumber and Dill Salad*

Black Bread and Sweet Butter

Beverage Suggestion: Pinot Grigio

◆

Ginger Pecan Bread*

Vienna Roast Coffee

*RECIPE INCLUDED

One of my favorite menus for a no-fuss fall lunch includes herring fillets with a rich, mustard-cream sauce, surrounded by crisp slices of Golden Delicious apples and red onion rings. With it, I usually serve piping hot buttered new potatoes in their skins, and cucumber slices tossed with dill and a sweet dressing made slightly piquant with a pinch of cayenne pepper.

The whole menu is so quick and easy to put together that there's time left to bake something sweet and warm for dessert, such as this Ginger Pecan Bread.

If you're making the whole menu, start by preparing the bread. While it bakes, put the potatoes on to steam, then salt the cucumbers and assemble the herring. Take the bread from the oven as you sit down to eat; it will still be warm when you're ready for dessert and a cup of rich Vienna roast coffee.

THE GAME PLAN

- Preheat the oven to 350°. Prepare and bake the Ginger Pecan Bread.

- Meanwhile, put the potatoes on to steam.

- Salt the cucumbers and let them drain. Make the dressing.

- Make the mustard-cream sauce for the herring; arrange the remaining ingredients as directed.

- Toss the cucumbers with the dressing and dill.

- Toss the potatoes in the butter and seasonings and serve hot with the salad and herring, accompanied with black bread and butter.

- Remove the pecan bread from the oven and let cool slightly during lunch.

- **If Time Allows:** The pecan bread, the mustard-cream and the cucumber salad can be made ahead. Serve the pecan bread at room temperature or reheat before serving.

Four to Six Servings

Herring in Mustard-Cream with Apples and Onions

2 tablespoons Düsseldorf or Dijon-style mustard
½ cup heavy cream
3 cups finely shredded romaine or leaf lettuce
3 jars (8 ounces each) pickled herring fillets in white wine, drained
2 Golden Delicious apples, cored and sliced into thin wedges
½ large red onion, cut into ⅛-inch rounds

1 In a small mixing bowl, beat the mustard and cream together with a wire whisk until slightly thickened.

2 Spread the lettuce on a serving platter or individual plates and arrange the herring fillets on top. Spoon the mustard-cream over the herring and surround with the apple slices. Separate the onion rings, scatter over the herring and serve.

Parslied New Potatoes in Their Skins

12 to 18 small red potatoes, unpeeled (about 2½ pounds)
2½ tablespoons unsalted butter, melted
½ teaspoon coarse (kosher) salt
Freshly ground pepper
2 tablespoons chopped fresh parsley
1 teaspoon fresh lemon juice

1 Steam the potatoes until tender, about 15 minutes.

2 Drain the potatoes and place them in a large bowl. Pour the melted butter over the potatoes and toss until well coated. Season with the salt and pepper to taste. Add the parsley and lemon juice and toss.

Sweet Cucumber and Dill Salad

3 medium cucumbers, peeled and thinly sliced
Salt
2 tablespoons white wine vinegar
1 tablespoon sugar
⅛ teaspoon cayenne pepper
2 tablespoons chopped fresh dill

1 Place the cucumber slices in a colander, sprinkle very lightly with salt and toss. Let drain for about 15 minutes.

2 In a small bowl, combine the vinegar, sugar and cayenne.

3 Pat the cucumber slices dry and toss with the dressing and dill. Serve chilled or at room temperature.

Ginger Pecan Bread

¼ cup light, unsulphured molasses
½ cup cold unsalted butter, cut into slices
½ cup boiling water
2 cups all-purpose flour
½ cup sugar
2 teaspoons ground ginger
1¼ teaspoons baking soda
1 egg
½ cup golden raisins
⅔ cup coarsely chopped pecans

1 Preheat the oven to 350°. Butter an 8-inch square cake pan. In a large mixing bowl, combine the molasses, butter and boiling water and mix until the molasses is dissolved and most of the butter is melted.

2 Sift the flour, sugar, ginger and baking soda together on a piece of waxed paper. Stir the dry ingredients into the molasses and butter mixture. Add the egg and beat with an electric mixer until thoroughly blended.

3 Stir in the raisins and pecans. Spread the batter evenly into the prepared cake pan. Bake for 30 minutes or until a toothpick inserted in the center comes out clean. Serve warm or at room temperature.

Seafood Pasta Dinner

Rum Collins with Honey*

Bananas Broiled in Bacon*

◆

Tomato Linguine with Poached Seafood*

Crusty French Bread

Tossed Green Salad

Beverage Suggestion: Muscadet de Sèvre-et-Maine

◆

Hot Fudge and Bourbon Sundaes with Pecans*

Espresso

*RECIPE INCLUDED

Thanks to the Great American Pasta Boom, there are now myriad possibilities for what colors and flavors the pasta as well as what goes on top of it. Cooks with a flair for experimentation can make garlic pasta or hazelnut pasta or can invent their own flavors. Busy cooks can pick up spinach or tomato pasta at specialty food stores and even in the gourmet refrigerator section of some well-stocked supermarkets. My choice for this menu is tomato linguine. Its delicate taste and muted color go particularly well with the lightly flavored seafood, flecked with bright green parsley.

The appetizer combines two familiar ingredients in a new way. Bacon is frequently wrapped around livers, oysters or even apples; in this twist, it's wrapped around green (underripe) bananas for an especially piquant flavor that's just right with a Rum Collins.

The main course needs no other garnish than crusty French bread to sop up the last drops of sauce. Follow with a simple green salad.

THE GAME PLAN

- Sauté the pecans for the dessert. Combine the chocolate and bourbon in a double boiler, but wait to heat it until just before serving.

- Preheat the broiler. Prepare the bananas up to the point of broiling.

- Assemble and prepare all the ingredients for the Tomato Linguine with Poached Seafood. Prepare the greens and dressing for a salad.

- Put the water for the pasta on to boil and the court bouillon on to simmer.

- Broil the banana, make the Rum Collins and serve together.

- Just before serving, finish the pasta, seafood and sauce; serve with the salad and bread.

- Just before serving dessert, heat up the sauce.

○ **If Time Allows:** The pecans for the dessert can be sautéed ahead.

Four Servings

Rum Collins with Honey

6 ounces (¾ cup) light rum
6 tablespoons fresh lime juice
4 tablespoons honey
Seltzer
4 lime slices, for garnish

Stir together the rum, lime juice and honey until the honey dissolves. Divide the rum mixture among four tall glasses filled with ice. Fill up with seltzer and stir to mix. Garnish each with a slice of lime.

Bananas Broiled in Bacon

1 large underripe banana or 1 medium plantain, peeled
2 tablespoons fresh lemon juice
7 to 8 bacon strips, cut crosswise in half
Hot pepper sauce

1 Preheat the broiler. Cut the banana in half lengthwise and then into 1-inch-long pieces. Place in a small bowl with the lemon juice and toss to coat.

2 Place a banana piece on each bacon strip. Season with a drop of hot pepper sauce. Wrap the bacon around the banana; secure with a toothpick and place in one layer on a baking sheet.

3 Broil until the bacon is browned on one side, about 3 minutes. Turn and broil until the second side is brown, about 1 minute. Pass as hot appetizers.

Tomato Linguine with Poached Seafood

1 cup (8 ounces) bottled clam juice
½ cup dry white wine
¼ teaspoon saffron threads
¾ pound large shrimp, peeled and deveined
½ pound sea scallops, quartered, or bay scallops
3 tablespoons unsalted butter
1 tablespoon olive oil
2 garlic cloves, finely chopped
2 scallions, finely chopped
1½ tablespoons minced fresh parsley
⅛ teaspoon hot pepper sauce
Salt
10 to 12 ounces fresh tomato or plain linguine
Lemon wedges and parsley sprigs, for garnish

1 Set a large pot of salted water to boil for the pasta. In a noncorrodible skillet, combine the clam juice, wine and saffron. Simmer for 10 minutes to make a broth.

2 Add the shrimp and scallops and poach gently over moderate heat, stirring occasionally, until just opaque, 4 to 5 minutes.

3 In a small saucepan, melt 2 tablespoons of the butter in the oil over moderately low heat. Add the garlic, scallions and parsley and stir together for 10 seconds. Add ¼ cup of the broth from the seafood and remove from the heat. Season with the hot pepper sauce and salt to taste.

4 Cook the pasta until just tender to the bite, about 3 minutes.

5 Remove the seafood from the broth, reserving the liquid. Place the linguine in a large serving bowl. Toss with the remaining 1 tablespoon butter and ½ cup of the seafood broth. Top with the seafood and pour the scallion-parsley sauce over all. Garnish with the lemon wedges and parsley sprigs.

Hot Fudge and Bourbon Sundaes with Pecans

1 tablespoon unsalted butter
½ cup whole pecans
¾ cup bottled fudge sauce
3 tablespoons bourbon
Vanilla ice cream

1 In a small skillet, melt the butter. When it begins to foam, add the pecans and sauté over moderate heat until barely toasted, about 1 minute. Let cool, then drain on paper towels.

2 Meanwhile, combine the fudge sauce and the bourbon in the top of a double boiler. Heat, stirring, over simmering water until hot, about 5 minutes.

3 Scoop the ice cream into serving dishes. Pour the hot fudge sauce on top. Sprinkle with the pecans.

Light, Louisiana Lunch for Four

Country Ham Biscuits*

Warm Crab Salad*

**Belgian Endive and Avocados with
Lemon-Tarragon Dressing***

**Beverage Suggestion: California French
Colombard, such as Parducci**

◆

Bananas in Rum Cream*

*RECIPE INCLUDED

When prepared the right way, jambalaya, Louisiana kin to paella, is as light, bright and welcome as a breeze is on the bayou. The Warm Crab Salad in this menu is inspired by jambalaya, filled with buttery lumps of crabmeat, fresh tomatoes, scallions and a touch of garlic and hot pepper sauce.

The biscuits are best when prepared with a flavorful dry-cured ham such as Smithfield. This type of ham can usually be found sliced and packaged in small quantities. It's also occasionally sold in small jars. If Smithfield or another country ham is not available in your area, use Canadian bacon; though it has a very different character, it makes a good substitute.

The economy-minded may wish to use one of several crabmeat substitutes now available such as Sea Legs, Sushi Sticks or Sea Shells, all of which look and taste a great deal like the real thing but cost a great deal less. They can be found in most well-stocked supermarkets.

THE GAME PLAN

- Put the rice on to boil.

- Blend the lemon juice and tarragon. Assemble and prepare the remaining ingredients for the Belgian Endive and Avocados, but wait to finish mixing the dressing until shortly before serving.

- Preheat the oven, make the biscuits and put them in to bake.

- Meanwhile, finish mixing the salad dressing, cook the remaining crab salad ingredients and toss with the hot rice. Serve with the salad and hot biscuits.

- Just before serving, assemble the Bananas in Rum Cream.

Four Servings

Belgian Endive and Avocados with Lemon-Tarragon Dressing

3 tablespoons fresh lemon juice
1 teaspoon tarragon
2 ripe avocados, peeled and cut lengthwise into thin slices
3 large Belgian endive, trimmed and cut lengthwise into ¼-inch julienne strips
¾ teaspoon salt
½ teaspoon powdered mustard
⅓ cup vegetable oil
Watercress sprigs, for garnish
Freshly ground pepper

1 In a small bowl, combine 2½ tablespoons of the lemon juice with the tarragon. Let stand for at least 10 minutes.

2 Sprinkle the remaining ½ tablespoon lemon juice over the avocado slices. Arrange with the endive on a serving platter.

3 Shortly before serving, whisk the salt and mustard into the lemon juice-tarragon mixture. Slowly whisk in the oil in a thin stream until well blended.

4 Drizzle the dressing over the salad, garnish with watercress and grind on pepper to taste.

Warm Crab Salad

1 bay leaf
1½ teaspoons salt
1 cup converted rice
¼ teaspoon hot pepper sauce
5 tablespoons unsalted butter
4 scallions, sliced
3 tablespoons minced, canned mild green chiles
1¼ cups peeled, seeded and coarsely chopped tomato
2 large garlic cloves, minced
½ teaspoon ground cumin
2 tablespoons fresh lemon juice
1 pound lump crabmeat, picked over to remove any cartilage
2 teaspoons minced parsley or fresh coriander, for garnish

1 In a large saucepan, place the bay leaf and 2½ cups water and bring to a boil over high heat. Add 1 teaspoon of the salt and the rice and let the water return to a boil. Reduce the heat to low, cover and cook for 17 to 20 minutes. Discard the bay leaf and stir in the hot pepper sauce.

2 In a large skillet, melt the butter over low heat. Add the scallions and chiles and stir for 1 minute. Stir in the tomato and garlic and cook for 3 to 4 minutes, until hot. Stir in the cumin.

3 Add the hot rice and toss with the sauce mixture. Gently fold in the lemon juice, crabmeat and remaining ½ teaspoon salt and let warm over low heat for 1 or 2 minutes. Garnish with parsley or coriander and serve hot.

Country Ham Biscuits

1 cup all-purpose flour
1½ teaspoons baking powder
⅛ teaspoon cayenne pepper
3 tablespoons cold unsalted butter, diced
¼ cup chopped country ham, such as Smithfield
1 teaspoon minced scallion
¼ cup milk

1 Preheat the oven to 450°. Into a large mixing bowl, sift together the flour, baking powder and cayenne. Cut the butter into the dry ingredients until the mixture resembles coarse meal.

2 Add the ham and scallion and blend thoroughly. Make a well in the center of the dough, pour in the milk and blend the dough in toward the center.

3 Turn the dough out onto a lightly floured work surface and knead for 60 seconds; do not overmix. Quickly roll out the dough to a ½-inch thickness. Using a lightly floured 2-inch biscuit cutter, cut out biscuits and place them on an ungreased baking sheet. Bake for 12 to 15 minutes, until lightly browned.

Bananas in Rum Cream

¾ cup heavy cream
¼ cup dark rum
2 teaspoons sugar
4 small or 2 large bananas, sliced
Shaved bittersweet chocolate

In a medium bowl, combine the cream, rum and sugar. Stir to dissolve the sugar. Add the bananas and toss gently to coat. Divide the bananas among 4 dessert dishes. Pour the remaining rum cream over the bananas. Garnish with shaved chocolate.

Easy, Elegant Dinner for Two

Avocado with Rum Vinaigrette*

◆

Red Snapper with Green Peppercorn Sauce*

Green Beans with Lemon Zest*

Crusty French Bread

**Beverage Suggestion: California
Chardonnay, such as Sebastiani**

◆

Baked Peaches on Brioche*

Espresso

*RECIPE INCLUDED

This is the perfect meal for those lovely summer evenings that demand an elegant dinner but are too serene to permit sacrificing hours in the kitchen. All the preparation for the meal and most of the actual cooking can be done in 45 minutes.

The focus of the menu is red snapper, baked to moist and tender flakiness in foil packets, served with a piquant green peppercorn sauce. Green peppercorns, packed in either brine or vinegar, are a popular item in most specialty food stores. Either way, they have a special peppery tang that is all their own and, like capers, are delicious with almost any bird, beast or fish. There's ample time to prepare the avocado and green beans while the fish and sauce are cooking.

For dessert, hot peaches contrast deliciously with ice cream or chilled crème fraîche. Blanch, drain and prepare the peaches up to the baking step ahead of time. Reduce the oven heat to 350° after the snapper is removed and place the peaches in the oven to finish cooking during dinner. Or, if you prefer, prepare the peaches in advance.

THE GAME PLAN

- Prepare the peaches up to the baking step.
- Preheat the oven to 400° and start preparing the sauce for the red snapper. While the sauce reduces, prepare and wrap the fish fillets.
- Prepare and assemble the avocados.
- Place the fish in the oven, drop the beans in boiling water and serve the avocados while the fish, sauce and beans cook.
- Stir the peppercorns into the sauce. Drain and finish the beans.
- Remove the fish from the oven and reduce the oven temperature to 350°. Place the peaches in the oven to cook during dinner.
- **If Time Allows:** The peaches can be blanched and the salad dressing made in advance. Or, if you wish to serve the dessert at room temperature, it can be baked in advance.

Two Servings

Avocado with Rum Vinaigrette

1 lime
1 ripe avocado, cut in half
Spinach leaves
1 teaspoon dark rum
1 tablespoon corn oil
¼ teaspoon salt
3 or 4 dashes of hot pepper sauce
Coarsely ground black pepper

1 Squeeze the juice from ½ of the lime over both avocado halves to prevent discoloration. Make a bed of spinach leaves on individual serving plates and place an avocado half on each.

2 Squeeze the juice from the remaining lime half into a small bowl. Stir in the rum, oil, salt and hot pepper sauce. Pour into the avocado halves. Sprinkle with black pepper to taste.

Green Beans with Lemon Zest

½ pound fresh green beans
1 tablespoon unsalted butter
1 teaspoon grated lemon zest
1 tablespoon fresh lemon juice
Salt

In a large saucepan of boiling water, cook the beans until bright green and crisp-tender, 6 to 8 minutes. Drain and return to the saucepan. Add the butter and toss until the beans are well coated. Add the lemon zest and juice and toss briefly. Season with salt to taste.

Red Snapper with Green Peppercorn Sauce

¼ cup bottled clam juice
¼ cup dry white wine
½ cup heavy cream
2 fillets of red snapper, about 6 ounces each
Salt
2 tablespoons unsalted butter
2 teaspoons green peppercorns packed in brine or vinegar, drained and rinsed

1 Preheat the oven to 400°. In a small saucepan, combine the clam juice and white wine. Boil over high heat until reduced to ¼ cup, about 5 minutes. Add the cream and continue to boil, stirring occasionally, until the sauce is reduced to ⅓ cup, about 10 minutes. Keep warm over low heat.

2 Meanwhile, butter two pieces of foil large enough to wrap each fillet. Place the fillets on the buttered foil, sprinkle lightly with salt and dot the fillets with the butter. Fold to seal the foil and place the packets on a baking sheet. Bake in the middle of the oven for 12 minutes.

3 Just before serving, add the green peppercorns to the sauce. Heat briefly to warm through. Remove the snapper from the foil and place on warmed plates. Pour the sauce over the fish and serve hot.

Baked Peaches on Brioche

2 peaches
4 slices brioche or thinly sliced firm white bread, cut into 3-inch rounds
2 tablespoons sugar
2 tablespoons unsalted butter
Greengage plum or raspberry jam
Crème fraîche or vanilla ice cream

1 Preheat the oven to 350°. In a large pot of boiling water, blanch the peaches for 30 seconds. Drain and rinse under cold running water; drain well. Slip the skins off and cut the peaches in half. Discard the pits.

2 Butter an 8-inch square baking dish. Place the brioche slices in the dish. Arrange the peaches, cut-side up, on top of the brioche. Sprinkle each with ½ tablespoon sugar and dot each with ½ tablespoon butter.

3 Bake in the middle of the oven for 30 minutes, until the peaches are tender and the topping is caramelized and bubbling.

4 Place a dollop of jam in the cavity of each peach half and top with chilled crème fraîche or vanilla ice cream. Serve hot or at room temperature.

Easy, Elegant Dinner for Two

PAGE 146

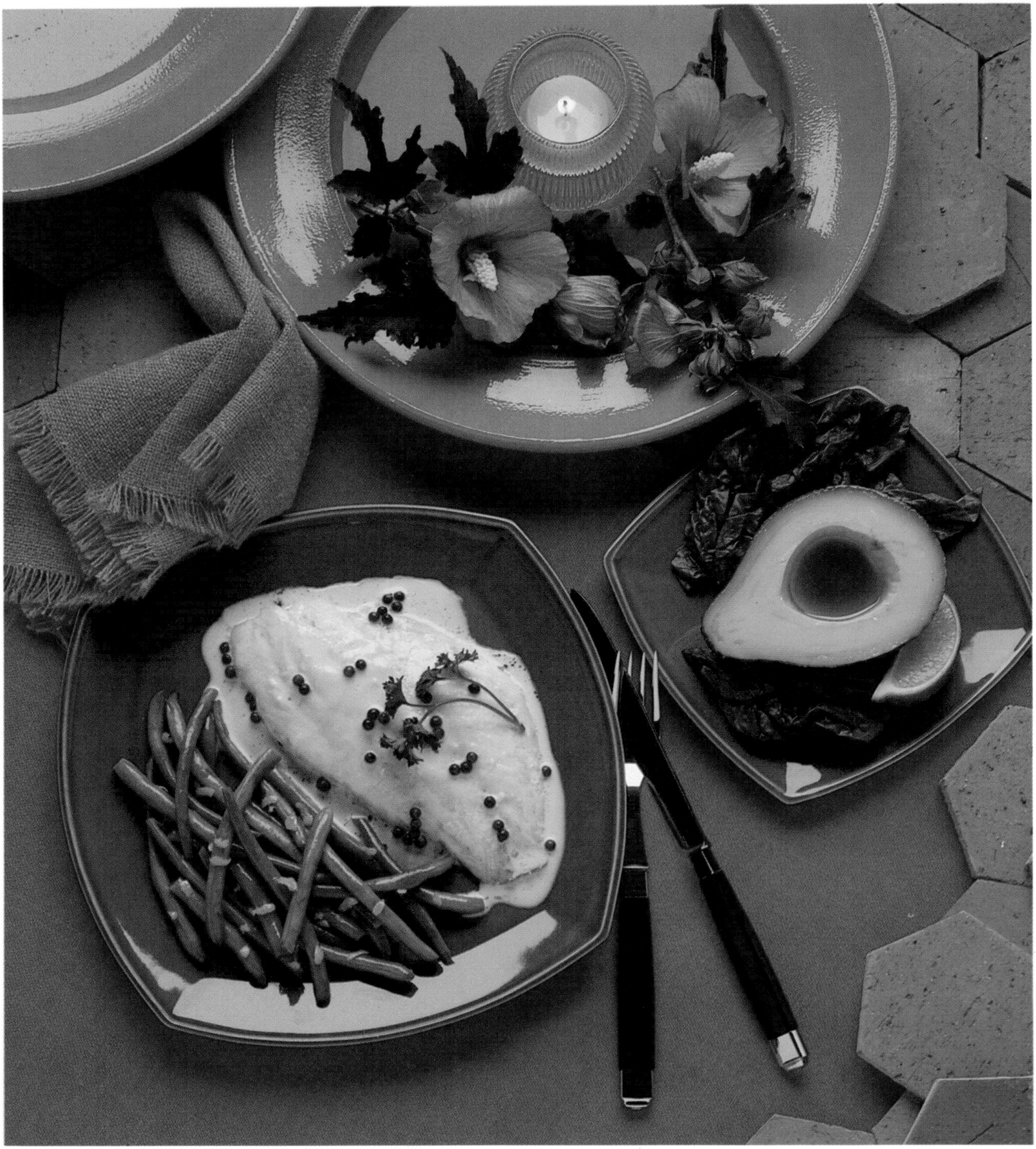

Mid-Winter Weekend Lunch

Pernod and Water

Red Pepper Almonds*

Calamata Olives

◆

Mediterranean Fish Stew*

**Salad of Montrachet Cheese, Romaine,
Watercress and Red Onion***

Crusty Peasant Bread

Beverage Suggestion: Torres Viña Sol

◆

Bartlett Pears

Amaretti Cookies and Espresso

*RECIPE INCLUDED

Here is an informal lunch menu sure to bring a glow of warmth and cheer to a mid-winter weekend. Begin the meal with spicy Red Pepper Almonds and Calamata olives to accompany a Pernod aperitif.

The Mediterranean Fish Stew, filled with the flavors of tomatoes, garlic, orange peel and herbs, is as bright and fresh as a sun-warmed breeze, with an underlying earthiness that's especially welcome in cold weather. It's wonderful with a crusty loaf of peasant bread. Follow the hearty stew with a light, aromatic salad of watercress, romaine and onion, made rich with the addition of Montrachet or another mild goat cheese.

Finish this leisurely afternoon meal with tiny cups of dark roasted espresso garnished with a twist of lemon peel. Ripe Bartlett pears and crunchy amaretti cookies pair perfectly with the bitter coffee.

THE GAME PLAN

- Make the Red Pepper Almonds.
- Start preparing the Mediterranean Fish Stew.
- While the stock simmers, assemble the salads and prepare the dressing, but wait to dress the salad until just before serving.
- While the stew finishes cooking, serve the almonds and olives with the aperitifs. (The stew can rest for 15 minutes or more.)
- **If Time Allows:** The almonds, the salad dressing and the stock for the stew can be made ahead.

Four Servings

Red Pepper Almonds

1 tablespoon unsalted butter
1 tablespoon vegetable oil
1 tablespoon Worcestershire sauce
⅛ teaspoon crushed hot red pepper
1½ cups (about 9 ounces) whole blanched almonds
½ teaspoon salt

1 In a medium skillet, melt the butter in the oil over moderate heat. Add the Worcestershire sauce, pepper and almonds. Cook, stirring often, until the almonds are well coated and golden, about 5 minutes.

2 Remove the almonds from the skillet and place in a single layer on a large plate. Sprinkle with the salt and let cool. Serve at room temperature.

Mediterranean Fish Stew

1 bottle (8 ounces) clam juice
1 cup dry white wine
1 onion, quartered
½ carrot, sliced
1 slice of lemon
1 piece of orange zest, about 1 by 2 inches
½ teaspoon fennel seed
½ bay leaf
¼ teaspoon thyme
¼ teaspoon marjoram
¼ teaspoon saffron threads
2 tablespoons olive oil, preferably extra-virgin
1 pound tomatoes, coarsely chopped
3 tablespoons chopped pimientos
5 large garlic cloves, minced
¼ pound capellini or vermicelli
1 pound firm white fish fillets, such as haddock, halibut, sole or red snapper
¼ pound medium shrimp, shelled and deveined
12 cherrystone clams, scrubbed
½ cup chopped fresh parsley
1 teaspoon grated lemon zest
½ teaspoon salt

1 In a large noncorrodible saucepan, combine the clam juice, wine, onion, carrot, lemon slice, orange zest, fennel seed, bay leaf, thyme, marjoram and saffron with 4 cups of water. Bring to a boil over moderately high heat. Reduce the heat to moderately low and simmer uncovered for 20 minutes.

2 Meanwhile, heat the oil in a large noncorrodible flameproof casserole. Add the tomatoes, pimientos and half of the garlic and sauté over moderate heat until the tomatoes are softened, 5 to 7 minutes.

3 Strain the stock and add it to the tomatoes. Bring to a boil over moderately high heat. Add the capellini and cook for 6 minutes.

4 Add the fish fillets, shrimp and clams. Reduce the heat and simmer for 6 minutes, or until the clams have opened, the shrimp are pink and the fish is opaque.

5 Add the parsley, lemon zest, salt and remaining garlic. Serve in deep soup plates.

Salad of Montrachet Cheese, Romaine, Watercress and Red Onion

1 small head of romaine lettuce
1 bunch of watercress, stemmed
½ pound Montrachet or other mild goat cheese, cut into ¼-inch slices
1 medium red onion, thinly sliced into rounds and separated into rings
¼ teaspoon thyme
Freshly ground pepper
6 tablespoons olive oil, preferably extra-virgin
1 tablespoon fresh lemon juice
1 tablespoon red wine vinegar
¼ teaspoon hot pepper sauce
¼ teaspoon salt

1 Arrange the romaine leaves and watercress on four individual plates.

2 Arrange the cheese slices over the greens. Scatter the onion rings on top. Sprinkle the salads with the thyme and a generous grinding of pepper.

3 In a small bowl, whisk the oil, lemon juice, vinegar, hot pepper sauce and salt until blended. Drizzle over the salads.

Rainbows for Six

Westphalian Ham with
Honeydew Melon*

◆

Sautéed Rainbow Trout in Rhine Wine*

Buttered Spinach*

Fresh-Herbed French Bread*

Beverage Suggestion: California or German
Riesling

◆

Chocolate Ice Cream with Hot Walnut
Fudge Sauce*

*RECIPE INCLUDED

Cool melon, rainbow trout in Rhine wine, young spinach, fresh-herbed bread and a chocolate dessert—what better way to reflect the freshness of spring? The menu is perfect for a little dinner or a late-and-leisurely Sunday lunch; serve it with a chilled California or German Riesling.

The preparation of this dinner will fit into schedules as fast moving and brimming over as a spring brook; the time required is well under an hour.

Prepare the melon first and keep it chilled until ready to serve. The bread, too, can be made in advance, up to the point of putting it in the oven. The spinach and trout are best prepared at the last minute, as is the hot walnut fudge sauce.

THE GAME PLAN

- Prepare and assemble the melon and ham and chill until serving time.

- Assemble the Fresh-Herbed French Bread.

- Start preparing the trout. As the trout sautés, cook the spinach.

- Preheat the oven to 350°

- Keep the trout and spinach warm (reserving the sauce to pour over the trout just before serving) while serving the Westphalian Ham with Melon.

- Put the herbed French bread in the oven just before serving with the trout and spinach.

- Make the Hot Walnut Fudge Sauce just before serving.

○ **If Time Allows:** The Westphalian Ham with Melon can be made in advance and the Fresh-Herbed French Bread can be assembled ahead and baked at the last moment.

Six Servings

Westphalian Ham with Honeydew Melon

1 large honeydew or Crenshaw melon
12 paper-thin slices of Westphalian ham or prosciutto
Freshly ground pepper

Cut the melon into 12 wedges; remove the rind and seeds. Place 2 wedges on each plate or arrange all 12 on a serving platter; lay the ham slices over the top. Garnish with a grinding of fresh pepper.

Fresh-Herbed French Bread

1 loaf of French bread
8 tablespoons unsalted butter, at room temperature
2 tablespoons minced fresh chives
2 tablespoons chopped fresh parsley

Preheat the oven to 350°. Cut the bread into slices and arrange on a baking sheet. Brush the tops with the butter and sprinkle with the herbs. Heat for 5 to 8 minutes and serve.

Sautéed Rainbow Trout in Rhine Wine

6 whole rainbow trout (about 1 pound each), cleaned but with heads intact
Flour
Salt and freshly ground pepper
4 tablespoons unsalted butter
½ cup Rhine wine or Riesling
½ cup heavy cream

1 Dust the trout well with flour and sprinkle with salt and pepper. Over moderately high heat, melt 2 tablespoons of the butter in each of two large skillets. When it begins to sizzle, add 3 of the trout to each skillet, reduce the heat slightly and sauté gently for about 5 minutes on each side. Transfer the trout to a platter and keep them warm.

2 Add the wine to one of the skillets, return to the heat and, as the wine boils, scrape the bottom of the pan with a wooden spoon to dislodge any brown bits. Then pour the liquid into the other skillet, repeat the deglazing procedure and add the cream, stirring until the sauce is well blended and slightly thickened. Taste the sauce and add a little more salt and pepper if necessary. Pour over the trout and serve.

Buttered Spinach

2 pounds spinach, stems removed
Salt
Freshly ground pepper
⅛ teaspoon nutmeg
Unsalted butter

1 Place the spinach in a deep saucepan. Sprinkle with a small amount of salt, cover and cook gently over moderate heat until the spinach is just wilted, about 5 minutes.

2 Drain the spinach well, and season it with a grinding of pepper, the nutmeg, butter to taste and, if desired, more salt.

Chocolate Ice Cream with Hot Walnut Fudge Sauce

4 tablespoons unsalted butter
¾ cup walnut or black walnut pieces
1 package (6 ounces) semisweet chocolate pieces
1 quart chocolate ice cream

1 In a heavy skillet, heat the butter. Add the nuts and brown them well over moderate heat.

2 Remove the skillet from the heat and stir in the chocolate pieces. When they have melted, spoon the sauce over individual dishes of chocolate ice cream.

East Meets West Dinner

Pork Dumpling Soup*

◆

Gingered Seafood Rice*

Stir-Fry of Broccoli with Oyster Sauce*

Beverage Suggestion: Sake or Kirin beer

◆

Sautéed Pear Slices with Cinnamon Sugar

Jasmine Tea

*RECIPE INCLUDED

East meets West in this quick, satisfying dinner menu, with Oriental flavors produced by streamlined American techniques. The meal is appropriate for guests or family and lends itself to enough advance preparation to avoid last-minute fussing.

Pork Dumpling Soup is a warming starter, with green vegetables and tiny dumplings in chicken stock. Gingered Seafood Rice is an adaptation of a *domburi*, the home-style Japanese meal-in-a-bowl composed of rice topped with meat, egg, fish and/or vegetables. For a simple family meal, serve the gingered rice mixture in individual bowls, Japanese style; for company, you might opt for an attractive arrangement on a platter.

Although *domburi* are traditionally accompanied with pickled vegetables for a contrasting taste, we suggest an easy Stir-Fry of Broccoli with Oyster Sauce, which provides a crunchy and slightly salty counterpoint to the rice-based dish. For maximum crispness, the broccoli should be stir-fried just before serving, although it may be trimmed up to 30 minutes earlier.

A light, aromatic fruit dessert, such as sautéed pear slices with cinnamon sugar, is in order after this meal. In keeping with the Oriental flavor of the meal, finish with fragrant jasmine tea.

THE GAME PLAN

- Mix and form the dumplings for the soup.
- Bring the water for the rice to a boil, add the rice, cover and cook.
- After the rice has cooked for 5 or 6 minutes, put the soup broth on to boil.
- Sauté the topping for the gingered rice and keep warm while finishing the soup and the stir-fry.
- Add the vegetables and dumplings to the soup broth, reduce the heat and simmer until time to serve.
- Stir-fry the broccoli.
- Top the rice with the warmed crabmeat mixture and serve.
- **If Time Allows:** The dumplings can be mixed, formed and refrigerated, covered, until time to prepare the soup. The vegetables for all these dishes can be trimmed and cut ahead of time.

Four Servings

Pork Dumpling Soup

½ pound lean ground pork
1 medium garlic clove, minced
1½ teaspoons minced fresh ginger
2 teaspoons dry sherry
2 teaspoons soy sauce
1 teaspoon cornstarch
½ teaspoon sugar
¼ teaspoon salt
Generous pinch of cayenne
  pepper
3 cups chicken broth
1 large broccoli stem, peeled and
  thinly sliced on the diagonal
1 small bunch of watercress, tough
  stems removed
1 scallion, thinly sliced on the
  diagonal

1 In a medium bowl, mix the pork, garlic, ginger, sherry, soy sauce, cornstarch, sugar, salt and cayenne pepper until blended. Form the mixture into marble-size balls.

2 In a large saucepan, bring the broth to a boil over high heat. Add the dumplings and reduce the heat to moderate. Add the broccoli. Simmer until the dumplings float to the surface; cook for 2 minutes longer. Stir in the watercress and serve, garnished with the sliced scallion.

Gingered Seafood Rice

2 garlic cloves, finely chopped
1 bay leaf
1¼ teaspoons salt
1 cup converted rice
¼ pound fresh spinach, stemmed
  and torn into bite-size pieces
3 tablespoons unsalted butter
1¼ pounds king crabmeat or Sea
  Legs (see Note), cut into 1-inch
  chunks
¼ cup thinly sliced scallion
1 tablespoon chopped fresh
  ginger
Generous pinch of cayenne
  pepper
Lemon wedges, for garnish

1 In a large heavy saucepan, bring 2½ cups of water, the garlic and bay leaf to a boil over high heat. Stir in 1 teaspoon of the salt and the rice. Cover, reduce the heat to low and cook until all the water is absorbed, 17 to 20 minutes.

2 Remove the bay leaf and place the spinach on top of the rice. Quickly cover the saucepan and set aside.

3 In a large heavy skillet, preferably nonstick, melt the butter over moderate heat. Add the crabmeat, scallion, ginger, cayenne and remaining ¼ teaspoon salt. Cook, stirring, until the seafood is hot, about 5 minutes.

4 To serve, toss the rice and spinach lightly to mix. Serve the rice in individual bowls topped with the seafood; or arrange in the center of a large platter and surround with the seafood. Garnish with lemon wedges.

Note: A mixture usually of crabmeat and pollock that appears under a wide variety of names, such as Sea Legs and Sea Shells. They often resemble a very neat crab leg and are far less expensive than king crabmeat.

Stir-Fry of Broccoli with Oyster Sauce

3 tablespoons vegetable oil
1 large bunch of broccoli,
  separated into florets
3 tablespoons Chinese oyster-
  flavored sauce

In a large skillet or wok, heat the oil. Add the broccoli and stir-fry over high heat for 3 minutes. Pour in ¼ cup of water and continue to stir-fry until the liquid has almost evaporated, about 2 minutes. Add the oyster sauce and cook, tossing, until all the broccoli is well coated with sauce, about 1 minute.

A Versatile, Satisfying Lunch

Oysters Poulette*

Canadian Bacon

Granny Smith and Kiwi Salad*
with Tarragon Dressing*

Beverage Suggestion: Chilled
Sancerre or Riesling

◆

Gooseberry or Plum Tartines*

Café Filtre

*RECIPE INCLUDED

This light and versatile lunch menu is just as satisfying for an easy Sunday supper. Although the dishes can be served in conventional courses, I like to spread them out on a buffet table and let guests help themselves.

Fresh oysters make all the difference in the Oysters Poulette, a delicate and savory stew served on toast points; have your fishmonger shuck the oysters for you and reserve the liquor on the side. Canadian bacon may be eaten with the main course or with the tart salad of Granny Smith apples and ripe kiwi that follows.

Impart a crisp Gallic finish to the meal with tartines—buttered slices of toasted French bread topped with caramelized jam—and steaming cups of café filtre.

THE GAME PLAN

- Prepare the fruit for the salad and make the dressing, but wait to dress the salad at the table.

- Prepare the tartines up to the point of baking.

- Start preparing the oysters. Meanwhile, warm the Canadian bacon and make the toast triangles. Serve all immediately with the salad.

- Preheat the oven to 400°.

- Put the tartines into the oven and serve hot with coffee.

○ **If Time Allows:** The salad dressing can be made in advance.

Four Servings

Granny Smith and Kiwi Salad with Tarragon Dressing

3 Granny Smith apples
Romaine lettuce
3 ripe kiwis, peeled and thinly sliced
Tarragon Dressing

1 Core and thinly slice the apples; dip them in lightly salted water to prevent discoloration.

2 Arrange the lettuce on a small platter or individual plates. Arrange the apples and kiwi in an attractive pattern on top of the lettuce. Before serving, drizzle the Tarragon Dressing over the salad.

Tarragon Dressing

MAKES ABOUT ⅓ CUP

2 tablespoons red wine vinegar
1 teaspoon tarragon
¼ teaspoon salt
⅛ teaspoon freshly ground pepper
¼ cup vegetable oil

In a small bowl, combine the vinegar, tarragon, salt and pepper. Let stand for 5 minutes. Gradually whisk in the oil in a thin stream.

Oysters Poulette

1½ tablespoons unsalted butter
¼ cup chopped scallions
1 tablespoon all-purpose flour
¾ cup heavy cream
24 fresh oysters, shucked, with their liquor reserved
1 egg yolk, beaten
¼ teaspoon salt
⅛ teaspoon cayenne pepper
4 slices of white bread, toasted and cut into triangles
2 tablespoons chopped fresh parsley, for garnish
Lemon wedges

1 In a heavy medium saucepan, melt the butter over moderately low heat. Add the scallions and sauté until softened, about 2 minutes. Add the flour; cook, stirring, for about 2 minutes without coloring to make a roux. Gradually whisk in the cream and cook, stirring, for 3 minutes longer, until the sauce is smooth and thickened. Remove from the heat and set aside.

2 Place the oysters and their liquor in a small saucepan over moderate heat. Cook until the liquid just begins to simmer, about 3 minutes.

3 Drain the oysters, reserving ½ cup of the liquor. Gradually whisk the reserved liquor into the egg yolk; whisk the egg yolk mixture into the sauce. Stir over moderately low heat until the sauce thickens again. Season with the salt and cayenne.

4 Add the oysters and cook until heated through, 1 to 2 minutes. Serve immediately in bowls over the toast triangles. Garnish with the parsley and serve with lemon wedges.

Gooseberry or Plum Tartines

1 loaf of French bread, cut into 1-inch slices
Gooseberry or damson plum jam
Unsalted butter

Preheat the oven to 400°. Spread each slice of bread with about ¾ teaspoon jam and place on a baking sheet. Dot each slice with 1 teaspoon butter. Bake until the bread is crisp and golden around the edges, about 10 minutes. Let cool slightly before serving.

Quick Company Menu

Bourbon Mists

Watermelon Pickles Broiled in Bacon*

◆

Broiled Swordfish Steaks with Horseradish Sauce*

Steamed New Potatoes with Butter and Dill

Spinach-Grapefruit Salad with Lemon Dressing*

Beverage Suggestion: white Châteauneuf-du-Pape, such as Château de Beaucastel

◆

Walnut Brownies

Coffee or Tea

*RECIPE INCLUDED

Swordfish serves as the focal point for this direct, delicious and simple meal. Begin nibbling on Watermelon Pickles Broiled in Bacon. Relax with a cool Bourbon Mist—bourbon poured over crushed ice, garnished with a sprig of fresh mint.

Dinner, prepared in less than half an hour, is surprisingly ample. I find swordfish a most satisfactory fish—its flesh firm and succulent, its flavor subtle. Lightly coating the fish with mayonnaise helps seal in its flavor and juiciness during broiling. A creamy Horseradish Sauce sets off the dish with added piquancy. Nothing else is needed but simple steamed new potatoes, tossed with butter and dill, if you wish.

The unusual Spinach-Grapefruit Salad, with its tart-sweet dressing, can provide a nice complement to the fish course or act as a pleasant refresher before dessert.

THE GAME PLAN

- Prepare the Horseradish Sauce.
- Assemble the salad and make the dressing, but wait to dress the salad until just before serving.
- Preheat the broiler. Assemble the watermelon pickles and bacon and put them in to broil.
- Meanwhile, prepare the swordfish for broiling.
- Serve the watermelon pickles and the Bourbon Mists.
- Put the fish in to broil and steam the potatoes. Serve hot with the Horseradish Sauce and salad.
- **If Time Allows:** Make the Horseradish Sauce, the salad dressing and assemble the watermelon pickles and bacon ahead of time.

Four Servings

Watermelon Pickles Broiled in Bacon

6 strips of bacon, cut into thirds
18 cubes (½-inch) of watermelon pickle (about half a 10-ounce jar)

1 Preheat the broiler with the broiler pan set about 4 inches from the heat.

2 Wrap a piece of bacon around each pickle cube and secure with a toothpick.

3 Place the skewered pickles on the hot broiler pan and broil for about 1 minute, until the tops are lightly browned. Turn over and broil until browned, about 1 minute longer. Serve hot.

Horseradish Sauce

MAKES ABOUT ¾ CUP

½ cup heavy cream, chilled
½ teaspoon salt
2 tablespoons prepared white horseradish, squeezed dry
Dash or two of hot pepper sauce

In a large bowl, beat the cream with the salt until stiff peaks form. Stir in the horseradish and hot sauce until well mixed.

Broiled Swordfish Steaks with Horseradish Sauce

1½ to 2 pounds swordfish steak (1 inch thick)—skinned, boned and cut into 4 pieces
½ teaspoon freshly ground pepper
¼ cup mayonnaise
1 teaspoon Dijon-style mustard
Parsley sprigs, for garnish
Horseradish Sauce

1 Preheat the broiler. Sprinkle both sides of the swordfish steaks with the pepper and place on a lightly oiled broiling pan.

2 Mix together the mayonnaise and mustard. Spread half the mixture on top of the steaks.

3 Broil about 4 inches from the heat for 6 minutes. Turn the fish over, spread the remaining mayonnaise mixture on top and broil for 4 to 5 minutes longer, until the fish has just lost its pinkness in the center.

4 Transfer to a warm platter. Garnish with parsley sprigs and serve with Horseradish Sauce on the side.

Spinach-Grapefruit Salad with Lemon Dressing

1 pound fresh spinach—stemmed, washed and dried
1 large grapefruit—peeled, seeded and sectioned
½ red onion, sliced into paper-thin rings
¼ cup vegetable oil
1 tablespoon fresh lemon juice
1 teaspoon sugar
¼ teaspoon paprika
⅛ teaspoon salt
Dash of cayenne pepper

1 Tear the spinach into bite-size pieces and place in a large salad bowl. Add the grapefruit sections and the onion rings; toss gently.

2 In a small bowl, whisk together the oil, lemon juice, sugar, paprika, salt and cayenne.

3 Before serving, pour the dressing over the salad and toss gently.

30-Minute Curry for Two

"Lilies" on Ice*

Salted Cashews

◆

Honeydew with Ginger*

◆

Curried Fillets of Flounder*

Rice with Fresh Coriander*

Cucumbers with Lime*

Beverage Suggestion: Riesling from Alsace

◆

Bananas Flambéed with Rum*

Coffee and Chocolate Cookies

*RECIPE INCLUDED

Most often, curry is thought of in terms of a long-cooking stew that serves a large number of people. However, this menu stars a curry for just two, which can be made in under half an hour.

Dishes fragrant with curry spices, although commonly Indian, also appear in Chinese, Indonesian, Middle Eastern and French cuisines. This curry of flounder is in the French style. French curry, or *cari*, is usually subtle and frequently includes a touch of tomato. My recipe might be considered a curry à la Normande, as it is baked in heavy cream.

Recommended accompaniments are low-keyed and designed not to overwhelm the delicate fish. The white rice is seasoned only with fresh coriander, the lightly salted cucumbers with just the juice of a lime. A light white wine such as a Riesling from Alsace would be in keeping with the other bright but gentle flavors.

THE GAME PLAN

- Prepare the Honeydew with Ginger.
- Salt the cucumber slices and drain.
- Put the rice on to boil.
- Preheat the oven to 350°. Assemble the curry up to the point of adding the cream.
- Make the "Lilies" and serve with the cashews.
- Finish the curry and place in the oven. Serve the honeydew.
- Toss the cucumbers with the lime juice and serve with the rice and fish.
- Prepare the dessert just before serving.
- **If Time Allows:** The melon can be prepared and the cucumbers salted and drained in advance.

Two Servings

"Lilies" on Ice

Crushed ice
6 ounces (¾ cup) gin
2 ounces (¼ cup) Lillet
2 thin lemon slices, for garnish

Fill two wine glasses half-way with crushed ice. Combine the gin and Lillet and pour over the ice. Garnish each drink with a lemon slice.

Honeydew with Ginger

2 wedges of honeydew melon, chilled
2 teaspoons finely chopped crystallized ginger
Lime wedges, for garnish

Place each honeydew wedge on a serving plate. Sprinkle each with 1 teaspoon of the ginger. Garnish with the lime wedges.

Curried Fillets of Flounder

1 tablespoon unsalted butter
½ teaspoon curry powder
1 small onion, chopped
½ small garlic clove, minced
2 flounder fillets, about 6 ounces each
Salt and freshly ground pepper
2 medium tomatoes—peeled, seeded and chopped
3 tablespoons dry white wine
½ cup heavy cream

1 Preheat the oven to 350°. Melt the butter in a small skillet over low heat. Add the curry powder and cook, stirring, for about 10 seconds. Add the onion and garlic and continue to cook until the onion is softened and translucent, about 5 minutes. Spread the mixture evenly over the bottom of a shallow baking dish just large enough to hold the fish in a single layer.

2 Season the fillets with salt and pepper to taste and place them in the baking dish. Scatter the tomatoes on top and sprinkle the wine over the tomatoes.

3 In a small saucepan, heat the cream until hot and pour over the fish.

4 Bake about 12 minutes, or until the fish is opaque throughout. With a wide spatula, transfer the fish to 2 dinner plates and pour the sauce over the fish. Serve hot.

Rice with Fresh Coriander

½ cup white rice
¼ teaspoon salt
¼ cup chopped fresh coriander or a mixture of minced fresh parsley and scallion

1 Place the rice, salt and 1 cup of water in a small, heavy saucepan. Bring to a boil over moderate heat; cover, reduce the heat to low and simmer for about 20 minutes, or until all the liquid has been absorbed and the rice is tender.

2 Remove the pan from the heat and let stand for about 5 minutes. Before serving, fluff the rice with a fork and sprinkle with the coriander.

Cucumbers with Lime

1 large cucumber, peeled and thinly sliced
Salt
2 to 3 teaspoons lime juice, to taste

Place the cucumber slices in a colander, sprinkle lightly with salt and toss. Let drain for 20 minutes. Toss again, place in a serving bowl and toss with the lime juice.

Bananas Flambéed with Rum

2 tablespoons unsalted butter
2 medium, firm bananas, sliced in half lengthwise
1 tablespoon brown sugar
¼ cup dark rum

1 In a medium skillet or chafing dish, melt the butter over moderately low heat. Add the bananas and sauté for 1 minute. Turn, sprinkle them with the brown sugar and continue to sauté until heated through, about 1 minute longer. (Do not overcook or the bananas will become mushy.)

2 Pour the rum over the bananas and ignite; shake the pan until the flames subside. Place the bananas on plates and spoon the sauce over them. Serve hot.

Apple-Walnut Betty and Baked Peaches on Brioche

PAGES 171 AND 147

Tostadas con Queso and Margaritas on the Rocks

PAGE 177

Special Occasion Dinner for Four

Sesame Canapés*

◆

Shrimp Dijon*

Green Rice*

Beverage Suggestion: Chilled California Chenin Blanc

◆

Honeydew and Green Grape Salad with Lime Vinaigrette*

◆

Coffee Ice Cream with Rum

Espresso and Amaretti Cookies

*RECIPE INCLUDED

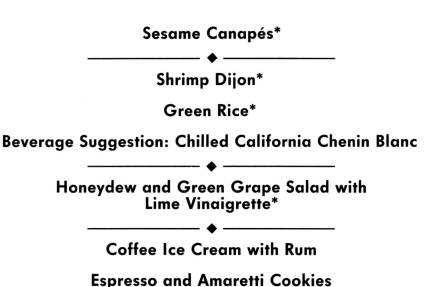

Shrimp, the perfect quick-cooking food, is easy and elegant; ideal for special occasions when you don't have time to labor over a complicated dish. Golden, fragrant Sesame Canapés are delicious crisp and hot from the oven. As an aperitif, you might enjoy an iced, light white wine, which can be sipped throughout the meal.

The shrimp are sautéed, then bathed in a lightly seasoned, brandy-spiked mustard cream. A simple accompaniment of rice flecked with fresh green herbs makes an attractive complement. For an unusual refreshing salad, summer-sweet honeydew melon is dressed with a lime vinaigrette and garnished with grapes. Dessert involves almost no work: coffee ice cream, doused with a splash of rum, and store-bought cookies.

When preparing the menu, assemble the salad and cook the rice before sautéing the shrimp. The rice can rest, covered, for at least 15 minutes, but the shrimp should be served immediately after cooking to retain tenderness.

THE GAME PLAN

- Assemble the melon and grapes and make the vinaigrette, but wait to drizzle the dressing over until just before serving.

- Preheat the oven to 425°. Assemble the Sesame Canapés up to the point of baking.

- Start preparing the Green Rice and assemble all ingredients for the Shrimp Dijon.

- Bake the canapés and serve with aperitifs.

- Make the Shrimp Dijon and serve with the Green Rice and salad, or serve the salad as a separate course, after the main course.

○ **If Time Allows:** The vinaigrette for the melon and grape salad can be made ahead and the canapés can be assembled in advance.

Four Servings

Sesame Canapés

16 unsalted melba toasts
2½ tablespoons unsalted butter, at room temperature
2 tablespoons sesame seeds
1 teaspoon coarse (kosher) salt

1 Preheat the oven to 425°. Spread each toast with about ½ teaspoon butter; then place them on an ungreased baking sheet.

2 In a small bowl, mix together the sesame seeds and salt; sprinkle the mixture generously over the buttered toasts. Bake in the bottom third of the oven 3 to 5 minutes, or until the sesame seeds are lightly browned. Serve warm.

Shrimp Dijon

16 jumbo shrimp (about 1¼ pounds), shelled and deveined
2 tablespoons fresh lemon juice
⅛ teaspoon nutmeg
3 to 4 grinds of pepper
3½ tablespoons unsalted butter
⅓ cup brandy
1 cup heavy cream
½ teaspoon Dijon-style mustard
Salt
2 teaspoons chopped fresh parsley, for garnish

1 In a medium bowl, toss the shrimp with the lemon juice, nutmeg and pepper.

2 In a heavy skillet, melt the butter over moderate heat. When the foam subsides, add the shrimp and sauté, stirring frequently, until they are just at the point of turning pink and opaque, about 3 minutes. Remove the shrimp and set aside.

3 Add the brandy to the skillet. Warm over low heat; then ignite. When the flames subside, whisk in the cream and mustard. Increase the heat to high and let the sauce boil for about 2 minutes, until slightly thickened. Season with salt to taste.

4 Reduce the heat to moderately low and return the shrimp to the skillet. Cook, stirring occasionally, until hot and opaque throughout, 2 to 3 minutes. Serve immediately, spooning the sauce over the shrimp and sprinkling with the parsley.

Green Rice

1½ tablespoons olive oil
1½ tablespoons unsalted butter
1 cup chopped scallions
1 cup chopped fresh parsley
1½ cups rice
2¾ cups chicken broth
⅛ teaspoon cayenne pepper, or to taste
½ bay leaf

1 In a medium saucepan, heat the oil and butter. Add the scallions and parsley and sauté over moderate heat, stirring, until wilted, about 1 minute. Add the rice and cook, stirring, until the grains are coated with oil and translucent, about 3 minutes.

2 Stir in the broth and cayenne; add the bay leaf. Bring to a boil, reduce the heat to low, cover tightly and simmer until the rice has absorbed all the liquid, about 20 minutes. Before serving, remove the bay leaf and fluff the rice with a fork.

Honeydew and Green Grape Salad with Lime Vinaigrette

½ medium honeydew melon
½ pound (1¼ cups) seedless green grapes, cut in half
2 tablespoons olive oil
1 tablespoon fresh lime juice
¼ teaspoon sugar
⅛ teaspoon salt
Freshly ground pepper

1 Cut the melon lengthwise into long, thin slices; trim off the rind. Divide the melon slices into four equal portions and arrange attractively on four plates. Sprinkle the grapes over the melon, dividing evenly.

2 Whisk the oil, lime juice, sugar, salt, and pepper to taste until blended. Drizzle about 2 teaspoons of dressing over each salad. Serve at room temperature.

Home-Style French Fare

Radishes with Sweet Butter*

———————— ◆ ————————

Salt Cod with Mashed Potatoes*

Cherry Tomatoes with Parsley and Chives*

French Bread

Beverage Suggestion: Beaujolais Villages

———————— ◆ ————————

Pears with Chocolate Sauce*

Café Filtre and Calvados

*RECIPE INCLUDED

French home cooking at its best is simple, satisfying and easy on the budget. In this pleasant menu, both the appetizer, Radishes with Sweet Butter, and the dessert, Pears with Chocolate Sauce, are traditional flavor combinations that require little work. The soul-satisfying main course, Salt Cod with Mashed Potatoes, is an old French favorite updated for modern tastes.

Those who live in France have the delightful option of bringing home from market a steaming dish of ready-made *brandade de morue* (creamy salt cod puree), fragrant with garlic. That is, if they don't want to undertake the considerable effort of making the dish from scratch, where preparations must start more than a day in advance in order to soak and pound the salt cod.

This modern, American version keeps preparations to a minimum by employing a commercially prepared shredded salt cod—available in many supermarkets—which needs only minutes of soaking. If you obtain a chunk of fish instead, I have found that finely shredding it first can keep the soaking time down to half an hour.

THE GAME PLAN

- Place the salt cod in a bowl of cold water to soak, and start steaming the potatoes.
- Make the chocolate sauce for the pears.
- Preheat the oven to 400°, prepare the salt cod and put it in to bake.
- Assemble and prepare all of the ingredients for the Cherry Tomatoes with Parsley and Chives.
- While the cod bakes, prepare the radishes and serve them with aperitifs, if desired.
- Cook the cherry tomatoes just before serving with the cod and French bread.
- Just before serving dessert, warm up the chocolate sauce gently and pour over the pears.
- **If Time Allows:** The cod dish can be prepared in advance up to the point of baking. The chocolate sauce can also be made ahead and reheated before serving.

Four to Six Servings

Radishes with Sweet Butter

2 bunches of red radishes
About ½ cup unsalted butter, at
  room temperature
Coarse (kosher) salt

Trim the radishes and cut them lengthwise in half. Arrange them decoratively on a plate or in a basket and serve with a small crock of butter and a bowl of salt. The radishes are spread with butter and sprinkled with salt to taste.

Salt Cod with Mashed Potatoes

2 boxes (2 ounces each)
  shredded salt cod or 4 ounces
  salt cod, finely shredded
4 large baking potatoes (about 2
  pounds), peeled and cut into
  ½-inch slices
11 tablespoons unsalted butter
½ pound mushrooms, sliced
2 garlic cloves, crushed through a
  press
5 tablespoons all-purpose flour
2 cups milk
Pinch of salt
Freshly ground pepper
¾ cup (3 ounces) grated Gruyère

1 Preheat the oven to 400°. Butter a 12-inch oval gratin or 7½-by-12-inch baking dish. Place the salt cod in a small bowl filled with cold water. Let commercially shredded cod soak for 15 minutes or as directed on package; soak cod shredded by hand for about 30 minutes, changing the water once, while you prepare the rest of the dish.

2 Steam the potatoes until tender, 20 to 30 minutes.

3 Meanwhile, melt 7 table-spoons of the butter in a medium skillet over moderate heat. Add the mushrooms and garlic and sauté until the mushrooms are tender, 4 to 5 minutes. Remove from the heat and set aside.

4 In a small heavy saucepan, melt the remaining 4 tablespoons butter. Add the flour and cook, stirring, over moderate heat for about 3 minutes to make a roux. Remove from the heat and whisk in the milk. Return to the heat and cook, stirring, until the sauce boils and thickens, about 3 minutes. Season with the salt and pepper to taste. Remove from the heat and set aside.

5 Drain the salt cod and squeeze out as much water as possible with your hands.

6 In a large bowl, mash the potatoes. Add the mushrooms and garlic butter, the drained cod and pepper to taste; mix well. Spread the potato-cod mixture in the gratin dish. Pour the sauce over the top. Sprinkle with the cheese.

7 Bake the gratin until the cheese is melted and bubbly, 15 to 20 minutes. Serve hot.

Cherry Tomatoes with Parsley and Chives

2 tablespoons unsalted butter
1 pint cherry tomatoes, stemmed
2 tablespoons chopped parsley
1 tablespoon minced chives

In a medium skillet, melt the butter over moderate heat. Add the tomatoes, parsley and chives and cook, shaking the skillet frequently, for about 3 minutes, or until heated through; do not overcook or the tomatoes will burst.

Pears with Chocolate Sauce

4 ounces semisweet chocolate
6 tablespoons milk
¼ cup sugar
2 tablespoons unsalted butter
1 tablespoon orange liqueur
  or 1 teaspoon vanilla extract
Pinch of salt
8 canned pear halves in syrup,
  chilled (29-ounce can)

1 Place the chocolate and milk in the top of a double boiler and heat, stirring, over simmering water, until the chocolate is melted. Add the sugar and cook, stirring, for about 4 minutes, until the sauce is smooth.

2 Remove from the heat and add the butter, orange liqueur and salt. Stir until the butter is incorporated.

3 Arrange 2 pear halves in each of 4 dessert bowls. Spoon the warm sauce over the pears.

A Sweet, Succulent Feast

Dry Martinis or Chilled White Wine

Melted Cheddar and Cumin Canapés*

◆

Bay Scallops in White Wine*

Sautéed Tomatoes with Cream*

Romaine and Apple Salad*

Beverage Suggestion: Dry Johannisberg Riesling

◆

Chocolate-Walnut Squares*

French Roast Coffee

Chilled Pear or Raspberry Brandy

*RECIPE INCLUDED

Of the scallops available in American markets, the smallest, most delicious and fastest to cook are bay scallops. Laced with wine, they make a wonderful dinner dish—one that is neither complicated nor time consuming.

If you intend to prepare the entire menu, make the chocolate-walnut squares first. (There is a new, very handy product on the market: pre-melted baking chocolate. It is a successful substitute for the hard squares in this recipe, and it saves a major cooking step as well as sparing you some of the cleanup afterward.) Next, ready the salad and dressing, but don't toss them together until you're ready to serve them. As mealtime approaches, pop the canapés in the oven. When done, serve them, have a drink and relax. Then, just minutes before dinner, prepare the scallops.

THE GAME PLAN

- Preheat the oven to 400°. Prepare and bake the Chocolate Walnut Squares.

- Make the salad and the vinaigrette, but wait to toss until just before serving.

- Preheat the broiler. Assemble the canapés and broil.

- While the canapés broil, assemble all the ingredients for the tomatoes and the scallops.

- Serve the hot canapés with the aperitifs.

- Just before serving, prepare the scallops and sauté the tomatoes; serve with the salad.

- **If Time Allows:** The Chocolate-Walnut Squares, the Cheddar mixture for the canapés and the vinaigrette can be made ahead.

Four Servings

Melted Cheddar and Cumin Canapés

¾ cup grated Cheddar cheese
½ cup coarsely chopped, pitted black olives
¼ cup thinly sliced scallions
2 tablespoons mayonnaise
Scant ¼ teaspoon ground cumin
⅛ teaspoon ground ginger
2 to 3 dashes cayenne pepper
¼ teaspoon salt
Melba toast rounds

In a small bowl, thoroughly combine the Cheddar, olives, scallions, mayonnaise and seasonings. Spread on melba toast rounds and broil for 1 to 2 minutes, or until the cheese begins to melt. Serve hot.

Sautéed Tomatoes with Cream

1½ tablespoons unsalted butter
4 slices of tomato, cut 1 inch thick
Pinch of thyme
Salt
¼ cup light cream or half-and-half

1 In a skillet, melt the butter and add the tomato slices and sauté until they are slightly soft. Season with the thyme and salt to taste.

2 Pour the cream into the skillet and boil until it has thickened slightly. Serve hot.

Bay Scallops in White Wine

1½ pounds bay scallops
About 2 tablespoons all-purpose flour
Freshly ground pepper
4 tablespoons unsalted butter
2 ounces salt pork, finely diced
2 shallots, chopped
¾ cup dry white wine
2 tablespoons chopped fresh parsley

1 Rinse the scallops, drain and pat dry with paper towels. Dust them with the flour and season lightly with pepper.

2 In a skillet, melt the butter and add the salt pork and shallots. When the salt pork begins to sizzle, add the scallops and sauté them, turning frequently, until cooked through, 3 to 5 minutes. Transfer the scallops to a warm serving dish.

3 Add the wine to the skillet and cook for 2 to 3 minutes over high heat, scraping up the bits that cling to the pan. When the wine sauce reaches the consistency of a thin syrup, pour it over the scallops. Sprinkle with the parsley and serve.

Romaine and Apple Salad

1 head of romaine lettuce, torn into bite-size pieces
2 Golden Delicious apples, cut into chunks
1 medium, red onion, thinly sliced into rings
½ cup vinaigrette dressing

Toss the lettuce with the apple chunks, onion rings and vinaigrette. Serve at once.

Chocolate-Walnut Squares

2 ounces (2 squares) unsweetened chocolate or 2 envelopes pre-melted chocolate
8 tablespoons (1 stick) unsalted butter, at room temperature
1 cup sugar
½ cup all-purpose flour
2 eggs, lightly beaten
½ teaspoon vanilla
1 cup walnut pieces

1 Preheat the oven to 400°. Line a 12-by-16-inch baking sheet with foil.

2 Melt the chocolate and combine with the butter, sugar, flour, eggs and vanilla. Beat with a fork until well blended. Stir in ½ cup of the walnuts.

3 Spread the mixture on the baking sheet, sprinkle the remaining ½ cup of walnuts over the top and bake for 15 minutes. While still warm and soft, cut into squares. Serve when cooled.

New England Chowder Supper

Vermont Cheddar and Common Crackers

Pickled Onions

Ale

◆

Fish Chowder*

Beet and Onion Salad with Escarole*

Buttered English Muffins

Beverage Suggestion: California Chenin Blanc

◆

Apple-Walnut Betty*

Coffee Laced with Rum

*RECIPE INCLUDED

Today, the most common New England chowder may be the type made with clams, but until the middle of the 19th century the word more commonly applied to a rich fish stew, usually prepared with cod or haddock, and traditionally including potatoes and salt pork.

The chowder for this warming winter supper menu follows the theme of those earlier piscatorial concoctions. It can be made with halibut, haddock or cod fillets and takes only about 40 minutes to prepare. Instead of the traditional salt pork cooked along with the stew, crisp pieces of bacon are sprinkled over the top at table in this version. A crisp Beet and Onion Salad with Escarole and buttered English muffins are all that's needed to make a fortifying supper, lunch or dinner.

The Apple-Walnut Betty, a real old-fashioned comfort food, can bake while you eat dinner.

THE GAME PLAN

- Assemble the salad and make the dressing, but wait to dress the salad until just before serving.
- Start preparing the chowder.
- While the chowder simmers, assemble the Apple-Walnut Betty. Preheat the oven to 450°.
- Finish preparing the chowder and cook the bacon. Meanwhile, serve the Cheddar and crackers, pickled onions and ale.
- Toast the muffins and serve hot with the chowder and salad. Put the Apple-Walnut Betty in the oven to bake while you eat the main course.
- **If Time Allows:** The Apple-Walnut Betty can be assembled in advance and the dressing for the salad can be made ahead.

Four to Six Servings

Fish Chowder

4 tablespoons unsalted butter
1 large onion, coarsely diced
4 medium potatoes, unpeeled and
    quartered
¼ teaspoon thyme
¼ teaspoon tarragon
2 teaspoons salt
¼ teaspoon freshly ground
    pepper
1 to 1½ pounds white fish (such as
    halibut, cod or haddock) fillets
    or steaks, fresh or frozen
2 cups half-and-half or 1 cup milk
    and 1 cup cream
1 pound bacon, cut crosswise into
    ¼- to ½-inch strips

1 In a large heavy pot, melt
the butter over low heat. Gently
sauté the onion in the butter until
it is soft and translucent.

2 Add the potatoes to the onion along with 2 cups of water,
the thyme, tarragon, salt and
pepper. Cover and simmer over
low heat for 15 minutes.

3 Place the fish on top of the
potatoes. Steam gently for about
10 minutes, or until the fish flakes
when touched with a fork. (Frozen fish will take a few minutes
longer.)

4 Add the half-and-half and
heat until the chowder is piping
hot. Do not allow it to boil.

5 Cook the bacon in a large
skillet over low heat until lightly
browned, stirring occasionally.
Drain on paper towels and place
in a serving bowl.

6 Serve the chowder in large
soup bowls and pass the bacon
pieces separately.

Beet and Onion Salad with Escarole

1 head of escarole, torn into
    bite-size pieces
1 can (1 pound) whole baby beets,
    drained
1 small red onion, thinly sliced into
    rings
½ cup vegetable oil
¼ cup vinegar
½ teaspoon Dijon-style mustard
1 teaspoon honey or sugar

1 Arrange the escarole in a
bowl and place the beets on top.
Scatter the onion rings over the
beets.

2 Combine the oil, vinegar,
mustard and honey and beat
well. Pour the dressing over the
salad just before serving.

Apple-Walnut Betty

1 can (1 pound, 5 ounces) apple
    pie filling
Juice of 1 lemon
½ teaspoon cinnamon, or more
    to taste
1½ cups walnut halves
4 double graham crackers
¼ cup unsalted butter
¼ cup firmly packed light brown
    sugar

1 Preheat the oven to 425° and
butter a deep pie pan or baking
dish.

2 Cover the bottom of the pan
with the apple pie filling. Sprinkle
the lemon juice and the cinnamon over the apples and stir
gently. Scatter the walnuts over
the apples.

3 Coarsely crumble the graham crackers into pieces about
the size of blueberries. In a small
pan, melt the butter. Off the heat,
add the crumbled graham crackers and sugar and stir until thoroughly mixed.

4 Spread the topping over the
apples and walnuts just before
placing the dish in the oven. (The
topping stays crunchier if you
add it at the last minute.)

5 Bake for 10 to 12 minutes, or
until the topping is crisp and
lightly browned. Serve warm.

ETHNIC

Informal Japanese Menu

Shiitake Mushroom Broth*

◆

Skillet Grilled Pork with Dipping Sauce*

Sauté of Shiitake Mushrooms*

Steamed Rice

Assorted Japanese Pickles

Vinegared Cucumbers with Sesame Seeds*

Beverage Suggestion: Kirin Beer

◆

Strawberries

Green Tea

*RECIPE INCLUDED

Japanese cooking—even everyday family style—can be at once both elegant and simple. Our menu includes a delicate broth based on *shiitake* (Japanese forest mushrooms) and lightly scented with lemon zest and scallions.

Tender, unseasoned grilled pork gets a brightly flavored dipping sauce. Sharp Japanese pickles make a good accompaniment to the pork, as do the Vinegared Cucumbers with Sesame Seeds.

Shiitake, *togarashi* (Japanese red pepper), *mirin* (sweet rice wine), Japanese pickles and Oriental sesame oil can be found in Oriental markets and in many gourmet shops. Sake is sold in wine and liquor stores. All the other ingredients are available in most food markets.

THE GAME PLAN

- Make the dipping sauce.
- Start making the mushroom broth.
- Meanwhile, prepare the ingredients for the cucumber salad and make the dressing, but wait to toss it until just before serving.
- Serve the broth.
- Sauté the pork and keep it warm while sautéing the mushrooms. Serve with the steamed rice, dipping sauce and the cucumbers.
- **If Time Allows:** The dipping sauce, mushroom broth and the dressing for the cucumbers can be made in advance. Just reheat the broth shortly before serving.

Six Servings

Vinegared Cucumbers with Sesame Seeds

1 tablespoon rice vinegar
½ teaspoon sugar
¼ teaspoon salt
2 cucumbers, peeled and sliced
2 teaspoons toasted sesame seeds
3 or 4 dashes *togarashi* (Japanese red pepper) or cayenne

1 Combine the vinegar, sugar and salt.

2 Just before serving, toss the cucumbers with the vinegar mixture and divide among individual bowls. Sprinkle with the sesame seeds and *togarashi*.

Shiitake Mushroom Broth

2½ cups chicken broth
1 small carrot, cut into ½-inch pieces
½ celery rib, cut into ½-inch pieces
1 small onion, sliced
3 or 4 sprigs of parsley
1 ounce dried *shiitake* mushrooms
1 tablespoon sake
2 teaspoons soy sauce
6 small spinach leaves
18 long slivers of lemon zest
1 tablespoon thinly sliced scallions

1 In a medium saucepan, combine the chicken broth, carrot, celery, onion and parsley with 2½ cups of water. Bring to a boil, reduce the heat and simmer for 10 minutes.

2 Snap off the stems from the mushrooms and add the stems and caps to the broth. Reduce the heat and simmer, partially covered, for 10 minutes longer. Remove from the heat. Remove the mushrooms and vegetables. Reserve the mushroom caps for the sauté; discard the vegetables and mushroom stems.

3 Season the broth with the sake and soy sauce. Strip the stems and back vein from the spinach leaves and tear each leaf in half. Place two pieces of spinach in each of 6 bowls and ladle broth over them. Garnish each with 3 slivers of lemon zest and ½ teaspoon scallion.

Sauté of Shiitake Mushrooms

Mushroom caps reserved from broth (see Note)
½ tablespoon vegetable oil
2 teaspoons soy sauce
Freshly ground pepper

1 Squeeze the mushrooms to remove as much liquid as possible; pat dry and cut into slivers.

2 In a small skillet lightly coated with oil, sauté the mushrooms over moderate heat. Season to taste with soy sauce and pepper. Serve as a side vegetable or garnish.

Note: If not making the broth, soak 1 ounce dried mushrooms in boiling water for 20 minutes and then stem them.

Skillet Grilled Pork with Dipping Sauce

2 to 3 tablespoons vegetable oil
1½ pounds boneless pork loin, trimmed of excess fat and cut into ¼-inch-thick slices
Dipping Sauce

Coat the bottom of a heavy skillet, preferably cast iron, with oil. Place over high heat. Working in batches, add the pork slices in a single layer and cook until the pork is lightly browned on the bottom and begins to color around the upper edges. Turn and cook for about 2 minutes longer, until just cooked through. Add oil as needed while the meat is cooking. Serve hot, with Dipping Sauce. (Do not season the pork; the dipping sauce provides all the flavor needed.)

Dipping Sauce

½ cup soy sauce
2 tablespoons sake
1 tablespoon *mirin*
    or 1 tablespoon sake plus ½ teaspoon sugar
1 large garlic clove, crushed through a press
Juice from 1½ inches of ginger squeezed in a garlic press
¼ teaspoon Oriental sesame oil
2 teaspoons minced chives or finely chopped scallions

Mix all the ingredients together and serve in individual bowls.

A Tex-Mex Meal

Margaritas on the Rocks*

Tostadas con Queso*

◆

Arroz con Camarones (Rice with Shrimp)*

Avocado Salad with Lime Dressing*

Beverage Suggestion: Chenin Blanc, such as Simi

◆

**Fresh Pineapple and Kiwi Slices Sprinkled with
Confectioners' Sugar**

*RECIPE INCLUDED

Cornmeal, peppers, avocados and tomatoes are all native to the New World. They lend distinctive character to southwestern regional cooking. When visiting friends in El Paso, I was served a memorable shrimp and rice dish that was as delicate as it was fresh and bright tasting. Preceded by margaritas and Tostadas con Queso, and accompanied with a tangy avocado salad, it completes a quick and easily prepared dinner or a leisurely lunch.

The growing interest in southwestern cooking has increased the availability of prepared ingredients. All sorts of Mexican sauces, relishes, pickled hot peppers and tortillas can now be found in supermarkets around the country. Canned or frozen tortillas can be used for the tostadas, though fresh are nicer if you can find them.

THE GAME PLAN

- Preheat the oven to 400°. Prepare the tostadas up to the point of baking.

- Start the Arroz con Camarones.

- While the rice is simmering, arrange the salad ingredients on a serving platter. Prepare the dressing and set aside to spoon over the salad at the last moment.

- Place the tostadas in the oven and make the margaritas.

- Stir the tomatoes and jalapeño peppers into the rice and serve the tostadas and margaritas while the rice simmers for 5 more minutes.

- Add the shrimp to the rice, let them heat through, garnish and serve with the salad.

○ **If Time Allows:** The tostadas can be assembled and the dressing for the salad made in advance. Cover the tostadas until baking time.

Four Servings

Margaritas on the Rocks

Coarse (kosher) salt
Ice cubes
1½ cups (12 ounces) tequila
¾ cup fresh lime juice
¼ cup Cointreau

Salt the rims of 4 old-fashioned glasses by dipping the rims in water and then in a dish of coarse salt. Fill the glasses with ice cubes. In a small pitcher, combine the tequila, lime juice and Cointreau and pour into the glasses.

Tostadas con Queso

4 tostada shells (see Note), quartered
4 generous teaspoons jalapeño relish or taco sauce
½ cup chopped tomatoes
¼ cup thinly sliced scallions
1 to 2 cups grated Monterey Jack cheese

1 Preheat the oven to 400°. Place the tostada shells on a baking sheet. Spread each with the jalapeño relish. Sprinkle with the tomatoes and scallions; top each tostada with ¼ to ½ cup cheese, to taste.

2 Place in the oven for 3 to 5 minutes, or until the cheese is melted. Serve immediately, with additional jalapeño relish or taco sauce if desired.

Note: To make tostada shells, fry 4 corn tortillas for 1½ to 2 minutes in ½ inch of oil, turning once, until crisp. Drain on paper towels.

Avocado Salad with Lime Dressing

1 small head of leaf lettuce
1 large avocado
3 tablespoons fresh lime juice
1 medium cucumber, peeled and sliced
½ medium red onion, thinly sliced
½ cup pitted black olives
1 tablespoon wine vinegar
1 teaspoon sugar
¼ teaspoon powered mustard
Pinch of paprika
Dash of salt
Hot pepper sauce
⅓ cup corn oil

1 On a chilled serving platter, arrange the lettuce. Peel and slice the avocado and toss to coat with 1½ tablespoons of the lime juice. Arrange the avocado, cucumber, onion slices and olives on the lettuce.

2 In a small bowl, combine the remaining 1½ tablespoons lime juice, the vinegar, sugar, mustard, paprika, salt and hot sauce to taste. Gradually whisk in the oil until blended. Spoon the dressing over the salad.

Arroz con Camarones (Rice with Shrimp)

1 tablespoon olive oil
1 small onion, chopped
2 garlic cloves, finely chopped
1 cup converted rice
2½ cups chicken broth
½ bay leaf
⅛ to ¼ teaspoon saffron threads, to taste
2 medium tomatoes—peeled, seeded and chopped
1 teaspoon chopped fresh or canned jalapeño peppers
¾ pound cooked medium shrimp, shelled and deveined
3 tablespoons chopped fresh coriander
Hot pepper sauce

1 Heat the oil in a large, flameproof casserole. Add the onion and garlic and sauté until the onion is softened and translucent, 2 to 3 minutes. Stir in the rice, mixing until evenly coated with the oil.

2 Add the broth, bay leaf and saffron. Bring to a boil, reduce the heat to low, cover and cook for 15 minutes.

3 Stir in the tomatoes and jalapeño peppers; cover and cook for 5 minutes longer. Arrange the shrimp on top of the rice. Cover the pan and continue cooking until the shrimp are heated through, about 2 minutes. Sprinkle with the coriander and serve. Pass hot pepper sauce or a dish of pickled hot peppers, if desired.

Greek Country Dinner

Ouzo

Herbed Feta* and Toasted Pita Bread

---◆---

Arní Souvlákia (Lamb on Skewers)*

Cracked-Wheat Pilaf*

Cucumber and Yogurt Salad*

Beverage Suggestion: Chilled Retsina or Castel Danielis

---◆---

Sugared Strawberries*

*RECIPE INCLUDED

Inspired by the richness, color and stimulating aromas of the Mediterranean, this menu features Calamata olives, golden olive oil, rosemary, marjoram, dill, garlic, bay leaves, limes, lemons, salty feta cheese, steaming pilaf, skewers of lamb and more. They are all brought together easily in a menu that offers the best of the Greek countryside and takes less than an hour to prepare.

If you have a terrace or a garden, as well as the time to get a good charcoal fire going, by all means do your grilling and dining outdoors. While the coals heat up, sip on an icy ouzo (a licorice-flavored Greek liqueur that when mixed with water and ice turns milky), munch on Calamata olives and rosemary-coated cubes of feta cheese, and dream of the golden isles of Greece while wafts of scented smoke from the sizzling herbed lamb float by.

Cracked wheat (bulgur) and feta cheese can be found in gourmet shops and stores specializing in foods from the Middle East. Natural-food stores also frequently stock bulgur; if it is not available, serve rice cooked in chicken stock with a bay leaf.

THE GAME PLAN

- Start the pilaf.
- Soak the bay leaves for the lamb.
- Make the herbed feta and the cucumber and yogurt salad.
- Toast the pita bread. Preheat the broiler
- Meanwhile, thread the lamb and bay leaves onto the skewers, season and place in the broiler (or on a hot grill).
- While the lamb cooks, serve the feta with the toasted pita and ouzo.
- Rinse the berries just before serving, shake off excess water and serve with sugar.
- **If Time Allows:** The herbed feta and the cucumber and yogurt salad can be made ahead of time. Cover and chill the salad. The feta should be covered and left at room temperature until serving time.

Four Servings

Herbed Feta

2 teaspoons rosemary
1 garlic clove
1 tablespoon fresh lemon juice
¼ teaspoon anchovy paste
2 tablespoons olive oil
½ pound feta cheese
¼ pound brine-cured Greek
  olives, such as Calamata
1 green bell pepper, cut into strips

1 Using a mortar and pestle or spice mill, grind the rosemary to a powder. Remove and set aside. Add the garlic to the mortar and mash to a paste.

2 In a small mixing bowl, combine the lemon juice, anchovy paste, garlic paste and rosemary. Beat in the oil one drop at a time.

3 Cut the feta into ½-inch cubes and place in a bowl. Pour the dressing over the cubes and toss to coat them evenly. Turn out onto a serving dish and surround them with the olives and green pepper strips. Serve with toothpicks.

Cucumber and Yogurt Salad

2 cucumbers—peeled, halved
  lengthwise, seeded and cut into
  half-rounds
2 cups plain yogurt
1 teaspoon salt
1 tablespoon chopped fresh dill
2 garlic cloves, crushed

Place the cucumbers in a bowl and add the yogurt, salt, dill and garlic. Mix well. If not serving immediately, chill.

Cracked-Wheat Pilaf

8 tablespoons (1 stick) unsalted
  butter
1 cup bulgur cracked wheat
2¼ cups boiling water
1 teaspoon salt

1 Melt the butter in a saucepan. Add the cracked wheat and stir for a minute or two over low heat.

2 Pour the boiling water over the cracked wheat and add the salt. Stir and cover. Cook over low heat for 20 minutes, or until the water has been absorbed.

Arní Souvlákia (Lamb on Skewers)

8 to 10 bay leaves, halved
1½ cups boiling water
2 pounds lamb (preferably from
  the leg), cut into 1-inch cubes
1 teaspoon marjoram
Salt and freshly ground pepper
1 lemon, halved
Shredded lettuce

1 Preheat the broiler. Place the halved bay leaves in a bowl with the boiling water; let rest 10 to 15 minutes and drain.

2 Dividing them equally, thread the lamb cubes, separated by bay leaf halves, on four metal skewers. Season with the marjoram and salt and pepper to taste and squeeze the lemon over them.

3 Turning the skewers at 3-minute intervals, broil 2 to 3 inches from the heat for about 12 minutes. Serve on a bed of shredded lettuce.

Sugared Strawberries

1 quart strawberries, rinsed
Confectioners' sugar

Arrange the strawberries in a circle on each plate. Place a few spoonfuls of confectioners' sugar in the center of each circle, for dipping. No cutlery is needed—only fingers.

Off-the-Shelf Italian Feast

Simple Antipasto* with Mediterranean Stuffed Eggs*

◆

Capellini Primavera*

Glazed Baked Tomatoes*

Beverage Suggestion: Chianti Classico, such as Palazzo al Bosco (Olivieri)

◆

Babas au Rhum with Whipped Cream*

Espresso

*RECIPE INCLUDED

Who says cooking great ethnic meals means hours of tedious shopping for expensive and exotic ingredients? Here is a sumptuous Italian menu, keyed to clever shopping strategy, for those days when you need to save time. It avoids side trips to the butcher, the baker and the greengrocer and enables you to do all your buying in one place—your local supermarket.

Some supermarkets stock more sophisticated cheese selections than others, but it would be rare to find one that does not carry Parmesan and an assortment of flavored soft cheeses, such as Boursin. Packaged, pre-sliced Genoa salami will do nicely for the antipasto. And while capellini, the finest "angel's hair" pasta, makes a lovely presentation, thin spaghetti is a fine alternative. Both cook in moments, and the entire main-dish recipe takes less than 15 minutes to prepare, counting the time required to bring a large pot of water to a boil.

If fresh asparagus isn't available, frozen may be substituted. Many supermarkets also carry *babas au rhum*—small cakes packed in rum-flavored syrup.

THE GAME PLAN

- Add the rum to the babas, whip the cream and refrigerate until serving time.
- Make the Mediterranean Stuffed Eggs and assemble the antipasto platter.
- Preheat the oven to 375° and prepare the tomatoes.
- Put a pot of water on to boil for the pasta.
- Prepare the asparagus and sauté the bacon.
- Put the tomatoes in the oven and serve the antipasto.
- Cook the pasta and heat the asparagus in the cream. Toss the pasta with the remaining ingredients and serve hot with the tomatoes.
- Spoon the whipped cream over the babas just before serving.
- **If Time Allows:** The stuffed eggs and the antipasto platter can be prepared in advance. Cover and refrigerate until serving time.

Four Servings

Simple Antipasto

Mediterranean Stuffed Eggs
4 ounces Genoa salami
Small (5-ounce) round of soft, garlicky herbed cheese, such as Boursin
Green olives
Breadsticks or Italian bread
Butter

Arrange the eggs, salami, cheese and olives decoratively on a platter. Serve with bread sticks, or bread, and butter.

Mediterranean Stuffed Eggs

4 hard-cooked eggs
2 tablespoons mayonnaise
1 teaspoon capers, drained and chopped
1 or 2 garlic cloves, to taste, crushed through a press
1 teaspoon fresh lemon juice
Salt and freshly ground pepper
8 rolled anchovy fillets, for garnish

1 Cut each egg in half lengthwise. Remove the yolks and mash them with the mayonnaise in a small bowl. Stir in the capers, garlic and lemon juice. Season with salt and pepper to taste.

2 Spoon or pipe the yolk mixture into the whites. Garnish each egg half with a rolled anchovy, if you wish. Serve as part of the antipasto.

Capellini Primavera

1½ pounds fresh asparagus or 1 package (10 ounces) frozen asparagus spears
2 tablespoons unsalted butter
¼ pound Canadian bacon, cut into 2-by-⅛-inch julienne strips
½ cup heavy cream
¾ pound capellini or very thin spaghetti
Chopped fresh chives
Freshly grated Parmesan cheese
Freshly ground pepper

1 Bring a large pot of salted water to a boil.

2 Meanwhile, prepare the asparagus. If using fresh asparagus, trim and cut into 1-inch pieces. Place in a medium saucepan of boiling salted water and cook for 3 to 4 minutes, or until tender but still slightly firm; drain. If using frozen asparagus spears, follow the package directions; drain and cut into 1-inch pieces.

3 In a skillet, melt the butter. Add the bacon and sauté over moderate heat until the bacon starts to crisp, about 2 minutes.

4 In a small saucepan, warm the cream over low heat. Add the asparagus and cook just until heated through. Remove from the heat and set aside.

5 Add the capellini to the large pot of boiling water and cook until *al dente*, about 1 minute. Drain and transfer the pasta to a large serving platter. Pour the butter and bacon over the pasta and pour on the asparagus and cream. Sprinkle with chives. Toss and serve immediately. Pass a bowl of Parmesan cheese and a pepper grinder at the table.

Glazed Baked Tomatoes

4 tomatoes, halved crosswise
2½ tablespoons light brown sugar
2½ tablespoons unsalted butter
¼ to ½ teaspoon cayenne pepper, to taste

Preheat the oven to 375°. Place the tomatoes, cut-side up, in a lightly buttered baking dish. Sprinkle a scant 1 teaspoon of brown sugar over the top of each, dot with butter and add a dash of cayenne. Bake for about 15 minutes, or until the tomatoes are heated through and the tops are glazed.

Babas au Rhum with Whipped Cream

1 tablespoon dark rum (optional)
1 jar (8 ounces) *babas au rhum*
½ cup heavy cream

1 If desired, for extra flavor, add the rum to the jar of babas, put the cover back on and turn the jar upside down once or twice to distribute the liquor.

2 Whip the cream until it forms soft peaks. Arrange 3 babas on each of 4 dessert plates and spoon the whipped cream over.

Provençal Lamb Dinner

Italian Vermouth and Soda

Radishes with Roquefort and Port*

◆

Baby Lamb Chops with Herbes de Provence*

Eggplant with Tomatoes and Parsley*

French Bread

Beverage Suggestion: Pinot Noir

◆

Orange Sorbet with Strawberry-Chambord Sauce*

*RECIPE INCLUDED

Perhaps the most unforgettable feature of the cypress-studded landscapes of France's Provence region is the pungent fragrance of the air there, laden with the scents of rosemary, lavender, marjoram, basil, thyme and a host of other herbs and spices.

Mixtures of these pleasantly potent *herbes de Provence* are available in packages at most specialty food shops and they should be kept close at hand, particularly when cooking lamb. They bring out the rich flavor of the thick baby lamb chops in this menu. If you can't find the pre-mixed variety, you can blend your own with dried thyme, rosemary, savory, marjoram, oregano or fennel and, if you can find it, a little lavender.

Provençal flavors and fruits—eggplant, tomatoes, olive oil and garlic—comprise the accompanying vegetable, a variation on ratatouille. And Roquefort and port make a creamy spread for radishes at the beginning of this flavorful meal. Serve an Italian vermouth with soda over ice as an aperitif with the radishes.

THE GAME PLAN

- Prepare the strawberries and oranges for the dessert.
- Make the radishes with Roquefort and port.
- Preheat the broiler. Prepare the lamb chops for cooking.
- Start the eggplant and tomatoes; when they've simmered for 3 or 4 minutes, put the lamb chops in the broiler.
- Serve the radishes with the vermouth and sodas while the lamb and eggplant finish cooking.
- **If Time Allows:** The strawberries, oranges and Roquefort and port mixture can be prepared ahead. The eggplant and tomatoes can also be made in advance and reheated or served at room temperature, but reserve the parsley to stir in just before serving.

Four Servings

Radishes with Roquefort and Port

4 tablespoons Roquefort or other blue-veined cheese
1 tablespoon port
16 radishes, both ends trimmed flat
Minced fresh parsley, for garnish

In a small bowl, blend the Roquefort and port until smooth and creamy. Heap a mound of the cheese mixture on one end of each radish, and stand the radishes on the other end on a serving plate. Sprinkle each radish with some of the parsley.

Baby Lamb Chops with Herbes de Provence

8 rib lamb chops (about 1½ inches thick), trimmed of fat
2 garlic cloves, halved
½ cup dry red wine
1 tablespoon unsalted butter
2 teaspoons *herbes de Provence* (see Note)
Coarse (kosher) salt
Freshly ground pepper
Watercress sprigs, for garnish

1 Preheat the broiler. Rub each chop with the cut side of a garlic clove. Place the chops on a disposable broiling pan.

2 In a small saucepan, combine the wine, butter and herbs and warm over low heat until the butter melts. Blend well and brush over each chop.

3 Place the chops in the broiler, 2 inches from the heat source and broil 3 to 6 minutes on each side, basting occasionally with the sauce. Season each chop with salt and pepper to taste and garnish with watercress.

Note: If you can't find *herbes de Provence*, blend your own with a mixture of any of the following spices: rosemary, fennel, marjoram, lavender, savory, oregano.

Eggplant with Tomatoes and Parsley

⅓ cup olive oil, preferably extra-virgin
1 medium eggplant, peeled and cut into 1-inch cubes
1 large tomato—peeled, seeded and coarsely chopped
2 garlic cloves, minced
1 bay leaf
½ teaspoon sugar
Pinch of cayenne pepper
Salt
⅓ cup chopped fresh parsley

1 In a large skillet, heat the oil. Add the eggplant and sauté over moderately low heat for 2 minutes, until the oil is absorbed.

2 Add the tomato, ¼ cup of water, the garlic, bay leaf, sugar and cayenne, and season with salt to taste. Bring to a boil, reduce the heat to moderately low, cover and simmer, stirring occasionally, until the eggplant is tender, about 15 minutes. (If the vegetables are still watery after simmering for 15 minutes, remove the cover and simmer for a few minutes more, until the excess liquid evaporates.)

3 Just before serving, stir half of the parsley into the vegetables. Sprinkle the remaining parsley on top. Serve hot or at room temperature.

Orange Sorbet with Strawberry-Chambord Sauce

½ pint fresh strawberries, sliced, or 1 package (10 ounces) sliced frozen strawberries, thawed
1½ to 3 tablespoons sugar (see Note)
1 pint orange sorbet or sherbet
4 orange slices, quartered
2 tablespoons Chambord liqueur
Crystallized violets, for garnish

1 If using fresh strawberries, place a few slices in a bowl with the sugar and crush with a fork. Add the remaining berries and toss together. (If using frozen, eliminate the sugar.)

2 Divide the orange sorbet among four dessert dishes. Spoon some of the berries over each portion of sorbet and top each with four orange quarters. Sprinkle each portion with 1½ teaspoons Chambord and garnish with violets.

Note: The amount of sugar will vary according to taste and the sweetness of the berries.

Chinese Family-Style Meal

Cold Noodles with Sesame Sauce*

◆

Stir-Fried Scallops in Garlic Sauce*

Braised Asparagus with Black Mushrooms*

Steamed Rice

Beverage Suggestion: Tsing Tao or Kirin Beer

◆

Strawberries with Raspberry Sherbet

Jasmine Tea

Fortune Cookies or Nut Cookies

*RECIPE INCLUDED

Here is a mouth-watering, family-style Chinese dinner, which can be expanded easily to feed extra mouths. As a starter course, the noodles serve four generously and six quite adequately. The scallop and asparagus dishes can satisfy four, five or six eaters depending on the amount of rice prepared to accompany them.

You should be able to find all the ingredients called for in this menu without much trouble. Chinese food products are increasingly available in markets other than specialty food shops and Oriental groceries. Many should be in your supermarket.

Several of the recipes have ingredients in common—ginger, garlic, scallions. To save time, chop or slice enough at one time for all the recipes.

THE GAME PLAN

- Soak the mushrooms.
- Make the two sauces for the noodles.
- Prepare all of the ingredients for the asparagus and the scallops: both will take about 6 minutes of cooking time at the last moment.
- Cook the noodles; drain, rinse and toss in the two sauces. Start the rice and serve the noodles.
- Start simmering the asparagus and mushrooms. Meanwhile, stir-fry the scallops.
- ○ **If Time Allows:** The black mushrooms can be soaked ahead and the noodles cooked and tossed with the sesame oil-soy sauce mixture. Reserve the sesame paste sauce and remaining ingredients to add just before serving.

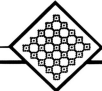

Four to Six Servings

Cold Noodles with Sesame Sauce

3 tablespoons Oriental sesame oil
5 tablespoons soy sauce
3 tablespoons rice vinegar or red wine vinegar
1 tablespoon plus 1½ teaspoons sugar
3 tablespoons Chinese sesame paste or tahini
3 tablespoons dry sherry
1 tablespoon plus 2 teaspoons Oriental hot oil
1 teaspoon hoisin sauce
1½ teaspoons minced fresh ginger
¾ pound fresh Chinese egg noodles or dried capellini
½ medium cucumber, cut into julienne strips
3 scallions, thinly sliced

1 In a small bowl, combine the sesame oil, 3 tablespoons of the soy sauce, 2 tablespoons of the vinegar and 1 tablespoon of sugar. In another small bowl, combine the remaining 2 tablespoons soy sauce, 1 tablespoon vinegar and 1½ teaspoons sugar with the sesame paste, sherry, hot oil, hoisin sauce and ginger; stir until blended.

2 In a large pot of boiling water, cook the noodles until just tender, 2 to 3 minutes for fresh, about 8 minutes for dried. Drain into a colander and rinse under cold running water to cool; drain well.

3 In a large bowl, toss the noodles with the sesame oil-soy sauce mixture. Add the sesame paste sauce, cucumber and scallions. Toss to coat the noodles with the sauce.

Stir-Fried Scallops in Garlic Sauce

1½ pounds sea scallops
1½ tablespoons peanut oil
1 scallion, cut into 1-inch lengths
2 garlic cloves, crushed
1 tablespoon minced fresh ginger
1 tablespoon cornstarch, dissolved in ½ cup water

1 Rinse and drain the scallops; pat dry on paper towels. Remove the small tough muscle on the side of each scallop. If the scallops are large, slice crosswise in half.

2 Heat the oil in a wok or large heavy skillet. Add the scallops and stir-fry over high heat for 1 minute. Add the scallion, garlic and ginger; stir-fry for 2 minutes. Stir the cornstarch mixture and add to the wok. Stir-fry until the sauce is thick and translucent, about 3 minutes.

Braised Asparagus with Black Mushrooms

4 medium dried black mushrooms
1 tablespoon unsalted butter
1 tablespoon vegetable oil
1½ pounds thin asparagus, cut into 1½-inch lengths
1 teaspoon soy sauce
½ teaspoon salt
¼ teaspoon sugar

1 In a small bowl, soak the mushrooms in hot water to cover until softened, about 15 minutes. Remove the mushrooms, squeeze out excess liquid and cut off the woody stems. Slice the caps into slivers. Strain the soaking liquid through a sieve lined with a double thickness of dampened cheesecloth; reserve ¼ cup.

2 In a wok or large heavy skillet, melt the butter in the oil over high heat; do not let the butter brown. Add the asparagus and mushrooms and stir-fry for 1 minute. Add the reserved soaking liquid, the soy sauce, salt and sugar, and reduce the heat to low. Simmer until the asparagus are crisp-tender, 4 to 5 minutes.

Italian-Style Spring Dinner

Half-and-Halfs (Sweet and Dry Vermouth on the Rocks with an Orange Twist)

◆

Giardiniera*

Sesame Breadsticks

◆

Calf's Liver alla Veneziana*

Saged New Potatoes with Parmesan*

Italian Bread

Beverage Suggestion: Valpolicella

◆

Honeyed Strawberry Granita*

Chocolate Cookies and Espresso

*RECIPE INCLUDED

Italian food remains the most popular ethnic food in America, and though the red sauces and strong flavors of the Southern-style food command a strong following, the subtler foods of the North, such as this Venetian-style calf's liver, are also much appreciated in this country.

This Northern-style menu hints at the coming of spring. A *giardiniera*—garden vegetables uncooked and pungently dressed—is for starters. The calf's liver is touched with the green of scallions and parsley and the fragrance of light white wine. Accompanying this are rosy, saged new potatoes with Parmesan. Dessert is a honeyed strawberry *granita*, which is springtime itself. All dishes are easily prepared and can be made in well under an hour.

THE GAME PLAN

- Dissolve the honey and hot water for the *granita* and stir into the orange juice. Set aside.
- Make the *giardiniera*. Start the potatoes.
- Meanwhile, make the calf's liver.
- Add the butter and Parmesan cheese to the potatoes and serve with the calf's liver and the *giardiniera*.
- Just before serving the dessert, process the strawberries with the honey-orange juice mixture and serve.
- If Time Allows: The *giardiniera* and the *granita* can be made in advance.

Six Servings

Giardiniera

1 medium zucchini, cut into 2-by-½-inch sticks
1 medium yellow squash, cut into 2-by-½-inch sticks
1 medium green bell pepper, cut into 2-by-½-inch sticks
1 large bunch of broccoli, broken into florets
2 tablespoons red wine vinegar
4 tablespoons vegetable oil
2 garlic cloves, crushed through a press
½ teaspoon oregano
1½ teaspoons salt
Large pinch of cayenne pepper

1 Place the zucchini, squash, bell pepper and broccoli in a large mixing bowl.

2 Combine the vinegar, oil, garlic, oregano, salt and cayenne and beat with a fork. Pour the dressing over the vegetables, toss well and serve. (If making ahead of time, store, covered, in the refrigerator until serving time.)

Calf's Liver alla Veneziana

6 tablespoons unsalted butter
2 bunches of scallions (white and tender green), sliced
1½ pounds very thinly sliced calf's liver, cut into 1-by-2-inch strips
1½ teaspoons salt
Freshly ground pepper
⅓ cup dry white wine
¼ cup chopped fresh parsley

1 In a large skillet, melt the butter. Add the scallions and stir them for 2 or 3 minutes over low heat. Add the liver, season with the salt and pepper to taste and cook over high heat, stirring and tossing, until all sides are browned, 3 to 5 minutes. Remove the liver to a serving platter and keep warm.

2 Add the wine and parsley to the juices in the skillet and bring to a boil. Pour over the liver and serve.

Saged New Potatoes with Parmesan

18 to 24 small new potatoes
Salt
½ teaspoon crumbled sage
3 tablespoons unsalted butter, melted
⅓ cup freshly grated Parmesan cheese

1 Place the potatoes in a steamer and sprinkle with salt to taste and the sage. Steam for 15 to 20 minutes, or until tender.

2 Drizzle with the melted butter and sprinkle the Parmesan cheese over them.

Honeyed Strawberry Granita

3 tablespoons honey
Juice of 1 orange
1¼ pounds frozen, unsweetened strawberries (see Note)

1 Dissolve the honey in 1 or 2 tablespoons of hot water and stir into the orange juice.

2 Place the unthawed strawberries and orange juice in a food processor or blender and process (in several batches if necessary) until the strawberries are the consistency of a smooth sherbet. Serve immediately. (If making ahead, store the granita in a covered container in the freezer. Just before serving, re-process it in a blender or food processor to soften to a scoopable consistency.)

Note: If the strawberries are solidly frozen, allow them to soften slightly before processing.

Southern French Supper for Two

Dilled Ricotta*

Peasant or Black Bread

◆

Giselle's Soup Provençale with Poached Eggs*

Pepper, Olive and Onion Salad*

**Beverage Suggestion: Dark Imported Beer,
such as Heineken Special Dark**

◆

Apple Raisin Crisp*

Café Filtre

*RECIPE INCLUDED

Giselle, a lovely young woman from Provence, first introduced me to this fragrant soup of tomatoes, herbs and spices, garnished with poached eggs. She prepared the dish as a simple but tasty supper for herself when alone, but it adapts well to a dinner for two: Giselle's Soup Provençale, thick-crusted peasant bread spread with dilled ricotta, and a Mediterranean flavored pepper, olive and onion salad make a lovely meal for you and a favorite friend.

To complete this easy menu in the least possible time, prepare the Apple Raisin Crisp first, then begin the soup. Serve the dilled ricotta as an appetizer spread by itself or, if you enjoy cheeses, group it with one or two others to be enjoyed throughout the meal.

THE GAME PLAN

- Assemble the Apple Raisin Crisp up to the point of baking it.
- Make the dilled ricotta. Start making the soup.
- While the soup cooks, prepare the salad and the dressing; wait to dress it at the table.
- Preheat the oven to 400° and put the dessert in to bake.
- Serve the dilled ricotta while the soup finishes.
- Serve the soup and salad.
- **If Time Allows:** This meal can be made almost totally in advance. Cover the assembled Apple Raisin Crisp with plastic wrap and let sit at room temperature until baking time. Store the dilled ricotta, covered, in the refrigerator. Assemble the salad and make the dressing; cover and refrigerate separately. Make the soup in advance up to the point of adding the eggs. Reheat gently and add the eggs.

Two Servings

Dilled Ricotta

¼ cup whole-milk ricotta cheese
2 tablespoons sour cream
2 tablespoons chopped fresh dill
2 teaspoons minced fresh chives
4 pickled cocktail onions, coarsely
 chopped
1 to 2 dashes hot pepper sauce,
 to taste
Salt to taste
4 slices peasant or black bread,
 cut into strips or triangles

Mix together all the ingredients except the bread. Serve at room temperature surrounded by bread to spread the cheese on.

Giselle's Soup Provençale with Poached Eggs

2½ tablespoons olive oil
1 medium onion, coarsely
 chopped
3 garlic cloves, finely chopped
1 can (35 ounces) Italian peeled
 tomatoes, crushed, with their
 juice
1 small waxy potato, finely
 chopped, or ¼ cup cooked rice
½ teaspoon fennel seed, slightly
 crushed
¼ teaspoon thyme
1 bay leaf
2 strips of orange zest, about 2
 by ½ inch
Large pinch of saffron threads
Dash of cayenne pepper
½ teaspoon salt
¼ teaspoon sugar
2 eggs
1 tablespoon chopped fresh
 parsley

1 Heat the oil in a medium saucepan. Add the onion and sauté over moderate heat until softened and translucent, about 3 minutes. Add the garlic and cook for 30 seconds longer.

2 Add the tomatoes and their juice, the potato, fennel, thyme, bay leaf, orange zest, saffron, cayenne, salt and sugar.

3 Bring to a boil, reduce to a simmer and cook, partially covered, for 20 minutes.

4 Remove the bay leaf and orange zest. Gently break the eggs into the soup, cover and poach until set, about 5 minutes.

5 Divide the eggs and soup between 2 bowls and garnish with the parsley.

Pepper, Olive and Onion Salad

1 large green bell pepper, cut into
 ¼-inch strips
10 imported black olives (such as
 Calamata), pitted and
 quartered
4 thin slices of red onion,
 separated into rings
½ cup canned chick-peas, rinsed
 and drained
2 tablespoons olive oil
2 teaspoons red wine vinegar
¼ teaspoon salt
¼ teaspoon coarsely ground
 black pepper
1 teaspoon chopped fresh parsley

1 Arrange the green pepper, olives, onion and chick-peas on a small platter.

2 In a small bowl, whisk together the oil, vinegar, salt, black pepper and parsley until blended. Pour over the salad and serve.

Apple Raisin Crisp

4 tablespoons unsalted butter
2 medium apples—peeled, cored
 and cut into ¼-inch slices
4 tablespoons packed dark brown
 sugar
¼ cup raisins
½ cup all-purpose flour

1 Preheat the oven to 400°. Butter an 8-inch square cake pan with 1 tablespoon of the butter.

2 Toss the apples with 1 tablespoon of the brown sugar and arrange in the pan in overlapping slices. Sprinkle on the raisins.

3 Rub the remaining 3 tablespoons butter and the brown sugar and the flour together until crumbly. Evenly distribute the crumbs over the apples and raisins and bake until the apples are soft, about 30 minutes. Let cool for about 15 minutes before serving.

A Hearty English Grill

Melon with Pepper and Lime

◆

English Grill*

Braised Onion Slices*

Toasted French Bread

Beverage Suggestion: Anchor Steam or New Amsterdam Amber or an English Ale

◆

Frozen Trifle*

Coffee and Cognac

*RECIPE INCLUDED

If anyone knows how to deal with dreary weather it's the English, so I've borrowed some of their traditional hearty dishes to warm up blustery winter evenings. Mixed grills have their roots in medieval England, when whatever meat was available was roasted on a spit and served on a trencher of bread. Nowadays, such grills are a staple on hotel menus and at home; the choice of meat includes lamb chops, bacon, kidneys, sausages and small steaks; and the plate of bread has shrunk to genteel slices of toast.

Grills can be dull colored, but this one is brightened by a bed of tangy watercress and a squeeze of lemon. A sharp English mustard, such as Coleman's, is the perfect accompaniment. If you don't like lamb kidneys, serve grilled sausages.

Braised onions in the place of potatoes lightens the meal, as does the melon with pepper and lime to start. Save room for frozen trifle, a pillar of the British Empire.

THE GAME PLAN

- Cut the melon and sprinkle with lime juice and pepper.
- Preheat the broiler.
- Prepare the trifle up to the point at which it can be covered and frozen, reserving the last four ingredients to add just before serving.
- Make the braised onion slices.
- Make the mixed grill and keep warm while serving the melon.
- Serve the mixed grill and onion slices.
- Just before serving the dessert, remove it from the freezer and top with the whipped cream, walnuts, ginger and cherries.
- ○ **If Time Allows:** The trifle can be made ahead.

Four Servings

English Grill

4 thick slices of bacon, cut in half
¼ cup plus 2 tablespoons olive oil
2 teaspoons white wine vinegar
½ teaspoon Dijon-style mustard
4 lamb kidneys, split lengthwise and cored
4 loin lamb chops, 1½ inches thick
1 garlic clove, cut in half
2 large tomatoes, cut in half crosswise
12 large mushroom caps
1 bunch of watercress
1 tablespoon fresh lemon juice
Coarse (kosher) salt
Freshly ground pepper

1 Preheat the broiler and broiler pan. Broil the bacon, turning once, until each side just begins to brown, about 1 minute a side. Set aside.

2 In a small bowl, mix 2 tablespoons of the oil with the vinegar and mustard until blended. Add the kidneys and toss to coat well. Wrap each kidney half in a piece of bacon and secure with a toothpick.

3 Rub both sides of the lamb chops with the cut side of the garlic. Brush the chops, tomatoes and mushrooms with the remaining ¼ cup olive oil.

4 Broil the lamb chops, tomatoes and mushrooms about 4 inches from the heat for 4 minutes. Remove the mushrooms and cover loosely with foil to keep warm. Turn the chops. Add the kidneys and broil for 3 minutes. Turn the kidneys and broil for 3 minutes longer.

5 Arrange the meats and vegetables on a bed of watercress. Squeeze the lemon juice over the lamb chops and season everything with salt and pepper.

Braised Onion Slices

2½ tablespoons unsalted butter
1 tablespoon brown sugar
¼ teaspoon salt
8 thick slices of onion, almost ½ inch
¼ teaspoon thyme
Pinch of pepper
1 tablespoon chopped fresh parsley

1 In a large heavy skillet, melt the butter, brown sugar and salt over moderately low heat until bubbling.

2 Add the onion slices to the skillet in a single layer. Cover and cook until softened, about 10 minutes. Turn the onions and season with thyme and pepper. Continue to cook, uncovered, turning once, until browned on both sides, about 5 minutes a side. Sprinkle with parsley before serving.

Frozen Trifle

8 ladyfingers
¼ cup medium-dry sherry
⅓ cup raspberry jam
1 banana, sliced
1 pint vanilla ice cream, softened
½ cup heavy cream, whipped to stiff peaks
¼ cup chopped walnuts
2 tablespoons crystallized ginger, chopped (optional)
4 to 6 glacéed cherries

1 Line the bottom of a 1½-quart glass bowl with the ladyfingers. Sprinkle with the sherry and spread with raspberry jam. Add the sliced banana, then spread the ice cream on top. (Cover and place in the freezer at this point if not serving right away in order to keep the ice cream semifrozen; the trifle may be held for up to 30 minutes.)

2 Before serving, top with whipped cream. Garnish with the walnuts, ginger and glacéed cherries.

Northern Italian Dinner

Orange and Red Onion Salad*

◆

Ham Steaks in Marsala Sauce*

Quick Polenta*

Creamed Spinach with Raisins and Pine Nuts*

◆

Beverage Suggestion: A Grignolino from Piedmont or California

◆

Coffee and Pistachio Ice Cream with Crème de Cacao

Espresso

*RECIPE INCLUDED

Several flavors of northern Italy are highlighted in this menu. It is food with a history.

Beginning in the 16th century, spinach was imported from the Middle East; soon thereafter, oranges, pine nuts and raisins began to grace a wide variety of the dishes served at royal feasts. Polenta, now made with cornmeal, is a descendant of the ground chestnut *pulmentium* of ancient Etruscan cooking. Parmesan cheese has been produced in the Enza Valley for almost a thousand years. And Marsala, a relative latecomer, is a fortified Sicilian wine, now popular with northern cooks.

Here these flavors have been combined in a hearty meal, designed to meet the time constraints of a thoroughly modern life-style.

THE GAME PLAN

- Assemble the salad and make the dressing, but wait to dress the salad at the table.
- Soak the raisins, sauté the pine nuts and steam the spinach for the creamed spinach.
- Start making the polenta.
- Preheat the oven to 200° and start the ham steaks.
- While the sauce for the ham steaks is reducing, assemble the creamed spinach and keep it warm, along with the ham and polenta in a low oven while serving the salad.
- Finish the Marsala sauce, return the ham to the skillet for a moment and serve with the creamed spinach and polenta.

Four to Six Servings

Orange and Red Onion Salad

1 bunch of watercress
4 navel oranges, peeled and sliced
6 thin slices of red onion, separated into rings
2 tablespoons olive oil
1 teaspoon red wine vinegar
¼ teaspoon salt

1 Make a bed of watercress on a serving platter. Arrange the orange slices on top. Scatter the onion rings over the oranges.

2 Blend the oil, vinegar and salt and spoon over the salad before serving.

Ham Steaks in Marsala Sauce

5 tablespoons unsalted butter
2 pounds ham steaks, cut ½ inch thick and trimmed of fat
½ cup chicken broth
½ cup dry Marsala
½ teaspoon grated lemon zest
2 tablespoons chopped fresh parsley

1 Preheat the oven to 200°. In a large skillet, melt 1 tablespoon of the butter. Working in batches, add half of the ham and sauté over moderate heat, turning once, until lightly browned, about 3 minutes on each side. Transfer to an ovenproof platter, cover loosely with foil and keep warm in the oven. Repeat with 1 tablespoon of butter and the remaining ham. Pour off any fat.

2 Add the broth, Marsala and lemon zest to the skillet and bring to a boil, scraping up any browned bits from the bottom of the pan. Boil until reduced to ½ cup, about 5 minutes.

3 Remove from the heat and swirl in the remaining 3 tablespoons butter, 1 tablespoon at a time; stir in the parsley.

4 Return the ham, along with any accumulated juices, to the skillet and turn to coat with the sauce. Serve the ham on a heated platter; pass the sauce at the table.

Quick Polenta

1 cup yellow cornmeal
1 teaspoon salt
2 tablespoons unsalted butter
⅓ cup freshly grated Parmesan cheese

1 Mix the cornmeal with 1 cup of cold water until blended.

2 In a heavy medium saucepan, bring 3 cups of water and the salt to a boil. Stir in the cornmeal paste and return to a boil, stirring constantly. Reduce the heat to low and cook, stirring occasionally, until the polenta is thick, 10 to 12 minutes.

3 Pour into a serving dish, dot with the butter and sprinkle on the cheese.

Creamed Spinach with Raisins and Pine Nuts

¼ cup golden raisins
1 tablespoon plus 1 teaspoon unsalted butter
¼ cup pine nuts
2 pounds fresh spinach, stemmed and washed
¼ cup heavy cream
Salt and freshly ground pepper

1 In a small bowl, cover the raisins with warm water and let stand until softened, about 15 minutes. Drain the raisins.

2 In a small skillet, melt 1 teaspoon of the butter over moderate heat. Add the pine nuts and sauté, shaking the pan occasionally, until lightly browned, about 4 minutes. Set aside.

3 In a large uncovered saucepan, cook the spinach in the water that clings to its leaves over moderate heat, stirring occasionally, until wilted, about 3 minutes. Drain and press out the excess moisture.

4 In a medium skillet, melt the remaining 1 tablespoon of butter over moderate heat. Add the cream, spinach and raisins and cook, stirring, until heated through, about 2 minutes. Season with salt and pepper to taste. Top with the pine nuts.

Festive Caribbean Dinner

Pork with Garlic, Green Chiles and Lime*

Black Beans with Fresh Coriander and Tomatoes*

Saffron Rice*

Orange and Bermuda Onion Salad*

Beverage Suggestion: Chilled Beer or Jamaican Ginger Beer

◆

Guava Shells with Cream Cheese and Crackers

Espresso

*RECIPE INCLUDED

The combination of earthy black beans and rice is both a staple and a savory delight in Latin American cookery. Inspired by a meal shared with close friends who live in the Caribbean, this menu features sautéed slices of pork loin topped with garlic, olives, chiles and thyme; black beans seasoned with fresh coriander and tomatoes, and saffron rice. A salad of sliced oranges and sweet onion is a refreshing accompaniment to these hearty foods. For a traditional Latin dessert, I suggest guava shells, served with cream cheese and crisp, salty crackers. Demitasse cups of espresso will finish the meal nicely.

Good quality canned guava shells packed in heavy syrup (guava shells resemble canned peach halves), canned black beans and bunches of fresh coriander—or *cilantro* in Spanish—are now available in many supermarkets. Of course, they are standard items in Latin American groceries throughout the country.

THE GAME PLAN

- Make the salad.
- Put the rice on to cook.
- Make the beans and keep them warm until the pork is ready to serve.
- About 10 minutes before serving time, start sautéing the pork.
- **If Time Allows:** The salad and the beans can be prepared a few hours ahead. Cover the salad with plastic wrap until serving time. Gently reheat the beans while sautéing the pork.

Four Servings

Black Beans with Fresh Coriander and Tomatoes

1½ tablespoons olive oil
1 small onion, chopped
5 plum tomatoes—peeled, seeded and chopped—or 1 can (14 ounces) Italian peeled tomatoes, drained and chopped
1 can (16 ounces) black beans, rinsed and drained
½ teaspoon hot pepper sauce
½ teaspoon salt
1 tablespoon coarsely chopped fresh coriander (cilantro)

1 In a small skillet, heat the oil. Add the onion and cook over moderate heat, stirring occasionally, until partially translucent but still firm, about 2 minutes. Add the tomatoes and cook, stirring occasionally, for 2 minutes more.

2 Add the black beans and season with the hot pepper sauce and salt. Cover and cook until heated through, about 2 minutes longer. Remove from the heat and stir in half of the coriander. Sprinkle the remaining coriander on top.

Pork with Garlic, Green Chiles and Lime

1 tablespoon unsalted butter
1 tablespoon vegetable oil
1 pound boneless pork loin, trimmed and cut into ¼-inch slices (about 12 slices)
Salt
2 small garlic cloves, minced
2 teaspoons chopped green olives
1½ teaspoons minced fresh green chile pepper (about 1 small)
¼ teaspoon thyme
1½ tablespoons fresh lime juice

1 In a large heavy skillet, melt the butter in the oil over moderately high heat. Add as many of the pork slices as will fit in a single layer and sauté, turning once, until lightly browned on both sides, about 3 minutes. Transfer to a heated platter, salt lightly and cover loosely with foil to keep warm. Sauté the remaining pork slices in the same way.

2 Drain off all but 1 tablespoon of the fat in the skillet. Return to moderately high heat and add the garlic, olives, chile pepper and thyme. Cook, stirring occasionally, until the garlic is light brown, 1 to 2 minutes. Sprinkle the garlic-chile mixture over the pork slices. Drizzle the lime juice on top.

Saffron Rice

2½ cups chicken broth
1 cup converted rice
¼ teaspoon saffron threads, crumbled

In a medium saucepan, bring the chicken broth to a boil over high heat. Stir in the rice and saffron and return to a boil. Reduce the heat to low and cover tightly. Cook for 20 minutes, or until all the liquid is absorbed.

Orange and Bermuda Onion Salad

3 navel oranges, peeled and sliced
4 thin slices of Bermuda or Spanish onion, separated into rings
¼ teaspoon coarse (kosher) salt

Arrange the orange slices, slightly overlapping, on a small serving platter. Scatter the onion rings on top and sprinkle with the salt.

Fettuccine for Four

Prosciutto with Pears*

◆

Fettuccine in Cream with Herb-Scented Mushrooms*

Fresh Tomato and Caper Salad*

Beverage Suggestion: Pinot Grigio, such as Santa Margherita, or Verdicchio, such as Fazi Battaglia

◆

Lemon Ice with Gin*

*RECIPE INCLUDED

The appeal of Italian food derives not only from its freshness and infinite variety, but frequently also from its beauty on the plate. This pretty repast, as appropriate for lunch as for dinner, is a perfect example. Deep-hued prosciutto is draped over pale thin slices of fresh pear. The fettuccine is light and fresh with cream and herb-scented mushrooms, and the accompanying salad is made of ripe red tomatoes and capers against dark arugula or watercress leaves.

For the pasta, a good quality dried fettuccine is fine, but if fresh is available, it's preferred. Remember that really fresh pasta cooks in the blink of an eye—usually less than a minute after the water has returned to a boil.

The dessert, a lemon ice sprinkled with gin, is American, but it's a pleasing, light end to this Italian-accented meal.

THE GAME PLAN

- Assemble the pears and prosciutto.
- Arrange the greens and tomatoes on a platter and make the salad dressing; wait to spoon on the dressing and capers until just before serving.
- Put the water for the fettuccine on to boil, make the mushrooms and keep warm.
- Serve the prosciutto and pears.
- Warm the cream and butter and cook the fettuccine. Drain the pasta and toss with the cream, butter and cheese. Top with the pepper and mushrooms and serve hot with the salad.
- Pour the gin and lemon zest over each portion of lemon ice just before serving.
- **If Time Allows:** The pears for the prosciutto and the salad dressing can be prepared a little in advance.

Four Servings

Prosciutto with Pears

3 firm-ripe pears, peeled and
    thinly sliced
3 tablespoons lime juice
16 thin slices of prosciutto (about
    ½ pound)
Freshly ground pepper

Place the sliced pears in a mixing bowl, sprinkle with the lime juice and toss. Divide them among four individual serving plates. Drape about four slices of the prosciutto over each portion of pears and grind a little fresh pepper on top.

Lemon Ice with Gin

1 pint lemon ice, sorbet or sherbet
6 tablespoons gin
2 teaspoons grated lemon zest

Divide the lemon ice among four dessert dishes. Pour 1½ tablespoons gin over each serving of ice and sprinkle each with ½ teaspoon of the lemon zest.

Fettuccine in Cream with Herb-Scented Mushrooms

4 tablespoons unsalted butter
6 scallions, thinly sliced
½ pound fresh mushrooms, sliced
¼ teaspoon *herbes de Provence*
½ cup dry red wine
¼ teaspoon salt
⅓ cup chopped fresh parsley
½ cup heavy cream
¾ pound fresh fettuccine or ½
    pound dried
½ cup freshly grated Parmesan
    cheese
Freshly ground pepper

1 Place a large pot of lightly salted water over moderately high heat and bring it to a boil.

2 Meanwhile, in a medium skillet, melt 2½ tablespoons of the butter over low heat. Add the scallions, mushrooms and *herbes de Provence* and sauté over low heat, stirring frequently, until the mushrooms have absorbed the butter, about 2 minutes. Stir in the wine and salt and simmer over low heat for about 3 minutes. Stir in the parsley and simmer 30 seconds longer.

3 In a large saucepan, combine the cream and remaining 1½ tablespoons butter and warm over low heat until the butter is melted and the cream is heated through.

4 Meanwhile, drop the fettuccine into the boiling water and cook until al dente, 45 seconds for fresh, 8 to 10 minutes for dried.

5 Drain the fettuccine and add to the warm cream. Add the grated cheese and toss until the pasta is well coated. Divide the fettuccine among four warmed serving plates and top each with a grind of fresh pepper. Divide the mushroom sauce evenly among the four plates and serve.

Fresh Tomato and Caper Salad

2 cups trimmed arugula or
    watercress
4 firm-ripe tomatoes, sliced
2 tablespoons olive oil
2 teaspoons fresh lemon juice
¼ teaspoon freshly ground
    pepper
Salt
1 tablespoon coarsely chopped,
    drained capers

1 Spread the arugula on a large serving platter. Arrange the sliced tomatoes on the greens.

2 In a small bowl, combine the olive oil, lemon juice and pepper and season to taste with salt. Spoon the dressing over the salad just before serving and sprinkle with the capers.

Saffron Rice with Pistachios

PAGE 127

Tuna Antipasto with Roasted Red Peppers

PAGE 207

Parisian Supper for Four

Cider Cup*

◆

Concierge's Soup*

Charcuterie and Cheese Board

Assorted Olives, Cornichons, Celery Sticks, Scallions and Radishes

Mustard and Horseradish

Warm French Bread and Sweet Butter

Beverage Suggestion: Côtes-du-Rhône, such as Gigondas

◆

Sautéed Apple Tart*

Café Filtre

*RECIPE INCLUDED

My favorite Sunday night supper is this simple French-style meal of steaming homemade soup, boards laden with cheeses and charcuterie.

The best thing about this meal, apart from its comforting qualities and the images and aromas of Paris it evokes, is the ease and speed with which it can be put together. A wide range of good French cheeses are available here: among my favorites are St. André and Brie. For the charcuterie, I like to include French-style pâtés and saucissons, Black Forest or Westphalian ham, Polish sausage and Italian mortadella and soppressata. Plan on ¼ to ⅓ pound of meat and ¼ pound of cheese per person.

The perfect companion to an array of these cold meats and cheeses is this hot leek, potato and watercress soup. I call it Concierge's Soup because it reminds me of the warming smells that frequently emanate from the apartments of French concierges.

THE GAME PLAN

- Preheat the oven to 375°. Start making the soup.
- Make the pastry for the tart and bake. Meanwhile, sauté the apples.
- Set up the charcuterie and cheese boards. Serve the Cider Cup.
- Cut the pastry as soon as it comes out of the oven and set aside. Finish the soup and serve with the charcuterie and cheese board.
- Gently rewarm the sautéed apples and assemble the apple tarts.
- ○ **If Time Allows:** The tart bottoms can be made in advance and the soup made to the point of adding the watercress.

Four Servings

Cider Cup

Ice cubes
6 ounces (¾ cup) bourbon
2 cups fresh apple cider
4 julienne strips of lemon zest
Freshly grated nutmeg

Fill four old-fashioned glasses with ice. Add 1½ ounces bourbon to each. Fill each glass up with cider and garnish with the lemon zest and nutmeg to taste.

Concierge's Soup

3 tablespoons unsalted butter
2 large leeks (white and tender green), sliced
3 cups chicken broth
2 large potatoes, peeled and sliced
Salt
1½ cups coarsely chopped watercress
Freshly ground pepper
Crème frâiche or heavy cream, for garnish

1 In a large heavy saucepan, melt the butter. Add the leeks and sauté over low heat, stirring occasionally, until softened but not browned, about 8 minutes.

2 Stir in the chicken broth and potatoes and season with salt to taste. Partially cover the pan and continue to simmer until the potatoes are fork-tender, about 10 minutes.

3 Using a wooden spoon, mash some of the potato slices against the side of the pan to thicken the soup. Stir in the watercress and simmer, uncovered, 1 minute more. Ladle into large shallow soup bowls. Grind fresh pepper to taste over each and garnish with a generous spoonful of crème frâiche or heavy cream.

Sautéed Apple Tart

1¼ cups all-purpose flour
⅓ cup plus 2 teaspoons sugar
½ teaspoon salt
9 tablespoons unsalted butter, at room temperature
3 Granny Smith apples—peeled, cored and sliced
1 teaspoon grated lemon zest
2 to 4 tablespoons maple syrup, to taste
4 to 8 tablespoons crème frâiche or heavy cream mixed with ½ teaspoon lemon juice (see Note)

1 Preheat the oven to 375°. In a medium bowl, combine the flour, ⅓ cup of the sugar and the salt. Cut in 6 tablespoons of the butter until the mixture resembles coarse meal. Press the crumbs evenly over the bottom of an ungreased 8-inch square baking pan. Bake for 25 to 30 minutes, until very lightly browned. Cut into four 4-inch squares or eight 2-by-4-inch rectangles while still warm; the crust will become too brittle to cut evenly when it cools.

2 In a medium skillet, melt the remaining 3 tablespoons butter. Add the apple slices and sauté over low heat until the apples begin to soften. Sprinkle with the remaining 2 teaspoons sugar and the lemon zest and season with salt to taste. Continue to sauté the apples until tender and lightly browned. Sprinkle the maple syrup over the apples to moisten.

3 Arrange the squares of crust on a serving platter or individual plates and divide the sautéed apples evenly among them. Serve warm or at room temperature, each portion topped with 1 or 2 tablespoons of crème frâiche.

Note: A small amount of lemon juice stirred quickly into cream will thicken the cream slightly and add a tartness similar to that of crème frâiche.

Instant-India Party Menu

Pink Gin*

◆

Madras Shrimp*

Boiled Rice with Hazelnuts

Raita of Bananas with Watercress Sprigs*

Beverage Suggestion: Premium Beer

◆

Honeydew Melon in Tawny Port*

Darjeeling Tea

*RECIPE INCLUDED

The cuisine of India is rich and varied, yet many of its deeply flavored dishes are not difficult to prepare. Certainly the most distinctive characteristic of this cuisine is the imaginative use and blending of spices such as cumin, coriander, cayenne, turmeric, cardamom, cloves and ginger, to name only a few. Many of these spices are put to good advantage in this menu, which delivers a maximum of intriguing flavors, colors and textures in a minimum of time.

The Madras Shrimp makes excellent party fare and takes only about 25 minutes to prepare from start to finish. There are many different versions of raita, a traditional, cooling, yogurt-based salad; this one includes bananas and watercress. Honeydew melon in tawny port makes a refreshing finale.

THE GAME PLAN

- Put the water on to boil for the rice.
- Meanwhile, make the melon and the raita and refrigerate both, covered, until serving time.
- Start cooking the rice.
- Make the Madras Shrimp.
- Keep the shrimp and rice warm in a low oven while serving the Pink Gin.
- Sprinkle the rice with chopped hazelnuts and serve with the Madras Shrimp and chilled raita.
- **If Time Allows:** Make the melon and the raita in advance.

Four to Six Servings

Pink Gin

12 ounces (1½ cups) gin
8 dashes Angostura bitters
Crushed ice

Combine the gin and bitters in a cocktail shaker, add a little crushed ice and shake well. Pour into four or six old-fashioned glasses filled three-quarters full with crushed ice.

Madras Shrimp

1 tablespoon ground coriander
½ teaspoon cumin
1 teaspoon turmeric
½ teaspoon powdered mustard
¼ teaspoon cayenne pepper
Juice of 1 lemon
4 tablespoons unsalted butter
5 or 6 scallions (white and tender green), cut into rounds
3 garlic cloves, minced
1 pound cooked shrimp, shelled and deveined (see Note)
1 to 2 tablespoons heavy cream
½ teaspoon brown sugar

1 In a small bowl, mix together the coriander, cumin, turmeric, mustard, cayenne and lemon juice. Set aside.

2 In a wok or skillet, melt the butter over moderately high heat. When the foam subsides, add the scallions and garlic and sauté for 3 to 4 minutes.

3 Stir in the spice paste and cook for another 3 to 4 minutes. Lower the heat to medium, add the shrimp, and toss until they are heated through, 2 or 3 minutes. Stir in the cream and brown sugar and cook for another minute. Serve the shrimp hot, accompanied with white rice, cooked with a bay leaf and garnished with chopped hazelnuts.

Note: Purchase cooked, shelled shrimp from a fishmonger, or use frozen cooked and cleaned shrimp, thawed.

Raita of Bananas with Watercress Sprigs

2 medium bananas, sliced into ¼-inch rounds
Juice of ½ lemon
2 cups plain yogurt
¼ teaspoon cayenne pepper
1 teaspoon superfine sugar
Watercress sprigs, for garnish

In a bowl, toss the banana slices with the lemon juice. Add the yogurt, cayenne and sugar and mix well. Refrigerate, covered, and serve chilled. Garnish with the watercress before serving.

Honeydew Melon in Tawny Port

1 honeydew melon—peeled, seeded and cut into 1-inch cubes
1½ cups tawny port
Fresh mint leaves, for garnish

1 Place the melon in a bowl and pour in the port. Refrigerate, covered, until serving time.

2 Serve the melon cubes, with some of the liquid, in a large chilled serving bowl or individual dessert dishes. Garnish with the mint leaves.

Southern Italian Supper

Tuna Antipasto with Roasted Red Peppers*

◆

**Broiled Eggplant with Three Cheeses and
Fresh Tomato Sauce***

Escarole Salad with Fresh Mint*

**Beverage Suggestion: Spicy Red Sicilian
Wine, such as Regaleali**

◆

Lemon Ice with a Squeeze of Fresh Lemon Juice

Espresso

*RECIPE INCLUDED

The flavors of Southern Italy dominate this menu for a satisfying supper without red meat. Broiled Eggplant with Three Cheeses and Fresh Tomato Sauce is a variation on the theme of eggplant Parmesan, a favorite throughout the South of Italy and in Sicily. The fresh tomato sauce is best when prepared with vine-ripened local tomatoes if you can find them.

To start, serve a colorful antipasto of roasted red peppers, tuna, anchovies, olives, radishes and scallions, accented with capers, parsley and a simple vinaigrette. Sweet fresh mint in the escarole salad takes advantage of the fresh herbs abundantly available in late summer. If you can't get fresh mint, you may substitute basil or coriander. Lemon ice, followed by espresso, brings this refreshing meal to a close.

THE GAME PLAN

- Make the tomato sauce.
- Assemble the antipasto up to the point of drizzling the oil and lemon juice over it.
- Prepare the salad greens and the dressing, but wait to toss until just before serving.
- Preheat the broiler. Slice the eggplant and sprinkle it with salt. Finish assembling the antipasto.
- Place the eggplant in the broiler and serve the antipasto.
- Toss the salad, finish broiling the eggplant and serve with the hot tomato sauce.
- o **If Time Allows:** The tomato sauce and salad dressing can be made ahead. The antipasto can be assembled to the point of drizzling the lemon juice and oil over it; refrigerate, covered. Reheat the tomato sauce just before serving.

Two Servings

Tuna Antipasto with Roasted Red Peppers

1 jar (4 ounces) roasted red peppers
1 can (6½ ounces) solid white tuna in olive oil, drained and flaked
4 flat anchovy fillets
1 tablespoon chopped fresh parsley
½ teaspoon capers (optional)
2 teaspoons fresh lemon juice
1 teaspoon olive oil
Coarsely cracked black pepper
6 Mediterranean olives, 4 small radishes and 4 small scallions, for garnish

1 Cut the roasted peppers in half lengthwise and arrange the pieces on 2 plates. Mound the tuna in the center, dividing evenly. Crisscross 2 anchovy fillets over the tuna on each plate. Sprinkle with the parsley and capers, dividing evenly.

2 Drizzle each serving with the lemon juice and oil. Season with black pepper to taste. Garnish the plates with olives, radishes and scallions.

Broiled Eggplant with Three Cheeses and Fresh Tomato Sauce

1 medium eggplant (about 1 pound)
2 tablespoons plus 2 teaspoons olive oil
½ teaspoon coarse (kosher) salt
½ cup shredded Monterey Jack cheese
½ cup shredded Italian Fontina cheese
2 tablespoons freshly grated Parmesan cheese
Fresh Tomato Sauce

1 Preheat the broiler. Cut the eggplant lengthwise into 4 thick, even slices. Cut the skin side of the 2 end slices to make them flat. Rub each side of the slices with 1 teaspoon of olive oil. Sprinkle with the salt.

2 Arrange the eggplant slices on a broiler tray or baking sheet and broil about 4 inches from the heat for about 5 minutes, until lightly browned on top. Turn and broil until lightly browned on the second side, about 2 minutes longer.

3 Mix the Monterey Jack, Fontina and Parmesan cheeses together. Sprinkle evenly over the tops of the eggplant slices. Return to the broiler and cook until the cheese is melted and bubbling, 1 to 2 minutes. Serve with the Fresh Tomato Sauce.

Fresh Tomato Sauce

1½ tablespoons unsalted butter
2 medium tomatoes—peeled, seeded and coarsely chopped
1 large garlic clove, finely chopped
Salt

In a small saucepan, melt the butter over low heat. Add the tomatoes and garlic; simmer, stirring occasionally, until thickened to a sauce, 10 to 15 minutes. Season with salt to taste.

Escarole Salad with Fresh Mint

1 small head of escarole, torn into bite-size pieces
2 tablespoons olive oil
1 teaspoon red wine vinegar
1 teaspoon fresh lemon juice
Salt and freshly ground pepper
1 tablespoon coarsely chopped fresh mint leaves, basil leaves, coriander or parsley, for garnish

Place the escarole in a chilled serving bowl. Toss with the oil, vinegar and lemon juice. Season with salt and pepper to taste. Scatter the mint leaves on top.

Country French Dinner for Two

Bifteck Haché with Chèvre and Beaujolais*

Red Potatoes in Sweet Pepper Butter*

Beverage Suggestion: Beaujolais or Beaujolais Nouveau, such as Georges Duboeuf

◆

Green Salad with Lardons*

◆

Poached Apples with Ice Cream and Walnuts*

*RECIPE INCLUDED

Certain ingredients in the right combination are so unmistakably French that they will always infuse a dish with the appetizing and intensely satisfying flavors we associate with French country cooking. Minced shallots, for instance, in a red wine sauce on broiled meat; *herbes de Provence*, that aromatic mixture of thyme, rosemary, summer savory, fennel and lavender; a simple green salad salted with those crisp matchsticks of bacon called lardons; pungent chèvre. All these flavors give a special touch to what is essentially a grandiose cheeseburger and green salad. To complete this cozy meal for two, steamed potatoes are garnished with colorful red and green peppers, and poached apples are served with ice cream.

The benefit to the busy cook is that the entire meal can be made in about 45 minutes. In fact, the lardons can be cooked at any time, and the poached apples are equally good warm or at room temperature. For a truly French accent, serve them with crème fraîche instead of ice cream.

Beaujolais is the ideal wine for this simple and hearty meal. Try the latest vintage of this fruity wine, or, in the fall, look for beaujolais *nouveau*, released every year on November 15.

THE GAME PLAN

- Make the poaching syrup for the apples.
- Meanwhile, make the lardons and the dressing for the salad. Prepare the greens and sprinkle with the onion and lardons, but wait to dress the salad at the table.
- Start steaming the potatoes.
- Make the biftecks hachés.
- Meanwhile, make the pepper butter for the potatoes and toss them in it.
- Ten minutes or so before serving dessert, poach the apples.
- **If Time Allows:** The poaching syrup for the apples, the lardons, salad dressing and the sweet pepper butter for the potatoes can be made in advance. Warm the pepper butter only until heated through; the peppers should remain bright and fresh-looking. The apples can be poached in advance if you plan to serve them at room temperature.

Two Servings

Bifteck Haché with Chèvre and Beaujolais

1 tablespoon plus 1 teaspoon unsalted butter
⅔ pound ground sirloin, shaped into 2 patties, ¾ inch thick
Salt (optional)
2 slices (½ inch thick) of Montrachet or other chèvre log
½ teaspoon *herbes de Provence* or equal parts of thyme, rosemary and summer savory
Freshly ground pepper
1 tablespoon finely chopped shallots
½ cup Beaujolais or other fruity red wine

1 In a heavy well-seasoned skillet, melt 1 tablespoon of the butter over moderately high heat. When the butter foams, add the patties and sauté for 5 minutes.

2 Turn the patties and season lightly with salt if desired. Place a slice of chèvre on each patty and sprinkle with the herbs and a grind or two of pepper. Gently press down the herbs and chèvre with a spatula and continue cooking the patties for about 3 minutes for rare meat. Remove to warmed plates.

3 Melt the remaining 1 teaspoon butter in the skillet. Add the shallots and sauté until softened and translucent, about 1 minute. Add the wine and boil, scraping the browned bits from the bottom and sides of the pan, until slightly syrupy and reduced to ⅓ cup. Pour the sauce over the patties and serve.

Red Potatoes in Sweet Pepper Butter

½ pound (6 to 8) small red potatoes, quartered
2 tablespoons unsalted butter
1 tablespoon thinly sliced scallion (white and tender green)
1 tablespoon finely chopped red bell pepper
1 tablespoon finely chopped green bell pepper
Salt and freshly ground black pepper

1 Steam the potatoes until tender, 10 to 15 minutes.

2 Just before the potatoes are done, melt the butter in a small skillet over moderate heat. Add the scallion and red and green peppers and sauté until warmed through, about 1 minute.

3 Place the potatoes in a serving bowl. Pour the butter and vegetables over the potatoes and toss to coat. Season with salt and black pepper to taste.

Green Salad with Lardons

2 thick slices of slab bacon, cut crosswise into ⅛-inch strips
1½ tablespoons corn oil
1½ teaspoons red wine vinegar
1 medium head of Boston lettuce, torn into bite-size pieces
Salt and freshly ground pepper
2 thin slices of red onion, separated into rings

1 In a medium skillet, fry the bacon strips over moderate heat, turning, until lightly browned and almost crisp, about 4 minutes. Drain well on paper towels.

2 In a small bowl, whisk together the oil and vinegar until blended.

3 Place the lettuce in a serving bowl. Add the lardons and the vinaigrette sauce and toss well. Season with salt and pepper to taste. Scatter the onion rings on top.

Poached Apples with Ice Cream and Walnuts

1 cup apple cider
3 tablespoons light brown sugar
½ teaspoon vanilla extract
1 teaspoon unsalted butter
2 tart, medium apples—peeled, cored and thickly sliced
Rum raisin or vanilla ice cream
2 tablespoons chopped walnuts

1 In a small saucepan, bring the cider, brown sugar and vanilla to a boil over moderately high heat and cook, uncovered, until reduced by half, 5 to 10 minutes.

2 Reduce the heat to moderate and add the butter and apples. Poach the apples, turning occasionally, until tender but not mushy, about 10 minutes.

3 Serve the apples and sauce warm or at room temperature over a scoop of ice cream. Sprinkle the walnuts on top.

Chinese Fare for a Winter Eve

Watercress-Pork Soup*

◆

Chicken with Cashews*

Steamed Rice

Beverage Suggestion: Ice-Cold Ale or Sancerre

◆

Sugared Pineapple with Kirsch*

Almond Cookies

Green Tea

*RECIPE INCLUDED

Confucius said that one should never ingest "anything overcooked, undercooked, deficient in seasoning or crookedly cut." Accordingly, our Chinese menu scrupulously attends to the basics of good cooking—although it is designed to give you, the cook, a bit of culinary relief. Though some slicing and chopping is required, precise sizing is not necessary, and you are permitted to get away with some uneven—if not actually crooked—cutting.

If you are preparing the entire menu, first do all the measuring, chopping, slicing, marinating and organizing required for both the Watercress-Pork Soup and the Chicken with Cashews. Icy ale or a chilled white wine, such as a Sancerre, will go nicely with the mildly exotic flavors of the meal.

THE GAME PLAN

- Assemble and measure, chop, slice and marinate all the ingredients for the soup and the chicken.

- Cut up the pineapple and arrange on the shells, reserving the sugar and Kirsch to sprinkle over just before serving.

- Make the soup.

- Put the rice on to steam and serve the soup course.

- Stir-fry the chicken and serve hot with the rice.

- Just before serving dessert, sprinkle the sugar and Kirsch over the pineapple.

- ○ **If Time Allows:** The pineapple can be cut in advance, covered tightly with plastic wrap and refrigerated until serving time. The ingredients for the pork and chicken can be prepared ahead.

Six Servings

Watercress-Pork Soup

4 slices (¼ inch thick) of peeled fresh ginger
3 large slivers of orange zest
1 tablespoon soy sauce
1 teaspoon salt
¾ pound pork butt, cut into 1-by-¼-inch strips
1 large bunch of watercress, tough stems removed
¼ teaspoon Oriental sesame oil

1 Place the ginger, orange zest, soy sauce and salt in a medium saucepan. Add 6 cups of water and bring to a boil over moderate heat. Reduce the heat to low and simmer, partially covered, for 10 minutes.

2 Add the pork to the broth and simmer, partially covered, for 5 to 7 minutes.

3 Coarsely chop the watercress. Add it to the soup and cook for 3 minutes; remove from the heat. Taste for additional seasoning. Stir in the sesame oil and serve.

Chicken with Cashews

1 egg white
¼ cup plus 1 tablespoon soy sauce
2 tablespoons cornstarch
1¼ teaspoons salt

2½ pounds skinless, boneless chicken breasts, cut into ¾-inch cubes
2 tablespoons dry sherry
1½ teaspoons sugar
1½ cups peanut oil
4 slices (quarter-sized) of peeled fresh ginger
2 scallions, thinly sliced
1 can (8 ounces) whole water chestnuts—drained, rinsed and quartered
2 medium green bell peppers, cut into ¾-inch squares
¼ pound mushrooms, quartered
1 cup (5½ ounces) unsalted, roasted cashews

1 In a medium bowl, combine the egg white, 1 tablespoon of the soy sauce, 1 tablespoon of the cornstarch, ½ teaspoon of the salt and 1 tablespoon of water and stir until smooth. Add the chicken and toss to coat with the marinade.

2 In a small bowl, combine the remaining ¼ cup soy sauce and 1 tablespoon cornstarch, the sherry and sugar to make a sauce.

3 In a wok or large heavy skillet, heat the oil over moderate heat until it registers 325°. Give the chicken a stir and add it, with its marinade, to the wok. Stir-fry until the pieces are white and do not stick together, 3 to 4 minutes. Turn off the heat and remove the chicken with a mesh skimmer or slotted spoon. Drain well on paper towels.

4 Remove all but ¼ cup of oil from the wok. Reheat the oil in the wok over moderate heat. Add the ginger and scallions and stir once; then add the water chestnuts, green peppers, mushrooms and remaining ¾ teaspoon salt. Stir-fry until the green peppers are heated through, 2 to 3 minutes. Stir the sauce to mix the ingredients and add it to the wok. Add the chicken and cook, stirring, until the sauce is thickened and slightly translucent. Transfer the mixture to a serving dish or platter, sprinkle with the cashews and serve immediately.

Sugared Pineapple with Kirsch

1 pineapple with unblemished leaves
1 to 2 tablespoons sugar, to taste
3 tablespoons Kirsch

Without removing the leaves, cut the pineapple lengthwise into 6 sections and remove the core from each. Run a sharp knife between the fruit and shell of each section. Cut the fruit into ½-inch slices and arrange them decoratively on the shell. Just before serving, sprinkle the pineapple with the sugar and Kirsch.

Quick Japanese Beef Dinner

Sliced Tenderloin with Sake and Scallions*

**Spinach with Lemon and Toasted
Sesame Seeds***

Rice with Sautéed Water Chestnuts*

**Beverage Suggestion: Cold Japanese Beer,
Hot Green Tea and Hot Sake**

◆

Raspberry Sorbet with Shaved Chocolate

*RECIPE INCLUDED

Spinach with sesame seeds is a Japanese classic. It's served cold in individual dishes and its flavors blend well with those of thinly sliced tenderloin sautéed with ginger, sake and scallions. Rice with crunchy, sautéed water chestnuts makes a clean-tasting side dish. The whole menu takes well under an hour to prepare. To add to the mood, serve the dishes Japanese-style on small plates or dishes and accompany them with hot green tea, icy cold Japanese beer or warm sake.

I prefer using Japanese soy sauce to Chinese in all cooking—it's lighter and less salty, and is found in supermarkets everywhere.

The spinach can be prepared well in advance, and the rice can sit, covered, for up to 15 minutes before serving. For best results, prepare the beef at the last moment and take care not to overcook it.

THE GAME PLAN

- Start cooking the rice.
- Marinate the beef.
- Make the spinach.
- Sauté the water chestnuts, toss with the rice and cover to keep warm while making the beef.
- Sauté the beef, transfer to a platter, make the sauce and serve, along with the rice and spinach.
- ○ **If Time Allows:** The spinach can be made in advance, covered and refrigerated until serving time.

Four Servings

Sliced Tenderloin with Sake and Scallions

½ cup plus 2 tablespoons sake
1½ tablespoons Japanese soy sauce
1 teaspoon grated fresh ginger
1½ pounds flank steak or boneless rib steak, about 2 inches thick, cut into ¼-inch slices
2 to 3 tablespoons unsalted butter
4 scallions—trimmed, quartered lengthwise and cut into 2-inch lengths

1 In a large mixing bowl, combine 2 tablespoons of the sake, the soy sauce and ginger. Add the beef and toss to coat. Let the beef marinate, stirring once or twice, for about 10 minutes.

2 In a large skillet, melt 2 tablespoons of the butter over moderately high heat until it foams but is not browned. Add the beef slices in a single layer, working in batches and adding more butter as needed, and sauté until browned but still pink inside, 1 to 2 minutes on one side and 15 to 30 seconds on the other. Transfer the beef to a platter and keep warm while making the sauce.

3 Add the scallions to the skillet and sauté, stirring, for about 15 seconds. Pour in the remaining ½ cup sake and simmer for 1 minute, scraping up any browned bits from the bottom of the pan. Spoon the scallions and sauce over the beef and serve hot.

Rice with Sautéed Water Chestnuts

½-inch piece fresh ginger, peeled
1 garlic clove
1 teaspoon salt
1 cup converted rice
2 tablespoons unsalted butter
1 can (8 ounces) sliced water chestnuts, drained and rinsed
Salt
⅛ teaspoon cayenne pepper

1 In a medium saucepan, place the ginger, garlic and 2 cups of water and bring to a boil. Stir in the salt and rice and bring back to a boil. Reduce the heat to low, cover and cook for 17 to 20 minutes.

2 Meanwhile, in a large skillet, melt the butter. Add the water chestnuts and sauté over moderately low heat until lightly browned. Season with salt to taste and the cayenne.

3 Remove and discard the ginger and garlic. Add the water chestnuts to the rice and toss well. Serve hot.

Spinach with Lemon and Toasted Sesame Seeds

2 pounds fresh spinach, washed and stemmed
1 tablespoon sesame seeds
1 tablespoon Japanese soy sauce
1½ teaspoons fresh lemon juice
1½ teaspoons sugar

1 In a large pot, steam the spinach, with only the water clinging to its leaves, over moderately high heat, covered, for 3 minutes. Rinse under cold running water, drain and squeeze out excess moisture.

2 In a small ungreased skillet, toast the sesame seeds over moderately high heat, shaking the pan, until the first seeds pop.

3 In a large mixing bowl, combine the soy sauce, lemon juice and sugar, stirring to dissolve the sugar. Add the spinach and toss well.

4 Divide the spinach among four bowls and sprinkle some of the toasted sesame seeds over each portion. Serve at room temperature or chilled.

Mediterranean-Style Lunch

**Grilled Chèvre with Fresh Rosemary on
French Bread***

◆

Salade Niçoise, My Way*

French Bread

**Beverage Suggestion: Provençal Rosé, such
as Bandol**

◆

**Honeydew Melon and Fresh Peaches with
Sweet Vermouth***

Iced Espresso

*RECIPE INCLUDED

Anchovies, capers, Calamata olives and their brine, fresh rosemary and rich, fruity olive oil—some of the famous products of the French-Italian Mediterranean coast flavor this light, colorful lunch particularly suited for leisurely alfresco dining.

My version of Niçoise salad has an Italian accent with its pungent and peppery arugula, and an extra kick from a few dashes of hot pepper sauce.

Goat cheese and olive oil are natural partners, especially when sprinkled with fresh rosemary sprigs and grilled on slices of French bread. Serve them as an appetizer with aperitifs, or along with the salad.

For dessert, fresh peach slices and decorative rings of melon are sweetened with a little sweet vermouth. In very warm weather, iced espresso is refreshing with or after dessert.

THE GAME PLAN

- Prepare the fruit for dessert, but wait to add the vermouth until just before serving.
- Steam the potatoes and prepare the remaining ingredients for the salad.
- Meanwhile, prepare the grilled chèvre slices up to the point of the final broiling.
- Assemble the salad and make the dressing, but wait to dress it at the table.
- Preheat the broiler and broil the chèvre slices. Serve hot either as an appetizer or at the same time as the salad.
- **If Time Allows:** The potatoes can be steamed and the fruit prepared in advance.

Four Servings

Grilled Chèvre with Fresh Rosemary on French Bread

8 slices (½ inch thick) of French bread
¼ pound goat cheese, such as Montrachet, at room temperature
8 sprigs of fresh rosemary or ½ teaspoon dried, crumbled
2 teaspoons olive oil, preferably extra-virgin

1 Preheat the broiler. Arrange the bread slices in one layer on a baking sheet, place in the broiler and broil until lightly toasted on one side.

2 Spread the untoasted side of each bread slice with some of the goat cheese. Top each with a sprig of rosemary or a pinch of the dried. Drizzle a little of the olive oil over the top of each bread slice and return them to the broiler until the cheese is heated through and the edges of the bread are lightly browned.

Salade Niçoise, My Way

8 medium new potatoes, quartered
Salt
3 tablespoons fresh lemon juice
6 cups arugula, tough stems removed
¾ cup thinly sliced celery
2 cans (7 ounces each) tuna, drained

2 tablespoons chopped celery leaves
12 bottled Calamata olives, drained, 3 tablespoons of brine reserved (see Note)
3 hard-cooked eggs, quartered lengthwise
2 teaspoons drained capers
1 can (2 ounces) rolled anchovies, drained
16 cherry tomatoes, halved
6 slices of red onion
½ cup olive oil
4 dashes hot pepper sauce
Freshly ground pepper

1 Steam the potatoes until tender, about 10 minutes. Season with salt to taste and sprinkle with 2 tablespoons of the lemon juice. Let cool slightly; the potatoes can be a little warm, but not hot when the salad is assembled.

2 Spread the arugula on a large platter or in a salad bowl. Arrange the potatoes on the arugula, sprinkle with the sliced celery and mound the tuna in the center. Sprinkle the chopped celery leaves on top. Decorate with the olives, eggs, capers, anchovies, tomatoes and onion rings.

3 In a small bowl, combine the remaining 1 tablespoon lemon juice, the reserved 3 tablespoons brine from the olives, the olive oil and hot pepper sauce and blend well. Spoon the dressing over the salad just before serving and top with a sprinkling of freshly ground pepper.

Note: If the brine from the olives is not available, substitute 2 tablespoons balsamic or red wine vinegar.

Honeydew Melon and Fresh Peaches with Sweet Vermouth

2 large peaches—peeled, pitted and sliced
Juice of ½ lemon
1½ tablespoons sugar, or to taste
8 wedges (½ inch thick) of honeydew melon, seeded and peeled
8 tablespoons sweet vermouth

Place the peaches in a mixing bowl, sprinkle with the lemon juice and sugar and toss well. Arrange two wedges of melon on each of four serving plates to form a ring. Divide the peaches among the four plates and pour 2 tablespoons of the vermouth over each.

MIX
&
MATCH

Menu planning is
something of an art,
a creative but balanced
approach to which is
almost as important to a
meal's success as the
actual cooking. With this in
mind, I have suggested
the following new menus
created by combining
the recipes and menu
elements from preceeding
chapters in new ways.
I hope they will be used
both as blueprints
and as inspiration for
your own menus.

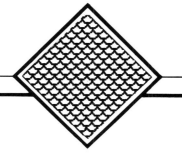

Margaritas on the Rocks
PAGE 177

Salted Walnuts and an Assortment of Olives

————————— ◆ —————————

Red Snapper with Green Peppercorn Sauce
PAGE 147

Parslied Rice

Cucumbers with Lime
PAGE 161

————————— ◆ —————————

Strawberries Marinated in Port and Red Currant Sauce
PAGE 47

---

4 SERVINGS

Grilled Flank Steak with Dill
PAGE 117

Braised Onion Slices
PAGE 193

Fresh Tomato and Caper Salad
PAGE 199

Toasted French Bread

————————— ◆ —————————

Walnut Brownies

---

6 SERVINGS

Dilled Veal Balls with Sour Cream and Caper Sauce
PAGE 99

Parslied New Potatoes in Their Skins
PAGE 141

Cucumbers Vinaigrette
PAGE 129

————————— ◆ —————————

Winter Fruit with Honey and Lemon
PAGE 43

---

4 SERVINGS

Arní Souvlákia
PAGE 179

Eggplant with Tomatoes and Parsley
PAGE 183

Green Rice
PAGE 165
or
Couscous

————————— ◆ —————————

Sultan's Yogurt
PAGE 113

Pernod and Water

◆

Fillets of Sea Bass with Sun-Dried Tomatoes
PAGE 137

Saffron Rice with Pistachios
PAGE 127

◆

Avocado Salad with Lime Dressing
PAGE 177

◆

Lemon Ice with Gin
PAGE 199

Café Filtre

---

4 SERVINGS

Sippin' Whiskey
PAGE 17

◆

Oyster Stew
PAGE 15

Cornmeal-Buttermilk Biscuits
PAGE 79

Raisin Pumpernickel and Sweet Butter

Romaine and Apple Salad
PAGE 169

◆

Brownies or Chocolate Cake

---

4 TO 6 SERVINGS

Red Wine with Soda and an Orange Slice

◆

Salt Cod with Mashed Potatoes
PAGE 167

Tomatoes Provençale
PAGE 117

◆

Apple-Walnut Betty
PAGE 171

Café Filtre

---

2 SERVINGS

Gin and Tonics

◆

Avocado with Rum Vinaigrette
PAGE 147

◆

Curried Fillets of Flounder
PAGE 161

Buttered Rice Garnished with Hazelnuts

Escarole Salad with Fresh Mint
PAGE 207

◆

Lemon Ice with a Squeeze of Fresh Lemon Juice

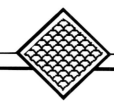

4 SERVINGS

Croque-Monsieurs
PAGE 55

◆

Broiled Sea Trout with Watercress-Watermelon Pickle Butter
PAGE 37

Croutons
PAGE 133

Salad of Belgian Endive, Apple and Walnuts
PAGE 105

◆

Chocolate Ice Cream with Apricot Brandy

Amaretti

---

6 SERVINGS

Skillet Grilled Pork with Dipping Sauce
PAGE 175

Rice with Fresh Coriander
PAGE 161

Orange and Red Onion Salad
PAGE 195

◆

Ice Cream with Honey

Jasmine Tea

---

4 SERVINGS

Warm Crab Salad
PAGE 145

Cucumbers in Cream with Basil
PAGE 107

Italian Bread with Parsley and Scallion
PAGE 65

◆

Chocolate Ice Cream with Kahlúa

---

4 BRUNCH SERVINGS

Chilled Riesling

Crisped Flatbread Parmesan
PAGE 107

◆

Sea Scallops with Orange Butter
PAGE 139

Toasted French Bread

Bibb Lettuce Chiffonade
PAGE 69

◆

Vanilla Ice Cream with Chestnuts and Brandy
PAGE 49

2 SERVINGS

Broiled Eggplant with Three Cheeses and Fresh Tomato Sauce
PAGE 207

Green Beans with Lemon Zest
PAGE 147

Whole Wheat Italian Bread

———————— ◆ ————————

Poached Apples with Ice Cream and Walnuts
PAGE 209

4 LUNCH SERVINGS

Sweet Vermouth and Soda

Sesame Canapés
PAGE 165

———————— ◆ ————————

Salade Niçoise, My Way
PAGE 217

French Bread

———————— ◆ ————————

Babas au Rhum with Whipped Cream
PAGE 181

Strawberries

Hot or Iced Espresso

4 SERVINGS

Dry Martinis or Chilled White Wine

Bananas Broiled in Bacon
PAGE 143

———————— ◆ ————————

Shrimp Dijon
PAGE 165

Gingered Rice
PAGE 69

Green Bean Salad with Balsamic Vinaigrette
PAGE 137

———————— ◆ ————————

Peaches with Apricot Sauce and Amaretti
PAGE 61

6 SERVINGS

Red Wine Spritzers

Prosciutto-Wrapped Breadsticks
PAGE 77

———————— ◆ ————————

Beef Salad Vinaigrette
PAGE 131

French Rolls

———————— ◆ ————————

Raspberry Sorbet or Rich Chocolate Ice Cream

Hot or Iced Café Filtre

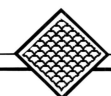

Mimosas with a Dash of Orange Flower Water

"Lost" Muffins with Sour Cream and Strawberries
PAGE 13

Glazed Bacon with Walnuts
PAGE 17

Jamaican Coffee

---

4 SERVINGS

Melon with Pepper and Lime

◆

Capellini Primavera
PAGE 181

Fresh Tomato and Caper Salad
PAGE 199

Italian Breads

◆

Miniature Grape Tarts
PAGE 63

Fresh Strawberry and Ricotta Barquettes
PAGE 123

---

4 SERVINGS

Manhattans

Ginger and Bacon Canapés
PAGE 139

◆

Medallions of Pork with Pommard Sauce
PAGE 103

Sautéed Apple and Lemon Slices
PAGE 29

◆

Bibb Lettuce with Golden Cream Dressing
PAGE 59

◆

Hot Fudge and Bourbon Sundaes with Pecans
PAGE 143

---

4 BREAKFAST SERVINGS

Campari Sunrises
PAGE 27
or
Fresh Orange Juice Flavored with Orange Flower Water and Lime
PAGE 13

Parslied Eggs in Baked Tomato Shells
PAGE 35

Sausage Patties with Fresh Ginger
PAGE 45

Vermont Pan Bread
PAGE 131

Coffee or English Breakfast Tea

Baked Eggs Fonduta with Three Cheeses
PAGE 27

Arugula and Romaine Salad
PAGE 123

───────── ◆ ─────────

Strawberries with Maple Syrup and Cream

Espresso

Chocolate Cookies

---

6 SERVINGS

Westphalian Ham with Honeydew Melon
PAGE 153

───────── ◆ ─────────

Shell Steaks with Caper Butter and Broiled Mushroom Caps
PAGE 83

Fresh-Herbed French Bread
PAGE 153

───────── ◆ ─────────

Oak Leaf Lettuce and Red Onions with Balsamic Vinaigrette

───────── ◆ ─────────

Vanilla Ice Cream with Brandied Cherries

---

4 SERVINGS

Watermelon Pickles Broiled in Bacon
PAGE 159

───────── ◆ ─────────

Spirited Veal with Bourbon and Granny Smith Apples
PAGE 133

Bulgur with Scallions
PAGE 113

───────── ◆ ─────────

Bibb Lettuce and Mushroom Salad with Tarragon Dressing
PAGE 127

───────── ◆ ─────────

Sugared Strawberries
PAGE 179

Café Filtre

---

4 TO 6 SERVINGS

Radish Slices on Buttered Pumpernickel Toast

Fish Chowder
PAGE 171

Arugula and Romaine Salad
PAGE 123

───────── ◆ ─────────

Pears with Chocolate Sauce
PAGE 167

Calf's Liver alla Veneziana
PAGE 189

Steamed Red Potatoes with Cream and Nutmeg
PAGE 83

Green Beans with Lime Juice
PAGE 119

———— ◆ ————

Sautéed Apple Tart
PAGE 203

Ginger Sundae
PAGE 89

---

4 SERVINGS

Lemon-Roasted Breast of Chicken
PAGE 69

Green Rice
PAGE 165

Orange and Bermuda Onion Salad
PAGE 197

———— ◆ ————

Coffee Ice Cream with Honey

---

4 SERVINGS

Bluegrass-Style Fried Chicken
PAGE 57

Grits with Red-Pepper Butter
PAGE 17

Cherry Tomatoes with Garlic and Parsley
PAGE 27

———— ◆ ————

Sliced Peaches with Heavy Cream

---

6 SERVINGS

Radishes with Sweet Butter
PAGE 167

———— ◆ ————

Broiled Cornish Game Hens
PAGE 77

Quick Polenta
PAGE 195

Buttered Spinach
PAGE 153

———— ◆ ————

Boysenberry or Raspberry Sherbet Cassis
PAGE 99

4 SERVINGS

Skillet Ham with Speedy Creole Tomato Sauce
PAGE 107

Louisiana Spoon Bread
PAGE 57

Roasted Green Pepper Salad
PAGE 53

———————— ◆ ————————

Bananas in Rum Cream
PAGE 145

4 LUNCH SERVINGS

Sweet Vermouth on the Rocks

Crisped Flatbread Parmesan
PAGE 107

———————— ◆ ————————

Fettuccine in Cream with Herb-Scented Mushrooms
PAGE 199

Whole Wheat Italian Bread

———————— ◆ ————————

Green Salad with Anchovy-Leek Dressing
PAGE 19

———————— ◆ ————————

Honeyed Strawberry Granita
PAGE 189

4 SERVINGS

Rhine Wine Punch
PAGE 109

———————— ◆ ————————

Chicken Breasts with Cucumber, Basil and Cream
PAGE 73

Italian Bread with Parsley and Scallion
PAGE 65

Cornmeal-Buttermilk Biscuits
PAGE 79

———————— ◆ ————————

Watermelon Balls with Raspberry Sorbet

6 SERVINGS

Gingered Melon
PAGE 131

———————— ◆ ————————

Chicken with Cashews
PAGE 211

Steamed Rice

———————— ◆ ————————

Coffee and Pistachio Ice Cream with Crème de Cacao

Chocolate Cookies

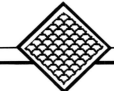

2 SERVINGS

"Lilies" on Ice
PAGE 161

Grilled Chèvre with Fresh Rosemary on French Bread
PAGE 217

◆

Giselle's Soup Provençale with Poached Eggs
PAGE 191

Green Salad with Lardons
PAGE 209

French or Peasant Bread

◆

Bananas Flambéed with Rum
PAGE 161

4 SERVINGS

Lime Rickeys
PAGE 69

◆

Broiled Swordfish Steaks with Horseradish Sauce
PAGE 159

Corn on the Cob with Cumin Butter
PAGE 107
or
Green Bean Succotash
PAGE 75

Tomatoes with Mustard and Brown Sugar Dressing
PAGE 73

◆

Fresh Blueberry Tumble
PAGE 107

4 SERVINGS

Chilled White Wine

Anchovy Toast
PAGE 117

◆

Chicken with Sun-Dried Tomatoes
PAGE 53

Rice with Fresh Coriander
PAGE 161

◆

Bibb Lettuce Salad with Vinaigrette

◆

Oranges on the Half Shell
PAGE 15

Chocolate Cookies

4 BRUNCH SERVINGS

Brandy Old-Fashioneds
PAGE 45

Deviled Eggs with Calamata Olives and Cayenne Walnuts
PAGE 73

◆

Poached Breast of Chicken with Autumn Vegetables
PAGE 55

Horseradish Sauce
PAGE 159

Apple Corn Muffins
PAGE 21

◆

Black Grapes and Ripe Pears

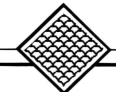

Fino Sherry

Red Pepper Almonds
PAGE 151

Calamata Olives

———◆———

Arroz con Camarones
PAGE 177

Honeydew and Green Grape Salad with Lime Vinaigrette
PAGE 165

———◆———

Coffee Ice Cream with Rum and Chocolate Cookies

Café Filtre

Concierge's Soup
PAGE 203

Herbed Feta and Toasted Pita Bread
PAGE 179

Prosciutto-Wrapped Breadsticks
PAGE 77

Lentil and Tomato Salad
PAGE 115

Mediterranean Stuffed Eggs
PAGE 181

Grapes and Pears

Chocolate-Walnut Squares
PAGE 169

Thermos of Coffee

Sweet Vermouth

Spiced Walnuts
PAGE 27

———◆———

Bifteck Haché with Chèvre and Beaujolais
PAGE 209

Warm French Bread

Pepper, Olive and Onion Salad
PAGE 191

———◆———

Vanilla Ice Cream with Chestnuts in Syrup and Whipped Cream

Black Coffee

Shrimp and Assorted Vegetables with Green Sauce
PAGE 77

———◆———

Lamb Chops Bar-le-Duc
PAGE 119

Parslied Rice

Braised Endive
PAGE 83

———◆———

Vanilla Ice Cream with Brandied Cherries

Café Filtre

Crystallized Ginger and Chocolates

INDEX

C

W-X-Y-Z

If you are not already a subscriber to *Food & Wine*
magazine and would be interested in subscribing,
please call Food & Wine's toll-free number
(800) 247-5470; in Iowa, (800) 532-1272.

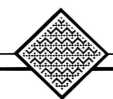